Ryan T. Pugh started writing at the age of fifteen. By the age of twenty he was forming whole sentences, mostly involving cats sitting on mats. He never looked back. Soon, not only were the cats sitting on mats, they were also receiving *gentle pats* and *chasing rats*. Within hours he had a Creative Writing degree from Britain's 115th best university (or 6th best, depending which way up you read the Times Educational Supplement).

Ryan harboured dreams of pop stardom until, one terrible evening, he caught his reflection in a toilet mirror before going on stage. He realised he had the hair, clothes, glasses and shape of Eric Morecambe. Upon this discovery, he relented and shifted his focus towards puns.

Ryan was born and raised in Norfolk. He is a teacher and general layabout. He has requested, in the event of his passing, to have his body quartered and sent to the four corners of Britain as a warning.

This is his second book.

Also Available

Amusements

Find out more at ryantpugh.co.uk

Kismet Quick

A Norfolk Odyssey

Ryan T. Pugh

To, Sarah, sorry!

No refunds.

Love,

[signature] x

Boo-Boo-Books

© 2015 Ryan T. Pugh. All rights reserved.

This book is sold subject to the condition that it shall not, by way of trade or otherwise, be lent, resold, hired out, or otherwise circulated without the publisher's prior consent in any form of binding or cover other than that in which it is published and without a similar condition including this condition being imposed on the subsequent publisher

The moral right of Ryan T. Pugh has been asserted

First published in Great Britain 2015 by Boo-Boo-Books

ISBN-13: 978-1508563914

Contact: *puede@hotmail.co.uk*

Cover by Sarah Ann Corlett

To Maureen and Jasmine. Norfolk girls.

Contents

Introduction 9
Note On The Text 19

Leg One
21 - Sheringham
31 - Weybourne
39 - Holt
46 - Fakenham
51 - Walsingham
67 - Wells-Next-The-Sea

Leg Two
77 - Blakeney
82 - Cley-Next-The-Sea

Leg Three
91 - Mundesley
95 - North Walsham
103 - Coltishall
109 - Norwich part I
117 - Wroxham (& Hoveton)
124 - Aylsham

Leg Four
134 - Bacton & Happisburgh
143 - Stalham

Leg Five
148 - Cromer
164 - Burnham Thorpe
185 - Burnham Market

191 - Heacham
199 - Hunstanton
205 - King's Lynn
218 - Downham Market

Leg Six
232 - Norwich part II
235 - Hingham
242 - Watton
246 - Swaffham
252 - Dereham

Leg Seven
262 - Martham
265 - Winterton-On-Sea
271 - Caister-On-Sea
275 - Gorleston-On-Sea
279 - Great Yarmouth

Leg Eight
291 - Thetford
306 - Attleborough
309 - Wymondham
316 - Horning

Leg Nine
323 - Diss
334 - Harleston
337 - Loddon
344 - Norwich part III
352 - Filby
355 - Reedham

Epilogue 359

Introduction

Scan the 'Local Books' section of your nearest library and you'll see any number of queer looking tomes. As corners of libraries go, this is usually the wackiest.[1] It's where books with names like *South Walsham & District II* and *Edwardian Attleborough* loiter, largely undisturbed by the hands of borrowers. They're loaned out so infrequently that to try and prise them apart sometimes requires gentle force. Their pages crackle on separation, as though glued together by time (and hopefully nothing else).
I've always been fascinated by local books. Especially the ones stuffed full of old photographs; there's a curious ecstasy in seeing long-dead, bearded fishmongers staring at you from the doorway of Poundland, or seeing your town hall, now a

---

[1] Its nearest rival is that bit with row upon row of large print Westerns. Do people with struggling eyesight predominantly enjoy Westerns? It's hard to imagine that they would. Then again, the main characters are usually called things like 'Deadeye' Jack and 'Blind' McGrew. Maybe they find them relatable.

BetFred, hosting a celebratory tea party in honour of Queen Victoria's diamond jubilee. Why is it so captivating to see these things? I'm really not sure. Maybe it's the feeling that the ever-fading images represent our past desperately stretching out an arm to us. Or it could be, more simply, that it's just exciting to recognise parts of our lives in *any* form of media, however marginal it may be.[1]

A local book is something you might buy your gran for Christmas, with mixed results. After unwrapping it, she usually proceeds to weep at a photograph of the town cricket team circa 1933. She then tells everyone that she's crying because the spin bowler ('A smashing fella. Dead now. Faulty liver') used to be her milkman. This is then followed by a thoroughly awkward silence, punctuated only by her sobs. You stand beside her, arm on shoulder, regretting that you didn't just get her a tin of Quality Street and the *Countryfile* calendar you'd seen in WHSmiths. Meanwhile all the youngsters in the room sit staring into the void, wondering what a milkman is.

As well as making elderly relatives yearn for the sweet release of the grave, local books can also be frightening. Black & white photographs of zombie-eyed Victorians staring directly at the camera are seldom a joy to behold. On weaker days, such pictures are enough to send you to bed convinced that one of the subjects has eyed you up and is currently ghosting his way along the garden path with the intention of coming to watch you sleep.

---

[1] I've lost count of the times I've leapt out of my seat when I've seen a character on television using similar crockery to my own:
'Oh my God! They've got the *exact same* cup as me!'
I then fight to refrain from calling every guest I've ever had and getting them to switch their teles on so that they, too, can delight in seeing the *exact same* cup in action.

It's not just the pictures that gently raise the arm hairs. The text can be full of horrors, too. It's not much fun to discover that the park you routinely saunter across during twilight was once a pit into which freshly-hanged murderers were dumped. And it's equally chilling to find out that your house used to form part of the town lunatic asylum, with your bedroom a detaining point for the particularly disturbed. Such trivia, I'm sure you'll agree, is often best left unread.

Local books have a wealth of good points, too, of course. They can be gloriously niche. It's one thing dipping into a potted history of Swaffham, but another to read exclusively about *Swaffham Roadways Of The 1860s*. That requires a rare dedication. After years of inner speculation about who the hell actually *read* these obscure books, I began to wonder who the hell actually *wrote* them.

After a moment's reflection, a cold perspiration formed on my ever-growing brow: they were written by people like me. They were written by balding, portly, hairy-faced corduroy-wearers who seldom left the county except to laugh at other counties.

I was then hammered by another thumping realisation: local authors were a dying breed. A quick scan of market town pubs on a Friday night told everything: there weren't too many potential local authors coming up through the ranks. The rural youth of today had loftier aspirations. Their dreams were of London media, Parisian au pair work, walking the secret beaches of Thailand, haggling in Indian marketplaces, getting drunk in Australian hostels, well-digging for Oxfam in Chad, networking at fairy-lit San Franciscan summer parties, drunkenly texting in New York waffle houses at 4am. They wanted the world and were likely to get it. These kids weren't going to be staying in Norfolk to bash out 300-page retrospective accounts of the Dereham-to-Wymondham steam railway. The future of local books was in peril. When the current crop of Norfolk scribes called it a day, who'd be there to pick up their pens?

I didn't know what I was going to write about, but I knew that Norfolk had to be the general theme of my next book. I'd lived in Norfolk for most of my life, it was my duty. In the name of research, I hit the 'Local Books' sections of every shop and library in the county, prising apart all the sticky pages I could lay my ever-stickier hands on.

I spent eight months reading of nothing but Norfolk. I began building my own collection of specialist literature. From *The Tram Routes of Great Yarmouth* to *The Back-Passages Of Felthorpe*, my collection swelled. They formed an ever-growing pile next to my desk. This tower of learning grew to such a height that it kept toppling over. I had to make shelf space. Into the shed went my last remaining video cassettes (*Tatie Danielle, Etre Et Avoir, Danny Baker's Own Goals & Gaffs 2*) and onto the shelf went my new loves.

During that eight-month period I became an oracle on Norfolk. I'd find myself single-handedly ruining parties by talking loudly about how Thomas Coke kick-started the British Agricultural Revolution[1] through farming reforms:

'It was a miracle,' I'd yell over the pulsating dance music. 'When he inherited Holkham Hall, he said that the land consisted of two rabbits fighting over one blade of grass. By the time he was done, they were growing wheat!'

No reaction.

---

[1] In need of a new type of headwear for the Holkham gamekeepers, whose top hats kept falling off, Coke's nephew asked a London manufacturer to develop a prototype for something smaller and sturdier. The family were so pleased with the innovative design that they ordered a job lot. The manufacturers referred to these new hats as 'cokes'. We now know them as 'bowlers'.

'Wheat!' I'd shout once more, thinking maybe I hadn't said it properly.

On each sticky page I found something fascinating. The stories were incredible. None more so than the story of Ellen Bird from the village of New Buckenham. She'd sailed on the Titanic. In total there were five Norfolk survivors of the disaster, but it was Ellen's story that made my heart skip. She'd been the maid of Ida Strauss, co-owner of Macy's department store in New York, who I'd written about in *Amusements*. I couldn't believe it. What were the chances? I'd written a chapter about a relatively forgotten Titanic passenger for my first book and stumbled upon the story of her Norfolk-born maid for my second. It was fate. Or kismet, if you will.[1]

I liked the idea of doing a tour. But if I wanted to tour the county I had to have a hook. That's what other travelogues had. Hooks. Wacky subplots. It wasn't enough for travel writers to just tour Scandinavia anymore: they had to do so carrying a tumble dryer. What could *my* wacky idea be? I thought about it for months. Inspiration struck whilst standing in the rain waiting for a train that would never arrive. Norfolk's public transport system. Of course! I could try and tour the county on it. Maybe I could do the entire journey using only buses and trains. What could be wackier? It would be like trying to get to Saturn on a donkey.

It was decided.

I then had to think of places to go and things to see. It was best that I didn't choose the places myself. If I did that, I knew I'd

---

[1] Ida Strauss refused to get into a lifeboat on the grounds that her husband wasn't allowed to join her. Ellen was encouraged to take the spare seat and save herself. Ida offered Ellen her lavish coat: 'Wear this. It will be cold in the lifeboat and I don't need it anymore.'

make things too comfortable. I'd only go to the easy-to-reach places (of which Norfolk has approximately six). I had to find a pre-existing list. Online search engines supplied links to lists of tourist attractions and landmarks but they all seemed too vague and dull. Then I happened upon an amiable website declaring itself the home of Norfolk Tourist Information. They'd compiled a handy list of forty towns and villages worth visiting. It had the obvious entries: Norwich, Cromer, Great Yarmouth, Burnham Market, Holt. But it also had a few rogue ones: Stalham, Martham, Downham Market.

The omissions were equally notable. There was no place on the list for Sandringham (birthplace of Lady Diana and death place of George V and his stuttering son, George VI); no place for Heydon (the most alluring village in the county, on which more later); no Walsingham (I visited it anyway); no Castle Rising (once represented in parliament by the diarist Samuel Pepys and former home to the French wife of the allegedly homosexual Edward II) and no Stiffkey, home of the most predictably defaced village sign in Great Britain.

Stiffkey was also the former home of an infamous rector called Harold Davidson, who, instead of organising raffles and penning thrilling articles for the *Stiffkey Church & Community Bi-Monthly Circular*, spent most of the working week cavorting with young London prostitutes. He claimed to be helping them see the light (whilst simultaneously trying to switch the light off). The British press went to town. They published a picture of him in a compromising position with a shapely-bottomed lady of the night. Davidson claimed to have been set up. He may have been telling the truth, although he was clearly playing a dangerous game (it would be hard to imagine, for example, John Sentamu, Archbishop of York, getting caught in a similar 'stitch up'). I should also point out that the rector seemed largely preoccupied with wrapping young *female* prostitutes under his caring wing. Male prostitutes don't appear to have had much of a look in.

The rector died, if you can believe such a thing, after being mauled by a lion in Skegness. He was part of a sideshow skit recreating Daniel in the lion's den. Such was Davidson's fame, he'd toured the country performing similar sketches. Skegness was his last. Lions are notorious for their unwillingness to read scripts through to the final page. They get two-thirds in and tend to ad-lib. Thus fell the final curtain on that strange little story.

Despite its wild omissions, Norfolk Tourist Information's list covered enough of the county to appease me. I rather liked the fact it was lopsided. I made the call. This would be my forty.

First, I had to establish some rules. I wasn't going to write about zoos and theme parks, leisure centres and museums. I wanted to just *go* to the forty places. I wanted to capture their essence. I would dig into local history but only if it interested me.[1] I didn't want to focus too much, or at all, on geographical features. Nor, if possible, did I want to use the word *silting* at any stage, or refer to locals as being *earthy*.

Whilst on a date in 2013 (on an evening which, readers of *Amusements* will be relieved to know, I *didn't* accidentally piss on myself in a disabled toilet) my companion informed me that when she'd announced she was moving to Norfolk one of her friends had snorted, 'Ooh, hard luck. It's horrible. A backwater.' It was enough to make my Norfolk blood boil. Then, weeks later, another cold-hearted fiend informed me that Norfolk was boring. (I later found out this person had travelled down from Yorkshire to come and look at a rare steam engine. She was obviously some sort of insatiable party animal.)

---

[1] For that reason, there would no doubt be some glaring historical omissions, among them, it turns out, the Burston School Strike and anything to do with the weaving industry.

Was this really what people thought? I'd always imagined that Norfolk was seen as an Eden to outsiders. If not, why were there so many holiday homes? I wasn't aware that some people hated the place. I'd often heard disparaging Norfolk jokes (incest, flat landscapes, tractors, sheep etc) on *Mock The Week* but had taken it as a given that viewers understood fully that anybody who went on *Mock The Week* had their every thought and action made void by default. Yet this clearly wasn't the case. To some, Norfolk was a joke, a boring backwater, a nothing.

I don't want to taint my introduction with spoilers but I ought to confess that my travels didn't necessarily disprove all of the above theories. There were places I visited that fell firmly onto the bullseye of the backwater dartboard. And there were others that contained more than their fair share of amusingly shaped heads, each questioning the legality of the relationship that birthed them (I'm not stupid enough to name the places though. You might be able to do a little detective work yourself as the book goes on). And, lastly, yes, there were some exceptionally quiet - I refuse to say boring – places, where the biggest upcoming events were the W.I tombola and next Thursday's visit from the mobile library. But even in those rare, dimly lit corners of the county, there was always something to love.

Norfolk has much to boast about (but seldom does so): it's the safest place to live in the UK (the Broadland district had eight reported violent crimes in one year – for a population of 125,000); the Millennium library in Norwich is the most visited and used library in England; north Norfolk has been voted the second best place to raise a family in the UK (2014); it's the happiest place for children to grow up (2014); it has the most museums per county (2009); the best beach in Britain (Holkham) and the happiest, hippest university students, forty percent of whom, once graduated, build careers in the county. 'It is not a place,' wrote J.B Priestley, 'in which to make money quickly and then plan a sudden exit. It is not filled with people who are there because they have never been offered a job elsewhere.'

Going back to that crime rate briefly, Norfolk is the fifth largest county by area and the fourteenth largest by population in the UK. It is served by just fourteen police stations. Its nearest counties, by population, are Nottinghamshire, Staffordshire and Hertfordshire. These are served by 20, 22 and 21 stations respectively. Around a third more. Why are there so few police stations in Norfolk? Why are there so few crimes? One obvious answer would be that fewer crimes go unrecorded due to the spread of the population and lack of police. Yet, in 2013, it was reported that Norfolk police had a 36pc detection rate. The national average was 28pc. If anything, Norfolk police were spotting more crimes than most.[1]

During the national riots of 2011, when it seemed the youth of England were all hell-bent on nabbing as many free televisions as they could squeeze into their bedrooms, the total amount of damage done to Norfolk was an upturned wheelie bin and an egg thrown at Matalan. And it's never even been proved if these heinous acts were linked to the wider national turmoil. The perpetrators are still at large.

Still, it's pretty boring, though, right? Nowhere near as exciting as places with high crime rates and disaffection. Having your bathroom window jimmied open by a crackhead is a hoot.

*

---

[1] Two of the officially reported 'violent crimes' in 2014 included a woman throwing a biscuit at a man, and a child brushing a stinging nettle against another child's arm. Seriously.

My tour of the county started on a beautiful morning in April and was completed on an equally beautiful afternoon in late October. I had to try and work the trips around my actual job, hence the dramatic time leaps between certain legs of the tour. This had the unforeseen benefit of allowing me to see the county through the changing weathers. The glorious thing about the English countryside is how clearly the seasons are defined. I hope I managed to capture some of it in these pages. If I haven't, I'm sorry. Actually, I'm not. If you wanted skilled pastoral writing you shouldn't have picked up a book called *Kismet Quick*. What on earth were you expecting?

I hope you enjoy the story. My real hope is that people from beyond Norfolk enjoy it. They're the ones who need to know that Norfolk isn't really full of sixteen-fingered farmhands and violated livestock. It's as quirky as hell, but often in wonderful ways. It is a community where madness and sanity get along just fine. It is a farmer's county, it is a fisherman's county, it is an artist's county, it is a student's county, it is a gardener's county. It is also Nelson's County:

'I am a Norfolk man and glory in being so,' the great Admiral once declared, whilst standing in Suffolk and drawing glares.

Norfolk is worthy of glorification. The locals already know that, of course. Although it never hurts to get a gentle reminder.

May those *Mock The Week* comedians turn into pillars of salt.

Ryan, July 2015

NOTE ON THE TEXT

Without wishing to pre-judge, the likelihood is that many readers (oh, those stony-souled thugs) will flick through the book to find chapters about places they're familiar with. For this reason, I've kept each chapter a little longer than might be expected, lest any such 'location hunters' feel short-changed. However, for those who prefer a little chaff with their wheat (oh, those goodly, virtuous beings), I've tried to ensure that the book is also suitable to be read in whole.

So, those are the options: picking out your hotspots or reading straight through. Whichever route you take, I hope you consider me to be a passable companion.

Ready?

'The years fall off and find me walking back
Dragging a stick along the wooden fence'

Sir John Betjeman, *Norfolk*

Leg One

Sheringham – Weybourne – Holt – Fakenham - Walsingham – Wells

Sheringham

It is quite difficult to look afresh at a place that you've known for all of your life. Sheringham is where I went to primary school, high school and college. It's also where I've been living for the last six years. I know it inside and out. I've seen it from the windows of trains and the windows of Geography classes. I've walked up and down each street a thousand times. All twelve of them. But my role was clear. From the moment I left my house, I was one of its many tourists. I was starting from scratch.
It was an early spring morning. The sun was on my back and there was zeal in my heart. You can't beat a bit of zeal. I decided to start with a part of the town I'd often walked past but never entered: the priory ruins. Technically, the priory was in the adjoining village of Beeston Regis, which is how it came by its catchy name of Beeston Regis Priory. But, as there was no noticeable dividing line between Sheringham and Beeston, I considered it fair game.
The ruins were wedged between a modern-ish housing estate and a busy main road. They were hidden amongst trees and overgrown hedges. You could easily walk right past without spotting them. Around the ruins was a body of water, privately owned. When I was younger it used to attract the occasional

fishing enthusiast. It was also a hotbed for discarded copies of *Reader's Wives* and *Penthouse*. They'd lay amongst the wild flowers, yellowed and half-torn, daring discoverers to peel apart their damp pages.

The adverts for adult chat-lines, towards the back of the magazines, always fascinated me most. They ranged from the shocking ('TOUCH YOURSELF WHILE I TALK') to the mundane ('BORED HOUSEWIFE LIKES TO CHAT') right through to the borderline depressing ('LONELY OLD WOMAN NEEDS COMPANY'). There were times when they even seemed to encourage readers to become embroiled in industrial disputes: 'MY BOSS THINKS I DESERVE PUNISHMENT FOR MY SHORT SKIRTS – WHAT DO *YOU* THINK?' It was all pretty strange.

I had a look in the hedge. The magazines had long been fished out.

The priory grounds were open to the public but surrounded by a number of 'Private' signs. Priory enthusiasts (for surely there *are* such folk) were kept from straying beyond the strip of grass inside the ruined walls. A 'Private' sign in Norfolk is not the same as a 'Private' sign in most other parts of the country. In, for example, Surrey, you become aware that you've strayed onto private property by the sound of a piercing, laser-triggered alarm. In Norfolk, you're likely to be alerted by the sound of a bullet whistling past your ear.

Fortunately, the non-private priory parts were spectacular. Despite going to the priory lake a few times as a kid, I'd never actually been amongst the ruins. They were truly grand. Effectively a large church with its roof removed: a convertible.

The priory was founded in 1216. I was walking between walls and under doorways that were 800-years-old. Within the original grounds (forty acres, in its prime) was once a brewery, a guesthouse, a wash-house, barns, a forge, and all manner of things. There was also a boarding school.

All wrecks that washed up on the Sheringham beach, as well as any additional flotsam and jetsam, once belonged, by default, to the priory. The monks may have worn wacky dresses and had the hairstyles of secondary school supply teachers, but they also had immense strength and power. They ruled the roost.

As I stood amongst the mossy stumps, looking up at the blue sky, my phone shook in my pocket. It was Vodafone asking if I would like to make international calls at local rates.

I wouldn't.

Beeston Priory was dissolved in 1538 when Henry VIII set about on his mission to ensure that all children of the future had plenty of ruined priories to visit on school trips. Henry decided that, despite already being pretty, the priories would look *even better* without doors. Without going too far into the sombre history of the Dissolution, suffice to say that there were more than enough commoners willing to help pull down the power-wielding monasteries and strip them of their riches (and jetsom).

Before its demise, Beeston Regis Priory had acquired something of mischievous reputation. Visiting bishops occasionally arrived to find canons skulking around off-duty, and, in one case, buggering off to Norwich without permission.[1] Visitors also reported that accounts weren't being kept ('But it's *really* hard to count flotsam!' may have been the monks' argument) and that the evening prayers were being said in the afternoon *and* that the school didn't have any teachers or any students. Other than that, everything was fine.

In 1317, one of the canons was sent to Rome after attacking a member of his diocese with a sword. Few facts about this

---

[1] The canon in question had allegedly gone to the city to 'celebrate Mass'. Something of a busman's holiday. That's like a London banker spending his vacation sitting in a branch of Natwest, reading the mortgage pamphlets and trying to nick the pens.

incident have survived, but it's safe to say that the next church newsletter was an absolute belter.

When the priory school ceased to be, it inspired one former pupil to build his own. His name was John Gresham. His school, Greshams, is in nearby Holt. It is a public school of some renown. John (Sir John, in fact) did not live to see it completed. Details of the building of the school and the investments Sir John Gresham made are sketchy at best. The majority of the documents containing such information were burnt in the Great Fire of London. Whilst people like Samuel Pepys rushed around digging holes in their back gardens to bury their favourite cheeses, reams of British history were turned to ash.[1] And they say the *modern* generation don't have their priorities right.

I decided that I couldn't spend all morning looking at priory ruins and getting annoyed about Samuel Pepys' cheese collection. Not if I wanted to get home in time to make those tempting international calls at local rates. I got on my proverbial bike and headed for the cliff-tops, towards something not often associated with Norfolk: a hill.

Beeston Bump was its name. It wasn't so much a hill as an oddly shaped, 15,000-year-old, grassy lump. It stuck out like, whilst not exactly a sore thumb, certainly a thumb in some degree of pain. Its presence dominated the Sheringham vista. There weren't many parts of the town where one could stand and not see it lurking in the background. There used to be two bumps before erosion had its say. The monks from Beeston Priory grew vineyards on them. (Perhaps their easy access to alcohol may

---

[1] 'I did dig another [hole], and put our wine in it; and I my Parmesan cheese, as well as my wine and some other things,' Pepys wrote in his diary, clearly unaware how tasty melted Parmesan is.

have contributed to the amount of laziness and stabbing that went on there.)

Sheringham was twinned with Otterndorf, Germany, and appeared suitably Germanic from atop Beeston Bump. The red, sloping roofs and winding roads gave the impression that I was looking at a little town in an unshaken snow globe. It looked like nowhere else on the Norfolk coast. Beyond the town, fields rolled away into a dark green horizon of spires and treetops. Behind me, the North Sea did likewise (minus the church towers and treetops).

Much of Sheringham was to be demolished and redesigned after World War Two in an attempt to give it a 'Skegness feel', as though Skegness were the gold standard in town planning. The high street was to be drastically widened, with the aim of driving pedestrians and traffic towards the beach. Fortunately such a thing never happened. Even from up here it would have looked ghastly. (Beeston's second bump had just about eroded entirely by the 1940s. Maybe Mother Nature was trying to implement her own 'Skegness feel'.)

During the war, secret Y stations were erected around Britain's coastline to intercept messages between German vessels. As the top of a hill is always a good place to hide a secret, Beeston Bump had a one plonked on it. The remains could still be seen: a concrete octagon embedded into the ground. I'd walked over it many times before in ignorance. As a child - an incredibly stupid child - I simply assumed that the octagon had been put there by Egyptians.

The messages picked up by the Beeston Y station were jotted down and sent, initially by motorcycle, to Station X at Bletchley Park, Buckinghamshire.[1] It was all very exciting.

---

[1] Station X sounds like one of those 'specialist' television channels where boss-eyed women talk on the phone whilst sucking their index fingers.

It seems romantic in retrospect. We ought not to think of it in such terms, but who could read the above lines about the scrambled messages and motorcycle rides to Bucks and not feel a fuzzy, nostalgic warmth? If you're anything like me, you've already visualised the whole story in the form of a BBC Sunday night drama.

Churchill said that the Y stations were 'The geese that laid the golden eggs but never cackled.' Which makes you wonder if the old man simply went around spouting memorable quotes, instead of doing any real work:

'Erm, Winston, we do need you to read this file really rather urgently.'

'And *you*, my dear, are ugly, but *I* shall be sober in the morning.'

'Eh?'

I walked down the bump. It's always more pleasing to walk downhill; it sends a gentle tingle up the nether regions. I walked as close to the cliff edge as possible. The sea was calm, the beach quiet.

Sheringham had always been a likely point for enemy attack. There were rumours of a Dutch invasion in the 17th century when unusual ships were spotted close to the shore. The townsfolk sent panicked petitions to the county chiefs:

'Our Town Joynes upon ye Maine sea, and we are afraid every night ye enemy should come ashore and fire Our Towne when we be in our Bedds... we have nothing to Resist them But one Gunn with a broken carriage and foure Musquetts which we bought at Our Owne cost.'

To which the council turned away, whilst muttering something about a Big Society.

In hindsight, the townsfolk should have just waited for the Dutch to invade and then scared them off with one of their countless Morris Dancing festivals. A couple of days of organised street merriment and the Orange army would have packed their bags and never returned. You must play to your strengths in moments of war.

Sheringham was a Frontline town during the Second World War. Windows were blacked out and the beach cordoned off with barbed wire. If you were to ever visit in late September, you might be under the illusion that the war was still on. Each year Sheringham stages a spectacular 1940s weekend in which people, young and old, dress up in 40s clothes and generally lark about as though the fire of war were still aflame. In an effort to get involved with the celebrations, the shops refuse to sell eggs, milk, sugar, meat and bread. Several of the town's young men are ceremoniously shot at random.

Larks aside, the town comes to life for the 40s weekend. It has become Sheringham's big event of the year. It easily surpasses the carnival and countless other nonsensical events which all seem to involve tambourines and people yelling 'Ho' in the middle of the road when I'm trying to cross it to buy a pint of milk. The 40s weekend draws everyone, from vintage-drenched hipsters to the borderline insane.[1] It really is something. I find it utterly charming that my hometown has a specific weekend dedicated to the 1940s, as though all its other weekends are rooted firmly in the 21st century.

Mindful of the fate of the second Beeston Bump, I backed away from the cliff edge. Standing over cliff edges makes me feel like one of those people at the start of an episode of *Casualty*:

---

[1] You're quite likely to overhear the phrase 'We could do with another war', or words to that effect, at least once over the course of the weekend. I heard it *twice* last year.

'Oh, I'll be fine, love! I'll just get a little bit closer to the edge so I can get a really good view of the... Nooooo!'

There were a handful of commemorative plaques in Sheringham but by far the most intriguing was just off the town centre. It read: *'The first bomb to be dropped on Britain in World War One fell in this yard at 8.30pm, 19th January 1915.'*

What makes the statement so interesting is that it isn't true.

The first bomb dropped on Britain was at Dover on Christmas Eve, 1914. The Sheringham plaque was actually meant to state that this was the landing site of the first bomb to be *dropped by a zeppelin*. Yet, this isn't true, either. The first zeppelin bomb was dropped further down the coast, just outside Great Yarmouth. Essentially, the plaque was commemorating the first bomb to be dropped *on Sheringham*, which was slightly less noteworthy. I'd suggest rewording the plaque so it says, 'Site of the first recorded attempt at flattening the town to give it that Skegness feel.'

Plaque inaccuracies aside, when it came to zeppelin trivia, Sheringham had one more card up its sleeve. In 1936, the German airship Hindenburg glided over the town, prompting rumours that it was on a spying mission of nearby Weybourne's new military camp. Just under a year later, the Hindenburg would catch fire and disintegrate in thirty terrifying seconds, taking the celebrated future of airship travel (and the ability to spy on Weybourne) with it. It also provided Led Zeppelin with a stonking album cover.

The seafront promenade was the only real blotch on Sheringham's aesthetic copybook. It was a mess of reinforced concrete. The postcards tried to avoid this Orwellian sight and focused more on the Victorian train station and silver sand beaches. There was also a disconcerting number of them which featured images of the war memorial. I don't know why.

'Oh, look, Brian. It's a postcard from Daphne's visit to Sheringham. I'm not sure but I think... it's of a war memorial.'

'How delightful. What does it say, dear?'

'Wish You Were Here.'

'Oh.'

When you live in a seaside resort, it's easy to forget just how fascinating the sea and the sea-trade are to people who rarely see either. I joined a growing crowd of tourists on a concrete bridge over a fishing boat slipway. They were looking below with great interest. At an old man hosing down a boat. We stood and watched him for about twelve minutes (although it felt considerably longer). Cameras flashed as though he were a member of One Direction.

It must have been strange for the old boy. I guess he'd been going to the same slipway every morning for the last fifty years or so, and he now had crowds of tourists filming him trying to do his job. I wonder if, as trades die out, future generations will look at other jobs with equal fascination. Will the people of tomorrow go on trips to see what a man welding looks like?:

'I've been welding round here since 2003,' he'll say, as the audiences applaud.

Three fishermen appeared. They were a couple of rungs further down the generational ladder. They pushed their boat down the ramp. The crowd went wild. The rest of 1D had arrived.

If you hadn't known any better you'd have thought the fishermen were purposefully re-enacting the olden times, like those American tourist attractions which recreate life in the early settlements. They were talking at a volume Brian Blessed would have been proud of. They were getting big laughs. It was pantomime. They were playing to the audience. I suddenly started to wish *I* was one of them. One of the lads. They were having a ball.

I changed my mind when I saw them push their boat off the pebbles and onto the waves. Even though it was mild and calm, the way their little boat rocked and swayed on the water made me yearn for the pleasures of the desk job. To think of the dangers faced every day by these men, the victims that their beloved sea had dragged into eternal nothingness. Incredible. Yet into their bouncing boat they hopped, laughing like naughty school children.

Allegedly, Sheringham's town motto was 'Mare Ditat Pinusque Decorat' which is Latin for 'The sea enriches and the pine adorns'. I must admit I'd never heard the phrase used in passing conversation. Certainly not in Latin.

Who do town councils, or whoever it is who selects these mottos, think they're fooling when they drop a little Latin in? Are they hoping casual passers-by will see the town sign and say to themselves, 'Ah, I see they're mainly speaking *Latin* in Sheringham now. I always knew they were a cut above'? You don't even see the phrase on novelty tea towels or mugs. They mostly say 'I'd Rather Be In Sheringham' instead.[1]

I don't know the Latin, but a translation of the phrase 'There are lots of good chip shops, pubs, and places to get ice cream' would be much more fitting.

I went home to check my Latin dictionary. The journey would start proper tomorrow.

My first trip was to include an early morning ride along the North Norfolk Railway. In *Around The World In 80 Days*, Phileas Fogg headed to Egypt first. With equal vigour, I'd

---

[1] A phrase that could easily give the ex-England footballer Teddy Sheringham the shudders.

plumped for Weybourne. The former being 2,344 miles away and the latter approximately three.

The train station was immaculate. I'd travelled back in time. Everything was from another era. In the ticket office, a fire crackled in the stove. Posters on the platform wall reminded you to have your ticket ready for the inspector and to *always* drink your cocoa and use Colman's mustard (preferably not at the same time). The only thing tainting the illusion of yesteryear was the massive Pay & Display car park on the other side of the track.

The sun shone. There was a rush of springtime in the air. The steam train was waiting. Forty towns and villages. I was one down already. Thirty-nine to go. Sheringham was always going to be easy, a gimme, a bye through to the next round. But now the call of public transportation had sounded. It could all get a little fraught. The adventure started here.

I placed my bag on the platform and bellowed, 'Porter, my luggage.'

Weybourne

I called 'Porter, my luggage' a good seventeen times before realising that the station hadn't decided to recreate that particular aspect of the Victorian train experience. I was going to have to deal with the luggage alone. And they call this progress, folks.

The thing with steam trains is that they peep and whistle and make a casual chugging noise even when stationary, so they constantly give the impression that they're about to depart. Even though I had ten minutes before the train was due to leave, and even though I was standing three feet away from my carriage, I still felt compelled to board as quickly as possible.

My sense of urgency was inspired by railway station scenes in black & white films. The characters were always in a rush. The moment the departing soldier shut the carriage door, the train would start pulling away, leaving his widow-to-be (we all know how these films end) weeping into her handkerchief. The soldier would then wave as his carriage disappeared into a noisy cloud of steam. I'd *never* seen an emotional farewell scene on a railway platform in which a lover boarded the train only for it to remain in the station another twenty minutes whilst said lover looked sheepishly out of the window. It just didn't happen like that. I'd been raised to believe that steam trains were nobody's fool. They pulled away. Fast.

So on I leapt. The carriage was empty. I wished it were this easy to get a seat on mainline trains. The carriage was more rugged than I'd expected. The wind whistled thinly through gaps in the doors and windows. I was on a *real* train. During Paul Theroux's tour of Britain's coast, he travelled on this branch line. He said that 'railway buffs were helping to dismantle British Rail' because they were never happier than 'when they were able to turn an old train into a toy.' The carriage didn't feel like a toy, although it certainly made me feel like a child again. I liked it. Weybourne wasn't even on my list of forty places, but I didn't want to just steam right through to Holt. I wanted to make the most out of the ride.

The carriage began to bounce up and down. We were on the move. It rocked with enough violence to shake the change in my pocket. This was excitement. I was on a rocket to Mars in an H.G Wells novel. The engine roared and screamed and off we went at that deceptive steam train pace; were we going fast or slow? Looking out of the window, I thought the NNR's owners would be wise to hire actresses to stand and weep into handkerchiefs as the trains pulled away. It was one for the Suggestion Box, at least. That, and a porter for my luggage.

Trains are a much more exciting mode of transport than buses and cars. Maybe it's the fact that railway lines use routes that no other forms of transport can, allowing you to see familiar things from unfamiliar angles. There is a certain romance to trains. Compare, for example, the lonely artistry of the last train home to the grim, ill-lit reality of the last bus. A delayed train is often cause for knowing shakes of the head and little jokes about privatisation. A delayed bus makes you question whether or not life is even worth bothering with.

Once away from the town centre, the view transformed from opulent townhouses and hotels to a panorama of Sheringham's cliff-top golf course. It was early but the course already had players. They were all performing that classic piece of golf body language: taking off their hats, rubbing their hair slightly, putting their hats back on. The North Sea provided the backdrop. It looked magnificent. It was dark blue. It made you want to jump in. If I'd been out on the course, I'd have thumbed my tee into a tuft of grass near the cliff and smashed golf balls into the sea all morning, shouting 'Fore' with each swing. Naturally, every now and then I'd stop to remove my hat, rub my hair slightly, and then put the hat back on. It would be a riot.

Pleasure, as we all know, is a short-lived thing. No sooner had I decided that the North Norfolk Railway was the *best thing ever* and that I really ought to ditch the day job and become a train driver than we arrived with a juddering, grinding halt at Weybourne station. The reverie was snapped. I had to get off and do some walking. I wandered along the platform. The reverie slipped back into view (unpredictable things, reveries). It was a beautiful old station, something you'd see in ITV family dramas about evacuees. It had been used as a location for an episode of *Dad's Army*. I can't say for sure which episode it was, but I think it was the one where things didn't go to plan.

The noticeable difference between this train line and a regular train line was that the North Norfolk Railway staff were clearly all delighted to be involved with the project. Every time I walked past two people wearing the official uniform, I'd overhear one say to the other, 'Well, nobody told *me* about it.' I'd heard the phrase used about ten times already that morning. It's a phrase people use when they care. It's also a phrase people use when they feel they ought to be involved with proceedings from a slightly higher position than that which they already hold.

I took my notebook out of my bag and realised that I'd forgotten to bring a pen. I was half an hour into my Norfolk odyssey and I'd already failed. Undeterred, I headed for the station gift shop. There was a box of NNR novelty pens just near the door. I took one to the till. It didn't have a price on it. This became a topic of great debate between the two elderly ladies assigned to deal with such purchases. I stood in silence as they deconstructed the crime:

'Someone hasn't priced the pens.'
'Aren't they all 75p?'
'I thought they were all a pound.'
'Whoever could have forgotten to price the pens!'
'I think all pens are a pound.'
'Well, nobody told *me*.'

I paid a pound and made my exit before it turned violent.

After five minutes' brisk walking, it became clear that the station was situated far enough from Weybourne for the name Weybourne Train Station to be seriously questioned by the Trade Descriptions Act 1968. The village church was still way over on the horizon. But at least it was downhill. For now.

The stiff breeze and enormous sky gave me extra zip as I strolled. I felt like singing aloud at the glory of it all. I passed a road sign that read 'Slow You Down'. There was something uplifting about it. Maybe it was the word 'You'. If the sign had said 'Slow Down', it would sound like a token gesture. The inclusion of 'You' added personality to a mere directive. 'Slow *You* Down' sounded like it was there for *my* benefit. It was, and is, a gentler, yet firmer, nudge. Anyone who's ever been asked to 'Sit you down' or 'Drink you up' in Norfolk will know of the warmth that the extra *you* gives.

For a village with such pleasant road signs, the origins of its name were darker. It derived from the term 'felon's stream'. Weybourne was where criminals were sent to be drowned.

Die You Now.

The church gate was locked and carried a warning that one entered the premises at one's own risk. 'Risk?' I thought, 'what nonsense.' I climbed over the adjacent one-foot wall with all the gaiety of a man who regularly laughed in danger's face. Two seconds later I was on the floor, wondering in precisely how many places my leg had been broken.

I was down. Done. Finished. Take me to the stream and drown me.

Disaster. I'd barely started my travels and I was already out for the count. As I'd climbed over the tiny wall, my left foot had slipped on the dewy grass whilst my right was lost in reverie and in no position to rush to the rescue. Whilst en route to my crumpled heap, I'd omitted a cry of pain similar to that of an old man upon seeing a ghost.

I grabbed onto the church gate and tried to pull myself up.

It worked. I was standing.

I was fine.

I'd survived my first scare. Regardless, it had served as a warning - I wasn't as nimble as I used to be. I made a note in my pad: 'Slow Me Down.'

The church was small and pretty, but, by Norfolk's high standards, not worth gawping at. The grounds were extremely well kept (I, for one, could vouch for the efficiency of the small wall around its perimeter). More noteworthy, perhaps, were the remains of a small 12th century priory at the end of the building. It had been founded by Sir Ralph de Meyngaren, which was the equivalent of the modern day Mainwaring. Stupid boy. The farmhouse behind it, incredibly, was still being used for its original purpose. It had been built in the 1300s.

I was pushed along by an ever-increasing wind. The beach consisted of steep shingle banks and little else.[1] Somehow it remained pleasing on the eye. I'd last been there on a Year 10 Geography field trip. We were sent home early after somebody stole some eggs from a nest. I've since toyed with writing the trip up in screenplay form and giving it to Ken Loach to direct.

The sea at Weybourne becomes dangerously deep dangerously quickly. You could dive in from two yards away. This is ideal for two things: one, for drowning criminals; two, for landing boats. It was the second of those perks that had occasionally caused concern. The following saying stemmed from the threat of the Spanish Armada:

'He who would all England win, should at Weybourne Hope begin.'

After the English soundly defeated the Armada,[2] the next genuine invasion threat came from Napoleon. Once he'd been thoroughly rogered and packed off to St Helena, Weybourne

---

[1] Smugglers used to bury themselves up to their necks in the Weybourne shingle whilst waiting for a delivery. Think about that the next time you complain about your job.

[2] They did this by arranging a wild storm to drive the enemy fleet up and around Scotland where nigh on half of it was shipwrecked. Clever, eh?

was left in peace until the threat of Nazi invasion. In 1939, the beach was treated to a refurb involving barbed wire and pillboxes, some of which were still on show. I spotted three on my journey along the cliff to the windmill. The doorways and rifle holes were bricked up, to stop teenagers getting in (although, having teenagers drinking in them is preferable to having teenagers shooting from them, if you ask me).

German Prisoners of War were later sent to seaside locations such as Weybourne to clear mines. In the summer of 1946, up to one hundred POWs worked on the beaches of Norfolk. 'We shall fight them on the beaches,' said Churchill, 'or, at the very least, get them to tidy up the beaches afterwards.'

Churchill twice visited Weybourne in the early stages of the war. He witnessed demonstrations of projectile firing at the Weybourne Camp (you might remember, this was the same camp that the Hindenburg came to have a cheeky butchers at). He was most displeased with the displays. He vowed to return seven days later, expecting to see an improvement. There wasn't one. He replaced the senior staff the following day. In the shadow of the Dunkirk retreat and those terrifying pictures of German soldiers eyeing up Kent from the French seaside, there was no time for messing about. 'Projectile Fire You Quickly' signs were hastily erected around the village.

I reached an isolated row of houses dangerously close to the cliff edge. The sea had almost claimed them. They couldn't have long left. One bad storm and they'd be gone. The building closest to the drop would soon be at the stage where it could advertise 'sea views' not only from the window of the master bedroom but also through the lounge floor.

Slightly further along, up a dirt road, away from the doomed houses, was Weybourne windmill, inhabited, during the early 1940s, by a Mr and Mrs Dodds. The couple were rumoured to have been involved in a German spy ring. Mrs Dodds, clumsily forgetting her first day's training at Spy School, had a thick German accent. People were suspicious. Policemen reported seeing lights flashing from the windmill's upper windows late in the evenings. If the couple *were* spies, they weren't in danger of getting a promotion anytime soon.

The final nail in the chances-of-getting-a-promotion coffin was hammered in on the evening Mrs Dodds left her bike unattended outside the village tennis court. It toppled over. A bag fell out of the basket. A radio transmitter fell out of the bag. The police were informed and the couple were taken away.[1]

I returned to the station with fifteen minutes to spare. Just off the platform was a model railway exhibit inside an old carriage. A sandwich board pointed the way.

'Is the model railway free?' I asked a porter.

'Yes, Sir.'

'Well,' I said, trying to fit in, 'nobody told *me*.'

Manning the model trains were a grandfather and grandson duo. The boy, no older than eleven, was bursting with excitement.

'Listen to that train, Grandad. That sound *rarely* real.'

It was the second week of the Easter holidays. Shouldn't he have been at home playing *Grand Theft Auto*? I didn't like to ask. It wasn't my place to interfere.

---

[1] Henry Williamson, author of *Tarka The Otter*, moved to nearby Stiffkey in the late 1930s to run a farm (arriving within weeks of the lion's-den-death of the village's 'prostitute's padre' - and even attending his funeral). When the war started, locals also accused him of being a spy. They had good reason to be dubious. Williamson's latest book, *The Story of a Norfolk Farm*, began with a charming quote about the spirit of the English age. Unfortunately the quote was by Britain's mercifully unconvincing Hitler impersonator, Oswald Mosley. Williamson was a fan.

The grandad was in charge of the miniature station, ensuring the little machines ran on time. The grandson was there to oversee proceedings; he ran up and down alongside the trains, knocking things off the shelves as he went, cheering as the engines buzzed around the tracks.

'That sound so real, Grandad! That's runnin' like a dream, that is.'

I asked the grandad if they'd had many visitors over the holidays.

'A few. Most people go to the Holt exhibit. It's bigger.'

In the distance a real steam train whistled its impending arrival. I was bound for the Georgian market town of Holt, where I would discover that the model railway was indeed bigger, but in no way was it better. How could it have been?

'Goodbye,' I said.

'Goodbye, Sir,' they replied.

I walked onto the platform and put my bag on the floor.

'Porter, my luggage.'

Holt

Just as at Weybourne, the train dropped me nowhere near the intended destination. You'd have thought with the stunning technological advances that locomotives represented in the 1800s, the least the blokes laying the tracks could have done was make the stations actually go where they were supposed to. I'd alighted in a village called High Kelling, on the edge of Holt.

Fortunately, there was an old red London bus to carry my weary limbs from the station to the town centre. It was called

The Holt Flyer. I couldn't tell if the name was supposed to be ironic.

I have no nostalgia for buses. They've caused me too much pain over the years. When I see these 'classic' ones get dolled up for re-use they remind me of cinema villains who just won't die. You know the type: they get shot in the head and tossed onto jagged rocks, then reappear in the finale with just a couple of bruises, and maybe a bandage around the eye.

The difference between old buses and old trains is that, in terms of comfort and grandeur, steam trains are finer machines than their modern day counterparts. Modern buses, on the other hand, are a vast improvement on the rickety nausea-inducers of the past. Sure, the oldies might be more aesthetically pleasing, but, if repeats of *The Waltons* on True Entertainment have taught me anything, it's that it's what's on the inside that counts.[1] And it's on the inside that the older buses fall short. The windows never open properly and they smell like dead farts.

The Holt Flyer got me to the town centre in minutes (although I must point out that it only flew *metaphorically*. I shall be having words with my MP). We passed the frankly enormous Gresham's school as we 'flew'. Cast your mind back to a few pages ago, and you'll remember that this was the public school founded by Beeston Priory's very own John Gresham. It began life as a school for boys but eventually felt the pull of history's tide and, after a mere four hundred years, began to educate smelly little girls.

Gresham's may have been slow to accept female students, but it was way ahead in other areas. It was one of the first public schools to abolish corporal punishment (doing so in the early 1900s). It was also the first to ban teachers from disdainfully

---

[1] *The Waltons* also taught me not to trust salesmen from out of town. They may initially seem very nice, but they're actually only interested in stealing your grandpa's civil war medals and trying to nob your eldest sister.

raising their left eyebrow when a child said something cheeky during morning register.

Gresham's alumni includes Sir Christopher Cockerill (inventor of the hovercraft - and the most common pub quiz answer in the UK after *Bohemian Rhapsody*); W.H. Auden ('Genius of the highest intellectual division which nobody could possibly be qualified to question,' was Morrissey's *qualified* assessment); Benjamin Britten (who, since death, has acquired the reputation of having perhaps taken an overly keen interest in boys); and Stalin's favourite spy, Donald Maclean (who worked doggedly alongside Churchill, Roosevelt, Atlee and Truman on Top Secret business during the daytime - then went home and traded these secrets with Russia at night, like twelve-year-old girls at a sleepover. It's not the same Don McLean who wrote the 1971 hit, *American Pie*). Other notable scholars were the founder of the BBC, Lord Reith (who once tried to escape the school on a bicycle), and Cromer-born multi-billionaire hoover enthusiast, James Dyson.[1]

My mum used to threaten to send me to boarding school if I kept misbehaving. It was a trick that usually worked. The idea of *living* at school and having to go in on *Saturdays*, sweet Lord, was always enough to temper my delinquency. If only I'd known then how difficult it is to get into boarding school, her threats would have landed on deaf ears. Gresham's would never have accepted a council house urchin like me, with my knotted hair and dreadful handwriting.

Imagine if my mum had gone through with the threat. Imagine her marching me up to Gresham's front office, knocking on the glass and saying, 'Take him in, will you? You can keep him for a year. I've had it up to here!'

---

[1] Although founded in 1555, it wasn't until the early 20th century that the school expanded and became nationally recognised. In fact, there were more students there in 1555 than there were in 1900.

The receptionist would look me up and down, then pull the prospectus out of the filing cabinet.

'Certainly, Madame. That will be £22,350.'

Holt was busy. It had a bypass but you wouldn't know it. There were cars *everywhere*. And not your average cars. Big cars. Big expensive cars; cars bought to manage the notoriously troublesome terrains of cul-de-sacs and gravel driveways - and to smash through the two inches of snow that blitzed the county every three or four years.

The town is famed for its independent shops and wandering celebrities. On any given day you might see Todd Carty down one alleyway and Les Dennis down the next. It's Rodeo Drive for the pantomime community. This was the first time I'd walked around Holt for two years. There were lots of new shops shoehorned into town cottages.

I went into four different nik-nak specialists. Little separated them. They all had a pretty, middle-aged lady on the till, busily cutting something with a pair of pink scissors. They all sold artificial flowers and things for children's bedrooms. They all had fairy lights around the square windows. They all smelt of fresh paint and perfume. They all sold decorative signs that read something along the lines of 'A Very Greedy Cat Lives Here' and 'Domestic Goddess In Action – Just Add Wine!' And in each was housed at least one strip of bunting. It was all frightfully independent.

I continued roving. I'd taken a packed lunch with me and eaten it too early (I've been doing that all of my life. I don't think I've ever eaten from a lunchbox after 11am). I was getting hungry but didn't feel in the mood to go into one of the many Holt eateries. They looked too trendy: places where boys called Tristan and Harry sat and decided whether or not to text Prudence and Ophelia. Stomping grounds for quilted jackets and new haircuts. I took my regular jacket and balding head as far as Albert's Fish Bar. The smell of salted chips blew into my face. Is there a nicer smell in all the world? I was sold. I took a table by the window and texted Ophelia. I told her that she could never hold a candle to Prudence and that whatever Tristan or Harry had said, it was all lies.

Holt was handsome. There was no denying that. It was a shame that so many of the fine townhouses were unlived in out-of-season. It was also a shame that the town centre was chock full of cars. But, still, it was attractive. The prominence of Georgian buildings was the result of a fire which razed the town to the ground in 1708. It tore through everything from the church roof to the butcher's market stalls. It was devastating (although many enjoyed the free barbecue). Had the fire not happened, Holt would have looked like the ethereal Lavenham in Suffolk.

I had to get to Fakenham. There are two must-see things in world travel. One is the Grand Canyon from the air. The other is Fakenham from a bus.

There was already a bus waiting at the stop. Whether it was the one I needed to catch, I couldn't tell. I was too far away. 'I hope that's the one,' I thought, as I lazed towards it at a pace usually adopted by bowls players during a particularly thoughtful shot. Then it dawned on me that if this *was* my bus, I'd need to get a move on. Missing a bus in Norfolk isn't like missing a bus in London or Manchester or Birmingham or anywhere. Missing a Norfolk bus is like missing a dentist appointment. You could be waiting months for the next.

I was still a good fifty yards away. I upped my pace, but not enough to look desperate. I didn't want to be *seen* running for a bus. It's depressing. Running for a train is poetic and evokes the golden age of romanticism. Running for a bus evokes grey Monday mornings and Job Centres.

In my haste, whilst making sure I avoided running, I strode in the manner of an Olympic speed walker: heel first, gyrating my hips with the vigour of Jayne Mansfield in *The Girl Can't Help It*. I was now close enough to the bus to hear its engine making those angry growls and hisses which inform the world that it's had just about enough of waiting around for latecomers, thank-you-very-much.

I still didn't know for sure if this *was* the bus I needed. I walked even faster, my backpack jumping about and sounding like house keys in a washing machine. I was so close. Close enough to read the bus number – it *was* the one I needed! Ten yards to go. I was going to make it! I gave myself to the moment and began running. Five yards. Almost there. Two. The bus door closed, making the following sound:

Piisssshhhhhhsssshhhh.

And off it went. I fell into a distorted heap. I looked up at an old woman sat on a bench. Lactic acid squeezed my muscles.

'Did you want that bus, love?' she asked.

'Ye...' I said, too bereft of air to put the 's' on the end. Why else would I have been sprinting towards it? To warn people of a bomb?

After ten minutes of quiet reflection on what it all meant, on whether life was all just a cruel joke, I regained composure. From the bus stop bench I visualised Holt how it used to be. I pictured the old market place in full swing (a market which began in the 1100s and ended in the 1960s). I wondered if the markets of the past sold similar stuff to the markets of today: primarily wolf fleeces and t-shirts depicting Native Americans riding Harley Davidsons.

Holt market was once a site for hangings. A royalist reverend was killed there on Christmas Day, 1650, and left to swing on a gibbet for the remainder of the festive period. He was left hanging as warning to anti-Cromwellians. Many came to stare at the corpse. Well, it was better than staying in and watching the repeats.

I had another meander around the town. I still hadn't seen any celebrities. Where were they hiding? Surely there was at least one *Emmerdale* cast member doing the rounds.
 At the far end of town was an obelisk with a pineapple-shaped apex. It was one of two gateposts from Melton Constable Park (a town once connected to Holt by train). The second pineapple topped obelisk was given to Dereham, where the townsfolk were so thoroughly delighted with the gift that they threw it down the nearest well, where it remains to this day. The Holt obelisk was bequeathed to the town in 1757. As there were no wells nearby, the locals kept it.

As we left Holt, the bus cut through a housing development on the other side of the bypass. It was Holt's very own *wrong side of the tracks*. As deprived areas go, Holt's wasn't the type you'd expect to hear Tom Waits sing about. There weren't any disused freight carriages or hobos in fingerless gloves. It all looked perfectly fine. But behind the façade was the reality that Holt, playground of the wealthy, also happened to be north Norfolk's child poverty capital.
 A recent national survey discovered that a quarter of Holt children were existing below the poverty line. The town was among the top ten percent of the *country's* most deprived areas. This little Georgian shopping hotspot for the affluent ('well-heeled' was the nicely diplomatic phrase used by the regional newspaper) was home to some of England's poorest children. It was almost laughable. Almost. Prudence and Ophelia weren't the only kids in town. They seldom are.

Fakenham

The chunk of land between Norwich, the fens and the coastal towns, represents Norfolk at its most raw. I'm tempted to say, with a touch of apprehension, that it's *real Norfolk*. It was to this chunk of land that I was headed next.

The bus passed through villages such as Briston and Melton Constable (original home of the pineapple obelisks, as you'll no doubt recall with a knowing raise of the eyebrow) and many more. Unlike the coastal towns, in these mid-Norfolk villages and hamlets you'd find few art galleries, bunting specialists or holiday homes. These were the places where people from Norfolk *lived*. It was a land of fields, Spar shops, bus stops, bungalows, allotments and war memorials. This was the part of the county where you were the most likely to see tables on pavements selling home-grown carrots, potatoes, runner beans, eggs, everything. Sometimes the food was given away:

'NEw PotAt's – tAke theM ThEiR FrEE.'

The bus travelled miles without seeing anything but farmland and would then zip past four isolated semi-detached council houses in a row, before the fields resumed their dominance. The pattern repeated itself. Nothing, then houses. Nothing, then houses. At least one in four houses had front gardens that had been converted into makeshift junkyards. Stripped cars and farm machinery engines were littered about their wisps of grass. The junkyard garden is *real Norfolk's* calling card. The great thing about them is they are usually next door to the owners of the world's tidiest gardens. On one side of the hedge are broken mopeds and canoes full of rainwater, on the other, perfectly pruned rose bushes and lawns trimmed with nail scissors.

To walk through this part of the county is to truly immerse yourself in it. I hoped to get a chance to do so during my tour. It is dreamily silent. Birdsong, yes. The bark of a dog, yes. A moth hitting a window, yes. BBC Radio Norfolk, yes. Little else. A car can be heard approaching five minutes before it arrives. The only other noise you'll hear is your own.

The isolated rows of houses became more frequent until they merged into one. We were in Fakenham. On the outskirts were hastily erected chain pubs and a Morrisons supermarket. There was also a bus depot. I packed my camera away.
It felt like a Sunday. I wasn't surprised. Fakenham lived in an eternal Sunday. It moved at its own tempo. I had the town to myself. Having spent the morning in Holt, being barged off the heaving pavement and into the even more heaving road, I initially found Fakenham's deserted feel liberating. After about ten minutes, however, it became a little worrying; this was precisely how films about the zombie apocalypse started.
Where was everyone? It was a glorious afternoon in the school holidays but could easily have been a cold night on the moon. I looked for signs of life. There were two people sitting outside a pub in the stately town square. An old lady walked by the war memorial. A car passed through. I could hear myself breathing. This couldn't be right. When was the last time you heard the sound of your own breath in the middle of a town? *The only other noise you'll hear is your own.* I cupped my ear and tried to hear moths hitting windows.
The town centre was a mixture of majestic open spaces and winding side-streets that, regardless of which direction I headed, invariably lead me to the back of Argos. I somehow made my way back to the centre and surveyed the scene. No Norfolk town could rival Fakenham for the sheer amount of empty shop

space. 'To-Let' signs hung in dusty windows. The rooms were empty.[1]

I walked up to the church. Positioned on a slight incline, it was the dominant feature of the town. I was halted by the sound of activity from inside. Surely this wasn't where everyone had been hiding? I approached the door but before I could move any closer it opened from within. Out came a coffin carried by pallbearers. Three mourners and a vicar trailed behind, their footsteps audible. Even the funerals were short on numbers. The casket may have been empty.

Fakenham hadn't always been so sleepy. It was formerly a thriving industrial centre. It had a gasworks (which was now the country's only surviving gasworks factory, despite having closed in 1965) and was a major wheel in the printing industry. Its main printworks, Cox & Wyman - who might sound like a progressive jazz duo, but were most definitely not - closed in the 1970s. The town still had a number of printing firms but not on the scale of centuries past.

For all its ennui, there was something about Fakenham that felt kingly. Maybe it was the open market place and tall, Georgian buildings. It was like walking around an unoccupied manor house. Echoes of the past bounced off the walls.

The gasworks had been converted into the intriguingly named Museum of Gas & Local History. (Gas and local history - not the most obvious bedfellows. It made me think what other unique combinations were out there: The Museum of Shakespeare & Windsurfing? The Magical World of Lamps & Horses?) It was shut. I'd vowed not to go to museums but this was one exception I was willing to make. According to its

---

[1] Except for the token copy of the *Yellow Pages* on the floor in the corner. Why do all empty shop premises have old *Yellow Pages* books in them?

website, it was 'Open Thursday Mornings' in spring. It staged an enticingly named 'Old Lorries Slideshow' and even had a room displaying second-hand gas cookers. I'm not making this up. I can't begin to tell you how upset I was that it wasn't Thursday morning. Long live the Museum of Gas & Local History.

I went for a cup of tea in a café. I was the only customer. I'd been the only person on the high street, except for the coffin carriers (and the person inside it, if there was one), so I expected to be the only customer wherever I went.
It was a cosy, angular little room. Every step I took I felt my backpack grazing against things, threatening to knock them over. I daren't move. I took it off and found a seat by the window from which I could sit and watch the world not go by. The waitress brought my tea over.
'Is it always this quiet?' I asked.
'In the afternoons, yeah. You couldn't move in here this morning.'
I didn't mention that I hadn't been able to move in there *three minutes* ago.
'The oldies come here in the morning,' she added. 'They go home after that.'
It was a sweeping generalisation but it did ring true. There are often more old people roaming about in the mornings than there are in the afternoons. Maybe they're all coming home from raves.
A middle-aged gentleman entered, possibly from having just competed in the World's Happiest Man competition. He had a bum-bag around his ample waist.
'Cuh, hass quiet!' he yelled.
'I know. We had pletty in this morning, though.'

'Oi dint! Hahahaha. Oi dint have hardly noo cussmers again! Cuh! Hahahaha,' he roared, before striding towards the exit. 'Si'yalata!'
'Yeah. Si'yalata, Brian.'
'Chairs.'
'Chairs.'
Silence returned. There aren't enough Brians in the world. How do these characters remain constantly elated? He'd effectively told us that his business was struggling yet had made it all sound like an enormous caper that was bound to have a happy ending.[1]
I'd spilt sugar granules over the tablecloth and left a puddle of tea from where I'd taken the spoon out after stirring.
'Sorry,' I said, paying the bill, 'I've made a bit of a mess of myself.'
It sounded like I'd soiled my underwear.
'Thass alright.'
'Si'yalata,' I said.
'Chairs. Si'yalata.'
I walked back onto the empty high street, through the market place. The sky was blue. Legend claimed that it rained on Fakenham market days because of a witch's spell. Apparently the Fakenham market was previously in the witch's hometown of Walsingham. The move annoyed her; she clearly had a

---

[1] He was the polar opposite of my mum, who can dress-up the most asinine news in catastrophic terms:
'Ryan,' she says, breathing heavily down the receiver, 'I've got some news. Don't worry, alright, don't worry.'
Oh, God. I instantly picture every other member of my family being trapped on an exploding mini-bus. I close my eyes and brace myself.
'It's bad news.'
Deep breath. 'What's happened?'
'It's the tumble dryer...'
End of conversation. My loved ones get back off the imaginary minibus until the next phone call.

partiality for local business not found in your average devil worshipper. She cast her spell, declaring, 'There will be more wet than dry days for Fakenham market!'

Rather than making it occasionally rainy, the witch may have been better off using her mystical powers to *stop the market from moving in the first place*. But, then, I don't really know how these things work. I'd need to go and bone up at the Museum of Markets & Witches before I could make further comment.

Walsingham

I spent the night at a friend's in a small village just outside Fakenham. The next morning I took an early bus from Fakenham to Walsingham (which consisted of two villages, Little and Great Walsingham). Fakenham *was* busier in the morning, with young people as well as old. It was market day, but the weather had held. The rainmaking witch clearly didn't have complete control over the meteorological situation.

The bus arrived on time. The landscape changed from relatively flat town sprawl to the type of green, hilly paradise usually depicted on tins of shortbread.

'Very flat, Norfolk,' wrote Noel Coward. The line might need amending. I suggest, 'Surprisingly hilly in places, Norfolk.' I'll submit the change to the Noel Coward Society and see what they say.

Incredibly, of the forty towns and villages listed by the Norfolk Tourist Information website, Walsingham didn't feature. After the larger urban areas of Norwich and Great Yarmouth, Walsingham was probably the county's most famous location. Outside of Britain, it was possibly *the* most famous. Every year hundreds of thousands of worshippers made pilgrimages to its numerous religious hotspots. Not only was it a holy destination for the global community of Catholics, Anglicans and Hindus, but the toilets on the high street were the only Grade I listed bogs in the country. I had to visit.

Walsingham's story began in 1061 when Richeldis de Faverches, a local noblewoman, saw a vision of the Virgin Mary, who proceeded to show her what Jesus' home in Nazareth had looked like. Richeldis was instructed by Mary to build a replica of the house. Richeldis then did what anybody would do in that situation: she grabbed the Black & Decker workbench out of the shed and got to work, possibly drawing some strange looks from villagers in the process.

'It's alright,' she said to the bemused onlookers, 'I'm just building a replica of the house of Jesus based on the design print given to me by the ghost of his mum.'

One night, whilst reading that month's copy of *WhichReplica*, Richeldis heard the sound of singing from the garden. She went out to discover that her replica had been moved two hundred yards away. It had also been completely finished.[1] She saw angels fly away from it. The Virgin Mary told her that the house should be a place of pilgrimage:

'Let all who are in any way distressed or in need seek me there in that small house that you maintain for me at Walsingham. To all that seek me there shall be given succour.'

As the apparition faded, Richeldis de Faverches vowed to spread word of the miracle. And to look up what 'succour' meant in the dictionary.

---

[1] It was ensconced in stone and contained a carving of mother Mary on a throne with baby Jesus in her lap (the classic family photograph pose).

The legend of the shrine grew. Miracles and healings occurred to those who visited it. Its popularity soared. It was said in the Middle Ages that every man in England should visit Walsingham at least once in his life. (History is quiet with regards to what was said about *women* visitors. Not much, I guess. After all, it only contained a statue of a woman based on a vision revealed to a woman by a woman.)

The earliest Walsingham pilgrimages are laced with mystery but we do know that the pilgrims returned to their hometowns with tales of miracles and answered prayers. Once news of Walsingham's wonders reached the royal court in Greenwich, its fame was complete. Soon every royal worth their salt was coming to pay Our Lady of the Shrine a visit. Walsingham quickly became world famous to all except the Norfolk Tourist Information website.

People travelled from around the globe, arriving in boats at nearby King's Lynn, Cley, Weybourne and Wells, before completing the journey on foot. They must have been delighted that the vision of Our Lady had chosen to appear in one of the parts of Norfolk that had hills; the first thing most pilgrims prayed for on arrival was that their feet wouldn't need to be amputated.

Walsingham became home to priories and friaries. It was known as England's Nazareth.[1] Among its visitors were Henry III, Edward I (the nasty king in *Braveheart* – who was actually not too bad an egg. He once stood up during a heated game of chess and a huge piece of stone fell from the ceiling and landed in his vacant chair. He said he had been protected by Our Lady of the Shrine), Edward II (the gay prince in *Braveheart* – who

---

[1] Walsingham would be a good name for a Nazareth tribute band. Although getting the reference does require a basic knowledge of key medieval pilgrim sites, which maybe the atypical Nazareth fan doesn't have listed in the Personal Interests section of their CV.

fathered five children by two different women. Although he did have homosexual relationships and was believed, by some, to have been murdered by having red-hot pokers inserted into his bottom. This allegedly happened in Castle Rising in Norfolk. It's all pretty unlikely, though. Hilariously, one historian, Michael Prestwich, claimed that Edward's grim death had been sensationalised and 'belonged to the world of romance rather than of history.' Romance!), Edward III, Henry VI and Henry VIII, who initially enjoyed the charming little village but would eventually adopt a spikier outlook. Other visitors included Anne Boleyn and Catherine of Aragon, both of whom came during their husband's 'You know, I actually quite like Walsingham' phase.

The 16th century thinker, Erasmus, also paid a visit, writing, 'Our Lady stands in the dark at the right side of the altar... a little image, remarkable neither for its size, material or workmanship.'

It was harsh criticism, considering the shrine was made by angels; building and labouring can't be too high on their list of set skills - they're better at harp playing and lending people money at airports. The UKIP candidate of the time suggested that if Erasmus didn't like it he could always bugger off back to Rotterdam. Erasmus tried to cool tensions by conceding that the water from the village's natural spring was 'efficacious in curing pains of the head and stomach.'

'Yeah,' the people replied, 'you're saying that *now*.'

The shrine was destroyed in the anti-Catholic rumblings of 1538. Our Lady was taken to Lambeth and burnt. The main priory was burnt, also, as was just about anything else with a Catholic bent. Walsingham was the hands-down winner of that year's 'England's Warmest Village' competition. The Slipper Chapel, on the periphery of the village, however, survived. It had often been the last port of call for pilgrims, the final stop on their journey to Walsingham. For me, though, it was the first.

I'd started my pilgrimage *in* Walsingham and I was walking *out* of it. I liked to do things differently.

It was ideal walking weather. Still sunny, still cool. The village was fast asleep.[1] The only noise was birdsong and distant farm machinery. The walk between the village and the Slipper Chapel was called the Holy Mile. After walking it for fifteen minutes, I began to wonder whether 'Mile' was the word they were after.

A stream ran alongside the lane. To my left were green hills, to my right, yellow fields of rape. There were no pavements so I was walking on a grassy verge. Even there, in the most beautiful of landscapes, scraps of litter were strewn. I saw a discarded can of Relentless and a packet of Skips dating, at a glance, from 2004.[2]

There was a Mars Drink bottle amidst the flowers, providing evidence that it had sold at least one unit since its creation. What kind of arsehole could walk through this idyllic English setting and bung a bottle of Mars Drink into a hedge? (Probably the same kind of arsehole who would think to buy a Mars Drink to start with.) The further I walked, the more litter I saw: Smarties tubes; Rizla papers; boiled sweet wrappers; scratchcards. It was maddening.

I'd walked a good two miles' worth of Holy Mile with no Slipper Chapel in sight. Maybe I was heading in the wrong

---

[1] I passed a friary under renovation. It was covered in protective plastic sheets and scaffolding. The monks at the village's main priory were sceptical of the friary when it was built in 1347. They thought that the friars would try and steal jewels from their shrine. Which is precisely what happened. The local Cash Converters had a field day.

[2] I could be wrong about the date. It's hard to say anything about Walsingham's history with certainty. It could have been a packet of Skips from 1623.

direction. To make matters worse, there were issues in my down-below region. The last thing I needed was more walking. I hadn't packed the Anusol. And even if I had, this was hardly the ideal location in which to try and apply it.

Then, as if sent from above, a Nissan Micra pulled up beside me. The window came down.

'Slipper Chapel?' asked an elderly voice.

'No, it's Ryan,' I answered. 'I think the Slipper Chapel is further down the road.'

Ignoring my hilarious quip, he asked if I'd like a lift. I hopped in. On the passenger seat was a ring-shaped cushion. Our Lady may have been torched in Lambeth, but she was still performing miracles in Walsingham.

'It's a lovely part of the world,' the driver told me. 'I retired here.'

As we talked it hit home just how long this Holy Mile was. My bottom would never have survived.

'Here we are,' he said, as we pulled into the car park.

I like it when old people let you know when you've arrived somewhere.

The chapel was fenced within the confines of a modern Catholic church, complete with neatly tended gardens and gift shop. I exited the car, sad that I'd never see the old chap again. I shook his hand. I wanted to take a picture of him for my collection but didn't have the nerve to ask.

'I'm ninety-years-old,' he told me with pride.

'Wow. And you've still got more hair than me!'

He laughed at this one. Everybody does.

The entrance looked the same as any one of Norfolk's many churches and chapels. It had a stone archway and a large wooden door. The door was locked. Visitors were required to use an alternative opening around the back of the building. Before doing so, I touched the main archway and thought of the people who had done so in the past. Had Henry III leant upon this arch whilst considering removing a stone from his shoe? Had Henry VIII leant upon this arch whilst considering removing a head from one of his wives?

The Slipper Chapel was built in 1340. It was where pilgrims removed their footwear in order to walk the Holy Mile barefoot to the Shrine of Our Lady. Some modern-day pilgrims still walked the journey barefoot, but I strongly recommend getting a lift in a Nissan Micra. It was named the Slipper Chapel not because you'd wish you had some slippers after walking to it, but because of the old word 'slype', meaning slide. One would *slide* out of England and into the Holy Land. (One might also slide quite effectively on slippers, but we won't go into that.)

After the Reformation, the chapel was used as everything from a poorhouse to a cow shed, proving that if you leave any building alone for long enough in Norfolk, someone will stick cows in it. It was bought in 1896 by a local and donated to the church. It was re-established as a shrine by the pope one year later. In 1934 it had its first public mass in four hundred years. Ten thousand people made the pilgrimage. It was renamed the Catholic National Shrine of Our Lady.

I slyped in via the all-new entrance. I was faced with two options. I could either go left into the chapel proper, or right, into a room of lighted candles. It was stony silent. There were one or two people walking around the grounds outside. I headed towards the chapel. My rubber shoes squeaked with every move.

It was tiny. Barely room to swing a catholic.[1] There was another person in there. He'd got straight down to business, praying on his knees. Next to the door was a Dimplex radiator. Had any kings or queens ever leant on that, too?

---

[1] Worst pun ever?

I tried to remain silent for the benefit of the praying man, but every time I flexed even the most minute muscle, my shoes squawked like an aggrieved parrot:

'Cawarkkkk! Eeeeeaaaccchhh! Awarrrrrkkkk.'

The man didn't flinch. I hoped he hadn't travelled too far to be there. He was praying to a stone statue of the Virgin Mary. The statue had been blessed by Pope John Paul II at Wembley Stadium in 1982. The blessing had to be hurried, though, as Spandau Ballet were keen to do their sound-check.

I squeaked along the passageway to the room of candles (I'm sure it had a proper name). It smelt of birthdays and magic. My shoes were so creaky that I was beginning to sound like a mobile haunted house. I lit a candle. As ever, my accompanying prayer was that I wouldn't drop it. I always think I'm going to accidentally burn down a church and become infamous in the respective area for having done so.

The candle was lit. No fire. This time.

A woman entered. She was wearing the single most daring pair of shorts I'd ever seen. They were luminous pink and green. They were so small that if you reworked the material there wouldn't have been enough to make a baby's sock. I tried not to look but didn't know how to resist. She bent down to pray. How, I'll never know. It was a miracle. A vision. But not worth commemorating in shrine form. It's one of life's cruellest jokes that people with the least desirable flesh are often the ones who are most eager to put it on display.

On my way out, the chapel bells began to toll. The sky was clear and everything sang. Ah, springtime. I walked back along the Holy Several Miles into Walsingham. It's not often you feel as though the world is good and that everything works out for the best, but that was my frame of mind. I felt like Brian from Fakenham. I wanted to belt out a song. Instead, I took a bottle of Mars Drink out of my bag, necked the contents, and tossed it into the nearest hedge.

*

I ate at a restaurant called Swallows. Spits was closed. The Swallows menu seemed to have been designed specifically with me in mind. I ordered Cornish pasty, chips and beans. Such cuisine may make many readers' toes curl, but this, my friends, is how your hero prefers to dine. I'd walked myself up an enormous appetite and the food tasted as only pasty, chips and beans can taste: heavenly. The place smelt of village primary school cafeterias. My serotonins gushed. The tea arrived in a pot big enough to drown a goose – and came with an *extra* jug of hot water. The waitress was also the chef. She took my order and headed straight to the kitchen. I was the only customer. It was as if I'd walked into someone's house and demanded they cook my lunch.

On the wall by the till were signed black & white headshots of equally satisfied clientele. Household favourites such as Beadle, Bruno, Tarrant, Schofield, the two off *Birds of a Feather* and Inspector Lewis peered across the room. The pilgrimage clearly still drew the higher reaches of society. Either that or Walsingham did a blinding panto.

I was tempted to hike back up to the Slipper Chapel and touch the archway again, visualising Pauline Quirke removing a stone from her shoe instead of Henry III. Or Chris Tarrant beheading his wife.

After settling up, I took a look around the village's ancient maze of side-streets. I lost track of what century it was. Was it 2014 or 1714? Two elderly nuns walked by, fully gowned. Their feet made a pleasant clopping sound on the pavement. They must have had heels on underneath.

I got lost several times. There seemed to be no logic to the alleyways. They never seemed to lead where I thought they would. It was as though the town was half made of mirrors.

Maybe it was all a trick of the mind. Walsingham didn't really exist. Somebody would shake me and I'd wake up on the bus.

A sign read that the Slipper Chapel was *precisely* one mile away. Nothing made sense.

At every turn I was confronted with an old market square or an old hall or an old hotel or an old school or an old red phone box. Tufts of weeds grew through gaps in the pavements and edges of the clumsily tarmacked roads. Up close, the buildings seemed in need of work. The paint was splitting on the window frames. The cement between the brickwork was cracking and crumbling. I'd never seen so many nets in windows. Behind them were dark, hollow rooms. The houses weren't unlived in but I got the impression that the owners were, like the village, aged and devout, expert in the economy of movement.

I found myself back where the bus had dropped me. At something resembling a high street from before the age of steam. It was a mixture of charity endeavours and religious iconography specialists (and, plonked on the end, a chain-store mini-market). Most sold postcards of the latest pope and classic popes. There were plastic recreations of Our Lady to go on the dashboard of the car or on top of the television set. This form of money spinning used to sit uneasily with the angrier, youthful version of myself, but I now felt affection for it. I went into one of the Christian charity shops. The lady on the till had a rich Irish accent. I mentioned the mystical atmosphere.

'Oh, yes,' she said, 'Walsingham does have a special air. You can feel God's presence here alright. You can also feel the opposite of it, too. There are battles in the air.'

I could have listened to her all day.

'I volunteer here. Isn't God great, Ryan? I'm retired now. I'm eighty-years-old. Would you believe it?'

She looked about forty. She was the second person in the village to have shared her age with me. We spend most of our lives hiding our age, treating it as though it were a prison

number that we'd rather forget, and then, at some point, it becomes an affirmation, shared with anyone who'll listen.
I told her about this book.
'Oh! That sounds splendid! What an adventure! Isn't life marvellous? What a time you'll have!'
'Maybe when I've written it I can come back and donate a copy for you to sell.'
'Oh, now! Wouldn't that be an occasion for coffee and cake?'
I agreed that it would. As I left the shop she called out, 'Enjoy it, Ryan! Enjoy it. Enjoy it.'

After the shrine had been built (by angels or otherwise), Richeldis' son, Geoffrey, left plans for a priory on the same site. It was built (by builders or otherwise) in the 12th century and burnt, of course, in the 16th. It had been at least 48 hours since I'd seen a ruined priory, so I decided to give it a visit. I had to enter via the Shirehall Museum. After missing out on Fakenham's museum of Gas & Roof Tiles, or whatever it was called, it felt right to have a little nosey.
After twenty minutes of myself and the lady on the till each trying to work out what the other was saying, in increasingly raised voices, I managed to buy a ticket.[1] The museum walls were covered in primitive photographs of the village. They were scary. Almost every one had at least one little girl lingering in the background, white gowned, with dead-looking eyes rolling in her head. Why must all black & white street photographs have a terrifying little girl in them?:
'I do believe the image is ready to be taken now,' says the photographer.

---

[1] She started the conversation by mishearing me: she thought I wanted to *know* about the abbey, whereas I actually wanted to *go* to the abbey. The conversation went downhill from there.

'Aren't you forgetting something, Sir?' asks his young assistant.
'Oh, my, yes! The terrifying little girl! I'd forget my head if it wasn't screwed on. Go and fetch her, would you, please?'

There was display of weapons used by Walsingham law enforcers of yesteryear. There was a mantrap on show. Like a rabbit trap, but for men. It was all a bit creepy.

The museum was once a courthouse. It had been used, on and off, from 1778 through to 1974. The courtroom was exactly as it had been left four decades ago. Visitors were permitted to walk around, to stand in the dock or sit in the judge's chair. I did so, alone. My footsteps fractured the silence. Many defendants were sent to a correction house down the road. And many were hanged. The room felt sickeningly alive. Battles in the air. I went outside.

In the vast, grassy abbey grounds, sunlit flowers were coming to life. Birds fluted their latest singles from the trees. The grounds were effectively a wild garden with the occasional chunk of priory wall popping out. A map of the original priory showed just how huge the thing once was. It was a city within a village. Standing in the heart of the grounds was the largest remaining piece. An arch. It was magnificent.[1]

I was walking with the past. Just how many other major and minor players in British history had walked these same paths? The girls from *Birds of a Feather* had, for one (or two). Walsingham monks and nuns were taught that the Milky Way pointed to Walsingham. Some villagers still referred to it as the

---

[1] For all the unpleasantness of the Dissolution, the literal tearing down of the monasteries was in itself an impressive feat. Imagine trying to knock a church down without modern machinery or dynamite. Where would you start?

Walsingham Way. No wonder the place felt special. Even the stars led towards it.

The year before the priory's destruction, eleven of its inhabitants had been tried for conspiring against the suppression of England's smaller monasteries. They'd had an inkling that seeing as the smaller monasteries were getting torched, the big ones were maybe going to be in for it, too. The eleven suspects were hanged outside the priory walls and chopped up as a warning to anyone who expressed concern at the way things were going. Within a year, their priory was no more. All of its gold and silver was taken to London and spent. Our Lady, as mentioned, was torched. The following lines were written (attributed to the Earl of Arundel) later that century:

Weepe, weepe O Walsingham,
Whose dayes are nightes,
Blessings turned to blasphemies,
Holy deeds to dispites

Sinne is where our Ladie sate,
Heaven turned is to hell,
Sathan sittes where our Lord did swaye,
Walsingham oh farewell

You may recall my mentioning of Walsingham's house of correction. It was where people generally went after a session in the courtroom and it was where I was headed next. I had to pick up the prison keys from the Shirehall Museum's front desk. This gave me a chance to have another protracted conversation with the lady on the till, in which neither party was entirely clear what the other wanted.

After ten minutes of loud talking and expressive sign language, I was given the keys. I was going direct to jail. The wind had settled and the air had started to warm. My trusty big coat became my enemy. Too hot to wear and too cumbersome to carry, I wore it unzipped, cape-like. I was the worst superhero ever created. Is it a bird? Is it a plane? No, it's CoatMan.

The more I walked, the stickier the air became. Where the hell was this prison? My back was pumping out enough sweat for it to become Walsingham's second natural spring. I was conscious of the time. My miniature train ride to Wells was going to be leaving soon.

'Excuse me,' I asked a teenaged girl, who, as far as I could tell, was watching a man from the council strimming grass. 'Do you know where the prison is?'

She gave up her vantage point of the grass-cutting action and walked me to the tall (unmissable, I might add) red brick prison. I had been about twenty yards from it the whole time.

'This is the way. Come on,' she said.

She darted around a corner. I followed her. I was confronted with a caged, padlocked door. For all the weather's clemency, the afternoon was starting to take on a slasher film aspect. As buildings went, this wasn't one for the front cover of *Town & Country* magazine. Where once there were windows: bricks. Where once there was life: dead air.

Clouds raced in front of the sun, creating fast moving shadows.

'Just unlock it and go in.'

'Is there anyone inside?' I asked.

'There might be.'

I couldn't deduce if this was her way of warning me about the neighbourhood throat slitter who liked to hang around the joint this time of year.

'Right. Thank you.'

'That's ok,' she said. She smiled and ran off. In the distance the strimmer kicked back into life, pleased to have its audience back.

I unlocked the door. Everything needed forcing. The key was stiff, the bolts were jammed, the door was heavy. I pushed it open and was confronted with a darkness punctuated by thin shafts of day from square, iron-barred windows. They gave just enough light for me to see a corridor of open cell doors. On the museum's website I'd read that the prison has survived 'virtually untouched.' This had seemed like a good thing. Before I was standing in there on my own.

I walked forwards in the gloom.

I approached the first cell, slowly. The metallic door was partly open. I craned my neck gingerly around to peek inside.

There it was! Horror. Flesh! An upright corpse! Good God! A mad, dead witch.

'Fuck my eyes!' I screamed.

I shall never know why I chose those specific words.

Relief. It was a dummy. Life-size. There were pieces of laminated text on the wall. She was a former inmate. That was as much as I read. I didn't fancy hanging around to learn the intricacies of the case. Maybe she'd tried to make it rain on Fakenham market day.

I carried on down the row of cell doors, expecting to see something equally horrific in each. They were all empty. This didn't relax me. I reached the end of the row. I was as far from the exit as possible. Then I felt it. An iced hand on the back of my neck.

I turned to see nothing but a cold cell door. It had merely brushed against me. Hadn't it? I must have caught it on my coat as I'd walked past. Mustn't I?

Then, from upstairs, footsteps! So there *was* someone in here. But, wait, *I* had the key.

Whenever you watch a horror film you spend most of it yelling, 'Don't go over there, you idiot! You're going to get killed!' If my trip was turned into a Hollywood movie, this would be the moment where everyone watching would shout, 'Just get out, you twat!' Yet, for some reason, I felt compelled to go upstairs and see who was up there. I don't know why. I guess it was similar to the phenomena of those perfectly normal people who fling themselves into Niagara Falls on family holidays. I was caught in the moment.

I crept up the stairs. I should let it be known that, even in the midst of terror, I was gently whistling *I've got the key, I've got the secret*' by the Urban Cookie Collective just because I had a key in my hand.

The sight at the top was familiar: a long row of cell doors, temptingly ajar in the manmade twilight.

'Hello?' I called.

Nothing.

Then a shuffling.

I recalled reading that the prison was built on the site of a leper colony. Maybe an old, chained leper was dragging himself towards me through the dark. Imagine that! A transparent Peter Beardsley covered in sores. No, thank you. I wasn't going to fling myself into Niagara Falls. I wasn't the type. I got my head down and marched towards the exit, refusing to look up. I made a complete pig's ear of locking the door. It's probably still open. Beardsley may have escaped.

Out in the daylight everything looked safe. I returned the keys to the woman on the Shirehall till and said I'd found it all incredibly interesting.

'No, we don't sell t-shirts,' she replied.

Wells-Next-The-Sea

When you've just had the shit scared out of you in a derelict 18th century prison, I often find that there's nothing to cool the nerves quite like riding along a miniature railway line.

Despite my initial worries, I arrived at the station[1] in time to see the train pop into view on the horizon i.e. about twelve yards away. Ten minutes later, it was halfway between the station and the horizon i.e. about six yards away. And a further ten minutes later it had arrived. Normally when a train pops into view in the distance, you have about twenty seconds to get your stuff together. With this train there was enough time to knit a scarf.

The station and the train were reassuringly busy. Nobody, and I mean nobody, likes to see a miniature train bereft of custom. They must lead a precarious existence. When regular railway lines are threatened with being pulled up, those doing the pulling are usually opposed by campaigns and strongly worded letters to newspapers. I can't imagine anyone ever fighting quite so valiantly to protect a miniature railway.

The engine had had a long day. Steam was wheezing from its little lungs. It was hard to believe something so small had the power to drag so many packed carriages. I became concerned that I might be required to pedal.

The carriages were, of course, also small. It was surreal seeing adults getting in them. It was even more surreal to join them. I genuinely don't know what I would have done if I were an inch taller. Maybe I could have laid on the roof, tied to it like a mountain bike on a Vauxhall Astra in high summer.

---

[1] Not so much a station as an embankment with a Walsingham sign hammered into it.

Miniature railways represent how the Industrial Revolution might have looked if it had ever hit Hobbiton. How did these little machines come into being? Who funded the miniature train business? Who, more importantly, agreed to drive the bloody things?

Whilst in situ, the conductor walked past each carriage, shutting the doors. A conductor shutting doors on a train carriage never fails to get me excited. It always gives a sense of adventure, even if, as in this case, the carriage wasn't big enough for me to check my watch without smashing the window with my elbow.

I wondered if there'd been a midget version of Dr Beeching who went around closing miniature railway lines in the 1960s. I asked the conductor but he neither knew the answer nor, it seemed, appreciated the question.

The engine gave a pathetic miniature peep and off we puffed. With a deep sense of regret, I realised I hadn't visited Walsingham's Grade I toilets. I almost jumped off the train and ran back.

We passed fields, secluded country manors, hedgerows, woodlands, farmland, dusty pathways. Sat opposite me was a look-alike and sound-alike of Lord Grantham from *Downton Abbey*. He was wearing salmon pink shorts. He had three sons with him. From what I could gather they were all called James. He spent most of the journey telling them off.

Go to any tourist attraction and you'll spend the majority of the day either telling children off or listening to someone else doing it. It's something that family attractions are keen to keep off their brochures. All pamphlets for zoos, theme parks, museums etc. should, by rights, include at least *one* colour photo - amidst all the shots of open-mouthed fathers and laughing mothers pointing at a tank of jellyfish - of a dad leaning into his child's periphery and pointing heatedly, whilst the mum searches her purse for a wet wipe. To omit such a picture would be flagrant false advertising.

The name Wells came about because its occupants used to tap into water reserves via the digging of, wait for it, *wells*. This practice wasn't unique to Norfolk. By the 19th century, so many English towns were called Wells that it was decided that the words *Next-The-Sea* should be added to clarify the situation.[1]

When not busy making wells, the locals of yesteryear used to enjoy the annual pleasures of the Wells Fair. It attracted a diverse range of performers. The most unusual of which was a husband and wife act who hit the town in 1863. Their routine involved eating live rats (we can only wonder what the couple's domestic life was like). Like all artistic pioneers, the rat gnawers weren't appreciated in their own time and were hounded out of town by the police. Their rejection may seem a trifle hypocritical when you consider that the nickname of Wells folk at the time was the 'Wells-Bite-Fingers'. Apparently they had a reputation for biting off the swollen fingers of dead seafarers who had washed up on the shores, because doing so made it easier to steal their wedding rings. No wonder the rat-eaters thought they'd found their audience.

The long walk from the station (again) took me past a large field containing approximately three geese and surrounded by an excessively sized electric fence. It was Norfolk's answer to *Jurassic Park*. Further down the road, on the left, was the church. In its graveyard rested the body of John Fryer: a sailing master on The Bounty's trip to Tahiti. Fryer was one of many Norfolk sailors aboard Captain Bligh's infamous ship. If you've got a minute, I'll give you the gist.

---

[1] I don't know what the town was called before people started using wells. How-Can-We-Obtain-Water?

*

Upon arrival in Tahiti, HMS Bounty's sailors were greeted by beautiful young women dressed as though on the set of *Blue Hawaii*. Not only were the girls pretty and vivacious, they refused to wear bras. They treated the sailors like gods. The days were long and the land was plentiful. Tahiti was the perfect climate; the average temperature, throughout the year, was a sumptuous 28 degrees. It didn't have winters. It was the planet's most agreeable climate: not too hot, but not cold enough for tribeswomen to cover their breasts.

The Bounty boys had a non-stop party. Within weeks of arrival, the travelling Brits had created a forerunner of the 18-30 holiday.

'Ooh, I say,' cooed one of the male Tahitians, whilst rehearsing for *Carry On Up Your Bounty*. 'There's English seamen everywhere!'

The sailors not only had sex with tribeswomen, they also ingratiated themselves into their communities by catching local diseases and having tribal tattoos jabbed into their newly sunburnt skin.

Their rep was nowhere to be seen.

The stay was due to last five months. When Captain Bligh decided it was time to leave, 18 of the 42 Bounty crew refused. They'd decided that instead of sailing home (the journey *there* had taken ten months) to a land of grey skies and labour, they would, instead, *not* go home. The captain's authoritarian manner had made him unpopular. The crew's loyalty to him and, by default, their country, was tested.

'There's always one, isn't there?' mused Bligh. Except in this case there were eighteen.

Those who stayed loyal to Bligh, despite being in the majority, were ruthlessly rounded up, with their captain, by the mutineers and bunged into a small boat and pushed out to sea. It was effectively a death sentence. The Bounty was then taken by the mutineers, with their Tahitian babes, to a new settlement on a distant, secret island (now known as Pitcairn Island). On arrival, the ship was set alight, lest it be discovered by the Royal Navy, who were bound to come looking for it eventually.

After being left for dead in what was no more than a dinghy, Bligh guided his loyal crew to Timor in the Dutch East Indies, casually mapping and charting new territory as he went. He managed this feat without a compass. It was a journey calculated at over 4,000 miles, during which they overcame raging seas, waning supplies, scary creatures ('a Very large Shark struck at one of the Oars,' wrote one crew member in his diary) and being chased by cannibals. From the relative civilisation of Timor they headed back to England. Two years and three months after leaving, Bligh returned on 15th March 1790. He couldn't wait to get his photos developed.

The Navy sent the HMS Pandora across the ocean to round up the mutineers. Incredibly, they found fourteen of them. On the long journey home the ship ran aground on the barrier reef and four of the fourteen were lost.[1] The survivors were shipped back to England to be hanged or acquitted.

The descendants of the un-captured mutineers still live on the island of Pitcairn. The population is currently 56. Its people speak a mixture of Tahitian and 18th century English. Their language is called Norfuk.

John Fryer was one of those bundled into Bligh's boat. It was he who wrote about the shark in his diary. He stayed loyal to his captain, despite disliking him. Bligh, in turn, was not loyal to Fryer. At the inquest he said that Fryer had pistols in his pocket at the time of the mutiny and could have stopped Bligh being bundled into the boat. Fryer's defence was that he was so surprised by the mutiny that he forgot he had the pistols. Bligh

---

[1] As were 31 of the completely innocent Pandora crew.

refused to acknowledge Fryer's loyalty and bravery. Despite this, Fryer went on to have a prosperous career at sea. He died in 1817. He was portrayed in a smarmy manner by Daniel Day Lewis in the underrated 1984 film, *The Bounty*.

I was surprised at how pleasant Wells was. My previous memories of it mostly involved boarded-up arcades and the smell of batter and cheap candyfloss. This was the first time I had properly walked it in years.

The streets were captivating. The buildings were freshly painted and well loved. The houses gave a possibly false, but no less pleasant, impression of being owned exclusively by seafarers. Signs in the windows read 'Gone Fishin'' and '*Sea* You At The Beach.'[1] In other towns, in other parts of the world, people desperately try and pretend they're home, lest some opportunistic scally prises their way in and helps themselves to the Blu-Rays. They leave the radio on and set the lights on a timer. Such deterrents are rarely required in Norfolk.

There was a picturesque, leafy square off the town centre called The Buttlands. It was surrounded by opulent townhouses and parked cars. Lots of parked cars. The Buttlands took its name from a 16th century requirement that all men practice their longbow technique in case of war. It was on this square of grass that the men of Wells did so.[2]

The high street led down to the quay. It was narrow and felt all the tighter for the amount of people walking it. There's

---

[1] It was reminiscent of the adoration received by the fishermen on the gangway at Sheringham. Are any professions looked upon as fondly as fishing? Has anyone ever put a rustic 'Gone Plumbin'' sign in the window?

[2] A butt, by the way, is the mound of earth behind an archery target. It's also another word for bum.

something about seaside towns that makes us Brits feel we no longer need to restrict ourselves to the pavement. The road is *ours*. A family of four, who might in, say, Leicester, walk single file, draw instant liberation from the sea air. They move out of single file and walk in a row instead, as though trying to play their dog offside. Wells had an abundance of such walkers.

The town had an unusual mixture of shops. Norfolk seaside towns are usually either up-market (galleries, delis, wax jackets) or down-market (beach balls, sandals, dog shit). Wells sat plump smack between the two. Its high street was a melting pot. There were galleries and bookshops slugging it out with their polar opposites, among them, impressively stocked beach paraphernalia stores with merchandise pouring out of the doors. Wells was crammed. Nobody knew where to look first.

The quay was Wells' main event. (*'I've got the quay, I've got the secret,*' I sang to myself.) The last time I'd visited (2006-ish) it was being lowered into the grave. It was in-season but felt out-of-season. Everything was boarded-up or in the process of being boarded-up. The local boarder-upper must have been rolling in it (he had a 'Gone Boardin'' sign in his window). But, now, in the sunlight, Wells seemed fit to burst. So much so that I started to worry about the plight of the Wells boarder-upper. Was *his* business now being boarded-up? And who would he hire to come and board it up for him?

It's curious how towns evolve. This was once one of England's most active ports. Mind you, all ports say that, don't they? In Wells' case, it's true. It welcomed visitors from all over the known world. They came in and out on the tide, dropping cargo off and picking cargo up. The town must have had a bit of a knockabout feel to it back then. It would have been constantly awash with sailors and thieves.

During the mid-Victorian era the town had approximately *forty* drinking establishments. Victorian pub-crawls through Wells were pretty extreme: people needed their stomachs pumped after twelve yards.

Everybody looked happy. People were laughing and joking and walking in the road. It was like those film reels of the VE Day celebrations.

I had ten minutes before the last bus. It was due to leave at 5pm. That was the problem with Norfolk. You couldn't really do much after *Countdown*. The town was heaving, the shops were packed, but the last, the *last*, bus was due. As an added bonus, I noticed that I didn't have any cash to buy a ticket home. I'd blown it on pasties in Walsingham.

A queue had formed by an arcade ATM. There was a questionable looking geezer holding it up. He may have thought it was a slot machine.

I looked at my watch. *Hurry up, you prick.*

The prick in question rubbed the back of his head with his hand, deciding whether to Hold or Nudge.

I visualised the bus pulling away. How quickly my rosy view of Wells would change were I forced to find last minute accommodation.

The man left the machine and I swooped in. It charged me somewhere in the region of six million pounds for the pleasure of withdrawing my own money. I power walked to the bus and hopped on just in time.

Maybe it was a good thing that I didn't have enough time to see the beach. Apparently there was a nudist area around there somewhere. I'd have hated to have wandered onto it. I don't like interrupting games of volleyball at the best of times.

Just down from the nudist beach was a natural pool used for pleasure boating and canoeing (which, ironically, both sound like terms nudists might find in the *Naturists' Glossary*). The pool was called Abraham's Bosom. The nudist beach was called Martin's Pleasure Boat. I think.

As the bus pulled away, I was sad that I'd only caught a glimpse of Ware Hall. The hall was originally built in Hertfordshire in the 15th century for a wealthy monk. It was bought in 1947 by May Savidge, a DIY fiend, with a view to restoring it. After years of work on the project, the council informed her that they were going to build a new road in the area:

'Oh, lovely,' said May. 'Now I'll be able to drive to my lovely Ware Hall with ease.'

'Er, yes...' replied the council, whilst looking at their shoes.

What May soon found out was that the new road was not going to be leading up to Ware Hall so much as it was going to be going *through* it. Thus began a fifteen-year fight with the council to keep the bulldozers at bay.

When the bulldozers eventually arrived (as they always do) in 1969, May decided that rather than let them smash her house to the ground, she would dismantle it piece-by-piece and rebuild it somewhere else. She chose Wells-Next-The-Sea.

A lorry made eleven trips from Hertfordshire to Norfolk, carrying the entire frame and brickwork. When the pieces arrived in Norfolk, May began assembling them from scratch. A carpenter installed the framework. May did the rest. She worked under the glow of old paraffin lamps and slept in a caravan in the garden. She didn't live to see her house completed. She left the job to her nephew. It was his wife, Christine, who took the baton and oversaw its completion.

May, you may not be surprised to learn, was a hoarder. Fortunately, her assortment of oddities, which ranged from service medals to notes from the milkman, helped fund the completion of the project. Many items were auctioned off or sold to antiquarians.[1] Ware Hall, fully restored, now runs as a bed & breakfast.

I'm desperately trying to think of a Ware Hall pun but can't work one out. I guess this is no great loss.

Hang on. Wait. I've got it. Ready?

So, you might say that May Savidge had the *wherewithal* to leave *Ware with hall.*

Sorry.

---

[1] There's no record of how much the milkman's notes went for. Millions, I imagine.

Leg Two

Blakeney - Cley

Blakeney

It was a grey morning. I'd woken up in a grump.

A letter arrived containing 'Important Information About My Gas Bill'. The important information wasn't about a price drop. I then seriously misjudged the milk situation. It looked like there was about half a pint left. I poured it on my cereal. There was a thimble's worth; I could have squeezed more milk from a lactating squirrel. I had a cup of black tea. It was grim. Judging by the stains on the inside of the mug, I might as well have had Bovril. Lastly, there was no toothpaste. My mouth felt like the inside of a rat's lair; it smelt as though a donkey had crept in whilst I was asleep, cocked his leg up and pissed in it. My molars had acquired an overnight fur. What was I going to do? When it comes to brushing, I'm a two-times-a-day man. Sometimes three. Lord, this was bleak. I didn't have time to go to the shop. I brushed my teeth with water and stuck some warm chewing gum, which had been in my coat pocket since Fresher's Week, 2002, into my mouth.

In short, I was in no mood to reflect on Norfolk's glory. If anything, Norfolk's glory could go hang.

In a generous effort to maintain the downcast feel of this chapter, the bus driver decided to get to Blakeney as slowly as possible. We travelled the coast at such a plodding rate that I yearned for the rapid thrills of the Wells miniature steam train. I was dropped off on the edge of the village. I was getting used to being dropped off on the edges.

There wasn't much to see: a stretch of relatively modern houses; some council developments; a playing park; a sloped football pitch consisting of long grass, daisies and two rusty, net-less frames. A man walked his dog across the pitch. I don't think I've ever looked at a village football pitch and not seen a man walking his dog across it. Even during matches.

The relative normality of the village's periphery came as a surprise. Blakeney had a reputation for being a cut above such triflings of the mundane. For those not in the know, Blakeney was a Wells-Next-The-Sea for the upper middle class of upper middle-age. I hadn't expected to see Ford Mondeos and satellite dishes, but there they were, those beacons of normality, hidden away like Quasimodo in the bell tower.

There were no beach shops or ice cream parlours or arcades on the quay. I asked a member of staff in a delicatessen if there was a chip shop nearby. She looked as if I'd asked for directions to the village crack den.

'We don't have a chip shop in *Blakeney*,' she purred.

'What about a crack den?'

Occasionally the normal folk of Blakeney's periphery had to nip to the stores to get bread and milk. They'd return home with falafels, mustard seed and two original prints, signed by the artist.

Blakeney's quayside wasn't too dissimilar to Wells', except there were fewer people, fewer gulls and fewer smiles. This was where serious people came to holiday. People who liked yachts and sandals. I ambled around trying to find things of interest. The houses along the front of the quay, and up its narrow, twisty lanes, looked empty. There was no denying their picture postcard beauty. The place was ripe to be used as a backdrop to a light-hearted serial starring Pam Ferris and Martin Shaw (called something like *Quay To Your Heart*). Looking at the immaculately presented empty rustic cottages and houses, it was hard to believe that these had ever been pubs, granaries, merchant offices and blacksmiths. Everything had been painted over.[1]

There was a book sale on the quayside. Having vowed not to buy any more books until I'd read the fifty currently sitting unread on my shelf, I thought it only right that I go in and test my willpower. Within three seconds I'd bought a biography of P.G Wodehouse and an absolute cracker called *Random Reflections of Blakeney*. The former I would save for a rainy day, the latter I intended to smash through as a matter of urgency.

I visited the remains of the Guildhall. It was just off the quay, embedded into a steep hill. There were a few theories as to what the Guildhall was originally used for. Nobody knew for sure. A sign on the wall stated that the remains were 'Open at any reasonable time' which was a policy that could lead to arguments (is 9pm a reasonable time? 6pm? 8am?). The stony cellar was all that remained of what was once, a prominent two-storey building. It was pitch black inside. The air was moist. Mice rustled about in the corners.

One of the theories was that the Guildhall had been used as a morgue for seafarers. It was predictably eerie: the kind of

---

[1] A smattering of the village's old cottages had been saved from their destiny as future holiday homes by a Mrs Nora Clogstoun. Her aim was to protect village property from being snapped up entirely by holidaymakers. She started a housing society. She alone bought five cottages for the exclusive use of Norfolk people. The society continues to this day and, in its own words, 'owns 39 houses and cottages in Blakeney or neighbouring villages and they are all let at affordable rents to tenants with a local birth tie.' Good on them.

building in which you might take a flash photograph of a wall and discover, upon developing, that you've also managed to get the spirit of a dead sailor in shot.

Amazingly, locals used the Guildhall as a place to grow rhubarb in the 1950s; proving that if you leave anything unoccupied for long enough in Norfolk, someone will start growing rhubarb in it.[1]

Blakeney was outrageously tasteful. A post-millennial re-imagining of the past.[2] I, being outrageously distasteful, was uncomfortable there. It felt too orderly and vacant. I was walking through a watercolour painting from *The People's Friend*. There were no edges to it (apart from the one the bus dropped me off at). Was this really the same Blakeney that once entertained pirates and stripped foreign ships of their goods whenever the chance occurred? Was this the same Blakeney that supplied warships for the Crusades and for the battle against the Armada? Where there were secret networks of smuggler's tunnels? Where the streets once heaved with children? If ever a place had muted its past, Blakeney was it.

The church of St Nicholas was situated away from the quay, inland, amongst the part of the village where normality reigned. It was next to a small school. Attendances there, as in many rural and seaside communities, had formerly been affected by the demands on children to assist adults in haymaking and fieldwork. The annual school holiday wasn't summer holiday,

---

[1] I know I've already done a variation on that gag, but I like it. I'll probably do a few more.

[2] Blakeney's evolution into an upmarket holiday destination began in the early 20th century. The influx of wealthy visitors from the Midlands grew as they invited more friends and family to their holiday homes.

but harvest holiday. It would occur at various times from year to year, depending on when the corn was ripe.

School children lived with the constant threat of illness. Outbreaks of diphtheria and smallpox meant that *all* children could be kept home for up to fourteen weeks, until the threat had completely faded. It wasn't until the 20th century that things started to improve: albeit rather late in the century. Blakeney school didn't have running water until 1949 or indoor toilets until 1976. By Norfolk standards, these facts were not unique. The entire village of Upper Sheringham, for example, didn't get running water until 1979. It is almost inconceivable. This was two years after *Star Wars* had been released.

I went inside the church and began reading *Random Reflections of Blakeney* by Margaret Loose. The highlight was a collection of sayings from the author's granny, a Norfolk Victorian.

Here are some of them:

'Sing at the table, die in the workshop' – I don't know what this means. Have fun while you can?

'A creaking door always lasts longest' – people who complain of ailments always live to old age

'Hulled into a buffle' – being confused

'He'd be better after he's been through the sheets' - I love this. It means after a good night's sleep

'Hinder part a-fore' – something is the wrong way around

Margaret's grandmother would run around the house during storms, covering the mirrors in case lightening hit them. When lighting a fire, she would shut the curtains because she believed a fire wouldn't start if the sun was shining on it (fortunately, she wasn't in charge of any fire safety initiatives at the village school).

The church was unusual in that it had an additional small tower at the opposite end of the large tower. Like the Guildhall, there was a little historical uncertainty about this. The accepted theory was that the small tower was built as a beacon to guide ships home. The theory falls short when you pose the following question: why not use the really big tower as a beacon instead of making a smaller one?

It had everyone hulled into a buffle.

Cley-Next-The-Sea

On the bus to Cley I found myself wedged next to somebody with the same voice as Ray Winstone. This in itself wasn't exactly disturbing, but became so once it was factored in that the person in question was female.

She was a gruff old sort. I waited for her to start giving me Bet365's latest odds on Aston Villa winning the next throw-in. She sat with her legs open, pressing me against the window, forcing my feet dangerously close to the rubber melting heat of the overactive floor heaters.

Mrs Winstone had boarded with her daughter. The daughter was about 25. *Miss* Winstone, unlike her East End thug of a mother, was stick-thin and pale. She had decided to sit at the front of the bus, whereas mater, born roustabout, had headed straight for the back. After several minutes of our bus pootling along at what Philip Larkin would call 'summer's pace', Miss Winstone stood and walked to the back. The bus driver eyed her suspiciously, as bus drivers often do when passengers stand up, in his rear-view mirror.

'Mum, I don't like it down there,' she said. Her voice matched her appearance. It was barely audible, like a little boy whimpering from the inside of a wardrobe.

'WHATCHOO CUM UP ERE FAW?' boomed Ray. 'DARE AIN'T NO SEATS UP ERE. I'M SQUASHED UP ENUFF AS IT IS!'

Well, I thought, you could try closing your legs, ma'am.

'But, Mum…'

'BUT MUM NUFFINK. GO AN' SIT BACK DAHN! OVAH DARE!'

She pointed at the girl's recently vacated seat.

The girl started to cry. I winced. Everybody looked out of the windows, pretending they couldn't hear. Pretending not to hear this particular conversation was akin to standing next to launch of Apollo XI and claiming you were listening out for the first starling-song of the season.

'There's too many people down there, Mum,' she whispered.

Ray sighed.

'FAHKIN' 'ELL. OH, ALRIGHT. COME 'ERE DEN.'

And with that, the girl, who, I stress, was in her mid-twenties, came and sat on Mrs Ray Winstone's ample lap. Next to me.

The effect of overusing words and phrases is that it can deaden their meaning when you truly need them. The classic example of this is the overuse of the word 'love'. It's hard to emphasise to someone how much you 'love' them when but moments earlier you'd also waxed lyrical about how much you 'love' the fact that you can now buy Frazzles in multi-packs. What is the currency of a word like 'love' when it is constantly spent on frivolities? In telling this story to you now, I am having a similar predicament with the phrase 'I didn't know where to look'. It's a clunky old platitude with almost no punch left in it. And yet, it is precisely the phrase I need. A woman was sitting on another woman's lap. Next to me. My friends, *I did not know where to look.*

Cley-Next-The-Sea wasn't particularly 'Next-The-Sea'. The constant evolution and silting[1] of the coast had left Cley further inland than its name suggested. A more suitable name would be Cley-Next-The-Marshes-Next-The-Sea. Or, even better, Cley.
It was certainly one of the prettiest villages along the Norfolk coast. It had an endless network of passageways and lokes, with rows of stunning flint cottages with chalk-red roof tiles. The gardens were immaculate and every angle, every view was eye-wateringly perfect. Each square foot seemed a potential bludgeoning spot for a truculent town councillor in *Midsomer Murders.*
Cley hadn't always been so far from the sea: it had occasionally found itself *in it*. December 2013 was the latest occasion when the sea broke the shingle barriers and raced its way across the marshes. Initially, it was feared that 2013 flood would surpass the damage caused by the flood of 1953. It didn't. Fortunately. The severity of the Met Office warnings and the improved sea defences allowed the wild January night of 1953 to remain the standard bearer.
All my life I'd heard old people talk about the 1953 flood but had never looked into just how devastating it was. It affected nearly every town and village on England's east coast, killing around 300 people – one hundred of them from Norfolk. Blakeney, Wells, Sheringham, and other places I'd yet to visit on the tour, were all decimated that night. The story of Cley's flood was typical of what had happened all along Norfolk's deadly stretch of coast.

---

[1] I got reasonably far without mentioning silting. You can't say I didn't try.

*

Nobody knew it was coming. On the evening of January 31st, people in the village commented on the sharp drop in temperature and the strengthening wind. This was nothing unusual. The weather here was predictably unpredictable (and has always been a conversational goldmine). What *was* unusual was the yellow tinge to the twilight.

This was a good night to get to bed early.

By this time, Scotland, like its Mars Bars, was already being battered. High winds were sending bagpipe tablature and treasured haggis recipes flying. Around the highlands and the lowlands, kilts were being wafted around Scotsmen's necks, like Marilyn Monroe in *The Seven Year Itch*, but not as sexy. The knock-on effect of the Scottish winds was that they drove the sea down the coast of England, where it was destined to smash into the first landmass it came across. This, as it always had been, and always would be, was Norfolk.

In preparation for this journey I'd acquired a great little book called *The 1953 & 1993 Floods* by the stupendously named Buttercup Joe. It wasn't too dissimilar from *Random Reflections of Blakeney* in terms of length, paper thickness, and use of staples as a binder. The cover had a picture of Buttercup Joe looking exactly as you would expect somebody called Buttercup Joe to look: he was wearing a Sherlock Holmes hat, had binoculars around his neck, was smoking a pipe and had sideburns to rival any member of Slade.

Joe's house had been behind Cley church, on the green, at the far side of the village. I walked over to the church. It was so far from the sea that I couldn't even hear it. I looked at the row of houses near the green and wondered which was Joe's. The sea level would reach almost five foot in his house that night.

It was the speed that caught people out. It was nigh on impossible to send warnings when the only people who knew about the problem were themselves marooned. The drowned couldn't save the drowning. Many first found out about the rising sea when it poured through the letterbox.

As the water hit the village, Buttercup Joe ran across the green to his allotment. With water around his knees, he began moving the chickens to higher ground. They had been 'floating quite happily' on the shallow water but began to look 'bewildered'[1] as it rose further. He threw them onto the roof of a nearby garage, turning to see a wall of sea rush towards him. He jumped onto the roof just in time. He watched as the icy water got higher and higher. Debris floated past, including the buffers from Wells railway station. They had travelled nine miles. The swelling of the sea rocked the garage. Joe knew he would be swept to his death eventually. He waited.

The water knocked out the village's power supply. Joe saw the houses in the distance disappear into darkness, one by one, as the sea extinguished the coal fires in the hearths. Knowing that the garage was doomed, he jumped onto a tree. He noticed that also hanging from the tree were hundreds of big, wet, black grapes.

They weren't grapes. They were rats. They were clinging desperately. Instinct kicked in. Joe shook the tree:

'The noise of their screams when they knew they were going back into the water was dreadful, something I can't describe.'

Time passed. It was snowing. The night sky was bright yellow. Joe wasn't sure if he was alive. After several failed attempts, a boat navigated its way to the tree. His body was considered a lost cause. He wasn't even sent to hospital. It was a waste of resources. He was rowed to a nearby cottage and had brandy forced into him. He was vigorously massaged by two nurses. This brought him back to consciousness (well, it would me,

---

[1] As chickens often do in moments of drama.

too). Other victims arrived at the cottage, including Gentle Annie, an elderly lady who had almost drowned in her bed.

Along the coast similar scenes were acted out. Buttercup Joe survived. Many didn't.

It's amazing that anyone would choose to live in a town or village that suffers Biblical floods every now and then. Where do they find the energy to redecorate when they know that they'll be doing the whole thing over again soon? Floods from burst riverbanks can create mayhem but seawater flooding really does the business. Not only does it destroy homes, it kills crops and habitations. And it moves with such force. The floods of 1953 took years of recovery. Around Cley were occasional markings of the sea levels from that night. It must have been petrifying.[1] If it weren't for the photographic evidence of north Norfolk looking as though it had been targeted by scores of bombers, I wonder if we could even believe the stories at all.

Like Blakeney, Cley was a former hotbed of criminality. In 1406, a ship called the Maryenknyght was captured by Cley pirates. After stripping it of cargo,[2] they found that the ship was harbouring an eleven-year-old boy called James. But not just any eleven-year-old boy called James. He was the son of the King of Scotland, Robert III. He was being sent to France amid fears that he would become a target for the English. The pirates, disappointed with their wool haul, captured the young prince instead. He was sent to London and thrown into the Tower at the request of Henry IV. The trauma killed Robert III.

---

[1] It was literally so for some of the animals. Two days after the event, Joe saw 'a large white cockerel sitting on a perch straight upright dead as could be.' It had frozen to the spot.

[2] The cargo was wool, which is never too high on a pirate's wish list.

Prince James was locked up for eighteen years, during which time he became James I.

And people think today's prisoners live like kings.

The most iconic Cley landmark was the windmill. It had been used in a number of movies, including 1949's long forgotten drag of a spy movie, *Conspirator*. What was it with Norfolk windmills and spies?

The film starred Elizabeth Taylor, who was sixteen at the time, and her on-screen squeeze, Robert Taylor, who had celebrated his own sixteenth birthday the same day that Prince James was hauled to the Tower. The plot revolved around a young girl falling for a Soviet spy. The age gap between its overly flirtatious stars caused a stir even in those simpler times.

The windmill was also used as a BBC ident in the late 1990s. The BBC One hot air balloon (remember that?) floated beside the mill whilst announcers told a national audience what they could expect to see that evening, which, in the late 90s, was usually *Changing Rooms* and fly-on-the-wall documentaries about airports.

The windmill was formerly owned by the parents of James Blount, AKA James Blunt. There was once a photograph of him in the toilet. I don't know if anyone's used it yet.

A slightly more highbrow visitor to the village than the talented Master Blount, was the poet Rupert Brooke, who visited fellow poet Frances Cornford there in 1914.[1] Brooke spent a Cley night having unpleasant dreams about war. When he woke the next day he was informed that the Great War had just started. It's not always for the best when dreams come true:

---

[1] Her husband was called Fran*ci*s Cornford. Imagine the hilarious misunderstandings that must have occurred. Every. Single. Day.

'Never mind,' said Frances. 'Maybe you can become a war poet and this story can feature in a crap little book about Norfolk.'
'Spiffing,' said Brooke, a tad ungratefully. 'Well, if I should die, think only this of me...'
'Think what?'
'I haven't thought of it yet.'
Rupert Brooke was dead within a year. He had avoided all bullets with his name on and had instead been infected by a mosquito with his name on. He received the fatal bite on his way to Gallipoli, where he would have been shot anyway. Death by infection was the tragic fate of many Norfolk soldiers stationed out East. The disease bit harder than the bullet.
Despite his sad dream in a Cley bed, under an English heaven, Brooke's poems were often more optimistic about the war than those of his contemporaries. His most famous being *The Soldier*, which I tastelessly lampooned above. The man described by Yeats as 'the handsomest young man in the country' was buried in a Grecian olive grove, now forever England.

The sky remained overcast. Even lovely old Cley could be gloomy in the grey. I stumbled around feeling more like Rupert Brooke facing the realities of war than I did James Blunt gaily cutting the windmill lawn.
 There wasn't much to look at with the clouds in full force. The weather wasn't raw enough to make the whole thing feel snug. The marshes during a storm can be quite a sight. This wasn't a storm. This was just unbroken, unbreakable, steely sheets of nothing cloud.
 I saw a house decorated externally with sheep vertebrae, which was quite unexpected. A house made out of sheep's bones was the sort of thing I'd expect to see on a road trip across the United States. It would be two towns down from the World's Largest Toothbrush.

Many people visited Cley to see rare birds. Its geographical location made it the bird equivalent of an inner city youth hostel. It attracted, according to one website, 'migrants, vagrants and rarities of all kinds.' The review almost made it sound exciting.

You have to admire ornithologists. There can't be a more unpredictable hobby. You can plan a birdwatching trip as thoroughly as you want, but you can never bank on the birds agreeing to sit and await your arrival. Birdwatching is trainspotting without a timetable. You can't knock it.[1] I can't be the only one who feels a twinge of envy upon seeing birdwatchers huddled together, drinking flasked tea and moistening pencils with their lips. They appear such a happy, dedicated community. They look so content with how everything has turned out.

Still walking. So many nooks and crannies. All beautiful and all asleep. Except for the delicatessen, located on the corner of the coast road's sharpest turn. Cley's sprinkling of shops and galleries had a secretive feel to them, whereas the delicatessen flashed its wears. Latest arrivals were proudly proclaimed in chalk, in neater handwriting than I could ever manage with a pen. The window displayed homemade jams and sauces, stacked artfully atop one another. Baskets out front contained fresh, raw, hand=picked groceries. I wanted to go in and ask if they did pickled onion Space Raiders but the force wasn't with me. The bus felt more appealing. So I got that instead.

A day that had started with grey disillusionment had just about evened itself out. I was looking forward to getting home, though. I'd be better once I'd been through the sheets.

---

[1] I've always believed that most hobbies and obsessions masquerade as an excuse to get us out of the house: sports teams, trainspotting, birdwatching, poetry, drama, dancing, fitness and so on. They all give us a reason to not to stay in and watch *The One Show*.

Leg Three

Mundesley – North Walsham – Coltishall – Norwich-Wroxham - Aylsham

Mundesley

I was looking forward to this. I'd lived in North Walsham in my late teens and the bus I had to catch, via Mundesley, was the one I used to ride to and from Sheringham Sixth Form. It was one of the few bus routes that I had any sentiment for.

My memories of those college journeys all take place on sunny mornings. The bus would be filled with Cromer High pupils. Most of them got on at Mundesley. I used to feel like a king because a) I was the oldest and b) I was in college and therefore didn't have to wear school uniform.

Back then I'd formed a kinship with two of the girls. They were in their final year of 'High'. They were laced with devilry. One of them had once phlegmed into the teachers' water jug in the cafeteria. The other had already had sex. They both wore the sweet, universal smell of teenage aerosol: a light, chemical vanilla. Freshly sprayed Impulse. It flowed in destructive waves, asphyxiating asthma sufferers within a six-mile radius. Theirs were the voices all obeyed. If I'd been any younger, a mere high school pupil, I'd have been just another one of their slaves. Yet, in my college armour, I was permitted entry into the kingdom. I couldn't even tell you their names now. But for two years we ruled the backseat and inadvertently acted our age by desperately trying to act older than our age. It was the only time I ever wore the crown.

There was another girl. She would get on at a unique stop, on a random Mundesley corner, no questions asked. She wore a Limp Bizkit jacket and had a streak of blue in her hair that had been applied with a Crayola felt tip. And there was a boy with natural red hair and even redder ears. Bright red. They looked as though they'd sizzle your skin if you touched them. They could melt headphones.

Where were these kids now? What did they look like? Were they happy? I don't know. The only thing I can confidently say, as I write this, is that the red haired boy is looking up from his office desk and saying, 'You know, I think somebody's talking about me.'

There was rain in the air. The sunny mornings of my memories were washed away. I'd asked to be dropped off on the periphery of the village because that was where the church stood and because I'd become accustomed to being dropped off on peripheries.

I'd passed Mundesley Church many times before but had never seen anyone going in or out. It didn't have a spire. It was an odd affair all round. I went in expecting it to be cold and silent. It was actually the most charming church interior I have ever seen. It felt as though I'd walked into the home of a friendly old woman;[1] the kind of old woman who made Eccles cakes and said 'Ooooh' when she found out about Janet from the bakery dying. There were soft furnishings and hand-knitted prayer mats. It was the first time I had ever walked into a warm church.

---

[1] I had to check to make sure that I hadn't.

A table had been laid out for Sunday school. On it were activity books and scraps of coloured paper. There was an old biscuit tin full of crayons and lidless felt-tip pens. Maybe this was where the Limp Bizkit girl first learnt to colour her hair. There was a bottle of Robinsons squash on one of the units, next to a stack of plastic cups. It could have made the sternest atheist repent and believe.

As villages go, Mundesley was a whopper. It had a population of almost three thousand: roughly as much as Weybourne, Walsingham, Blakeney and Cley combined. It was like a village from the 1960s. It had the amenities that most other villages had lost over the last fifty years. It had a pharmacy, a post office, a café, a bakery, a wool shop, a craft shop, a takeaway restaurant, a butchers, a mini-market, a hardware store, a florists and a charity shop. And that was just the village centre. Away from there, along the seafront, was an ice cream parlour, an arcade, a beach shop and a couple of greasy spoons, not to mention a range of pubs and hotels.

I tried to fathom how Mundesley's businesses had survived when the fate of many Norfolk village stores (Spar shops aside) had been largely disastrous. Village shops tended to survive by becoming clinically twee. Not in Mundesley. I don't know what it was doing, but everything was somehow thriving independently from the nearby market towns. The actress who played Pat Butcher in *Eastenders* had once lived there, but that couldn't account for everything.

The place seemed remarkably peaceful. I could have dropped a bomb on the village green and the best I'd have got by way of a response was a cursory glance from a dog walker:

'Good morning,' they might say. 'Lovely bomb.'

Talking of bombs, there was a massive bomb replica outside Mundesley's Maritime Museum on the cliff top. It formed part of a war memorial for those, and there were many, who had died clearing the coast of mines during and after the Second World War. It was good to see them remembered. Although maybe an enormous bomb wouldn't have been their preferred choice of symbolism.

The Maritime Museum was shut. I was curious to see inside. It really was tiny. If you wanted to sleep in it you'd have to lay diagonally. The *Women's Institute Book of Norfolk Villages* called it 'the smallest museum in the world.' Quite an exciting claim. *Bridgewater's Guide to Norfolk* threw cold water over this by saying that it was '*probably* the smallest museum in the country.' I didn't dare to read any more reviews lest it get demoted further. By the time I'd read my other Norfolk books it would be 'just about the fifth smallest museum on that particular street.'

The cold drove me away from the cliffs. I wasn't the first to find the Mundesley winds too keen. With no landmass between Norfolk and the North Pole, the sea breezes have always had a notable pinch. In 1795, the poet William Cowper (pronounced *Cooper*, for no discernable reason) moved to Mundesley because he believed the sea air would cure his melancholia. It wasn't long before he realised that the constant cold wasn't doing much to warm his spirits.[1] He moved to Dereham instead. And died of dropsy.

---

[1] According to one of his letters, the sand in the Mundesley breeze made his 'eyes swell'. They stuck out of his head like Bugs Bunny's did after seeing a sassy female.

North Walsham

Riding through my old haunt's back streets on the bus, seeing those modern builds again, under the blanket of Tuesday afternoon clouds, gave me a rush. I was seventeen again. I was awkward again; I was sweaty; I was savage; I was soft; I was wearing Brylcreem (I had hair!); I smelt of Brut Aquatonic and jeans that had been left in the washing machine too long.
Ah, the North Walsham sprawl. I wouldn't expect anyone other than myself to get dewy-eyed upon seeing it. It brought to mind Philip Larkins' *Afternoons*:

An estateful of washing
And the albums, lettered
Our Wedding, *lying*
Near the television

It was the definition of ordinary. Families were started there. First homes bought. Company cars driven. Targets met. Kitchens fitted. Sky remotes polished. Late library books returned. Complete normality. And yet, to me it looked like Wivenhoe must have looked to Constable. Only with fewer cows. I saw nothing but majesty.
It's difficult for some to see how hurried modern houses, with their poorly aligned wall sockets and polystyrene walls, can stamp any affection on the hearts of their inhabitants. But they can and they do. Countless times have I been in a random part of the country and a friend has leant across and said, 'While we're here, do you mind if we just drive by my old house? It's *lovely*. It's only five minutes down the road. God, it's so lovely, you're going to love it.' When we get there, the charming little

thatched cottage I'd envisaged after my compatriot's glowing review is no more than a 1980s two-bed on a never-ending housing development of 1980s two-beds of the exact same design (bar the front door occasionally being on the right-hand side of the house rather than the left).

Home is where the heart is and all that. A part of mine is in the discreet, captivating network of North Walsham cul-de-sacs.

In the town centre stood a tower-less church. I'd always assumed that the tower had been bombed. Actually, it just fell down one morning in 1734. There wasn't a Luftwaffe pilot in sight. Or any pilot for that matter, primarily because they didn't exist. The evening prior to the collapse, the bells rung out for four hours as part of a church fair (an annoying church fair, by the sounds of it). The vibrations caused sufficient structural damage for the walls to cave in. The remains were exposed to the elements and the tower fell into further disrepair. An 1836 storm brought more of it down, causing the ground to shake violently.

North Walsham Church was once the second tallest in Norfolk. It was now the 623rd. Approximately. Shades of its former glory could be seen in a solitary tower wall, which still stood at a mighty 85 feet. Had it survived, it would have been quite the landmark. Unfortunately, once it started to collapse, the people were *towerless* to stop it. Yeah?

The churchyard was occupied with students from nearby Paston Sixth Form. They sat on the cold grass, talking loudly and pretending it was summer. It was Paston's continual stream of students that kept North Walsham from going stale. If the college didn't exist, or if it were located a mile away from the centre, North Walsham would be unexceptional. It's easier to forgive a high street its inanity when it's full of young people. They possess the fresh air of hope.

I watched them like a film. They moved around the town in packs, invading charity shops and buying coffee-to-go, like they'd seen Americans do on the tele. The girls walked with eager steps and their voices sang. The boys trailed fifteen yards behind, being sarcastic and looking amazed at how tall they suddenly were. It was a joy. All town centres should have a college. That will be my first move as Prime Minister.

North Walsham high street was Georgian and handsome, like Holt. The buildings were rooted in history. Unlike Holt, North Walsham had been repeatedly kicked in the groin by a spate of factory closures, not least the one where my dad had worked. But there were changes afoot. Talks were in place to turn the town into one of the nation's most desirable places to live and shop. It would have regular farmer's markets and all derelict buildings would be renovated. The wheels were already in motion; scaffolding adorned buildings in the town centre. One extreme to the other. On the site of an enormous factory now stood a Waitrose and a museum of magic.[1]

Just off the high street was a concrete precinct. In the boom of the late 90s (when we all wore Union Jack miniskirts and sawed cows in two whilst listening to Kula Shaker), the precinct used to have a sports shop, a jeweller, a youth-orientated guidance office and a mattress store. None of these appealed to me in my younger years (nor would they now) and my memories of them are only semi-visible. What the precinct also had, however, and my memories of it are in 3D Technicolor with smell-o-vision, was a video shop called Cash Cut.

---

[1] If the museum covered the history of the factory, it could become the Museum of Magic & Trailer Construction. Fakenham's Museum of Gas & Local History would then have a major rival.

It had been ten years since I'd walked through this precinct. With a hint of sorrow, I discovered Cash Cut had gone. A café stood in its stead. Ditto for the mattress shop. The other premises were empty. England could conceivably be one giant cafeteria soon.

Cash Cut was extraordinary. It was a video rental that also sold trainers. Think about that. On reflection, maybe it was a trainer shop that also rented videos. I don't know what their priorities were. I don't think anybody did. You'd walk in and be drawn to either the wooden staircase up to the 'video room' or a wall full of new-ish looking trainers. What a choice.

I'd always wondered whether anyone ever left with both a new pair of shoes *and* a video:

'I'll take the Nike Air Max in a twelve and a copy of *Shadowlands*, please.'

'Yes, Sir. That will be £79.65.'

On each stair up to the 'video room' was a pink sticker in the shape of an alien footprint. They were promotional stickers for the 1988 film *Mac & Me*: a genuine contender for the worst film ever made. The last time I went into Cash Cut was 2004. The stickers were still there.

Cash Cut's upstairs 'video room' was big and creaky and smelt alarmingly like damp carpet. The 'Latest Releases' shelf was routinely the emptiest. Like most video shops, new videos were seldom in stock. Some bastard always got to them first. I always envisaged the bastard in question to be a morbidly obese twenty-something, sitting in an armchair in his dirty flat, laughing out loud to himself with a mouth full of wet popcorn. In my mind, he hadn't even put the video in the machine; he was just using it to hit his dogs.

Cash Cut would stock, at most, two copies of blockbusters, and one of everything else. By the time I'd seen a film from the 'Latest Releases' shelf, the sequel was out. I wasn't aware there was more than one *Police Academy* until 2003.

The older videos were stocked roughly according to genre. There were no signs saying which section was which, you had to decide for yourself by looking at the covers. The only genre this didn't apply to was pornography. These were scattered about with gay abandon.[1]

Video shops died without a trace. Even Blockbuster, the original Conquistadors of the likes of Cash Cut, was eventually wiped out by the armies of Amazon and Netflix. Blockbuster died with a mere whisper in the national news, silently dragging the very notion of video shops to the grave. If somebody asked where your nearest video shop was, what would you say? The library? I made it a point to find a real video shop during my tour. Hopefully there were still some out there, clinging on:

'Come on in, guys. You can rent this film out for one night for just £3.99, *plus* the cost in petrol of coming to pick it up - and returning it (before 11am, please). By the way, if you *do* fail to bring it back in time, we'll charge you again. Hey. Stop. Where are you going? Come back...'

Renting a film was always the pale nephew of a trip to the cinema, but wasn't without its charms. Sometimes you *did* manage to beat the morbidly obese dog-beater to the latest release, and, ah, the excitement of having the case in your hand as you made your way home.

Things change, of course. Now, when you rent a movie digitally, there's no faffing about or trawling through half-empty 'Latest Releases' shelves. Every film ever made is there already. Click. Done. Our countless devices do the legwork for us, freeing up more time to eat at all of those new restaurants and cafés. Still, I would have given anything to have seen Cash Cut on the precinct, going strong, selling Reebok Classics and telling me that *Mac & Me* was due for release in 1988.

---

[1] I think *Gay Abandon* might have been one of the titles, along *with Asian Rutting '97* and *Daylight Nobbery*.

*

On the way out of town, towards Coltishall, marked by a stone monument, was the site of the Battle of North Walsham. The battle formed part of the Peasant's Revolt. Rebellion was in the air. A man by the name of Geoffrey Litster (from the village of Felmingham), by no means a peasant himself, had become known as 'the King of the Commons' after forming an army of rebels to overthrow the ruling class.

Litster had been inspired by the story of Wat Tyler and his raids on London. It was a strange story to be inspired by. Tyler's initial successes had forced King Richard to agree to meet him to discuss terms. During the meeting, Tyler is said to have sipped his water in a derogatory manner. How it's possible to do such a thing with water is a puzzle I'm not qualified to solve. Anyway, to make matters worse, Tyler then had a pop at one of the king's party. Not one to take flippant witticisms lightly, the man in question returned the favour by stabbing Tyler in the neck. Tyler made a valiant attempt at escape but fell thirty yards from the scene. His cries for water were understandably rejected. Instead, he had his head stuck on a pole and paraded around London. Nobody in Litster's army thought this a disturbing omen.

Litster's Norfolk peasants were fighting against increased taxes and pay restrictions. At least, that's the consensus. Nobody truly knows what their motives were because nearly every rebel involved was either killed in the battle or had their head removed, and paraded, soon after. Some think that rather than fighting for the rights of the poor, rebel leaders were trying to grab more land for themselves. The revolting peasants weren't always *revolting peasants*, many of them, like Litster, were of noble birth. There was much to win and lose. On they marched. Litster's rebels did a similar Norfolk tour in 1381 to the one I was doing. The exception being that they set fire to things they didn't like, whereas I made sarcastic comments about them.

The peasants marched to Norwich. Upon arrival, they found the city gates open. Not ones to hang around, they seized control of the castle and went on a mission to cause general mayhem, mainly to those in positions of power. They also released all of their mates from the prison.

Unfortunately for the rebels, the Bishop of Norwich at that time was one Henry le Despenser: a noted gut-slasher who was more likely to set fire to his congregation with a torch than with a particularly passionate sermon. The bishop was at home in Burley, busily writing a tenuous extended metaphor for his *Pause For Thought* for the following Tuesday's Radio 2 breakfast show, when he heard of the troubles in his diocese. He spat out his tea. As problems in the diocese went, an invasion by rebels ranked considerably higher than a low turnout for the annual craft fair. Despenser acted immediately, running upstairs to find the silliest bishop uniform he owned. Once satisfactorily attired, he amassed an elite army of professional swordsmen and archers and headed to Norfolk to find the troublemakers.

The bishop's years as a soldier had prepared him well for any doings with rowdy commoners. Already that year he'd crushed similar rebellions in Cambridge and Peterborough. By the time he arrived in Norwich, his army had increased in size, picking up knights and landowners along the way. Litster's rebels retreated to North Walsham, possibly to find out what year *Mac & Me* was due to be released. Despenser continued the chase and caught up with the peasants. His army wiped the floor with them. Those who fled were chased into the woods and butchered as they ran.

The surviving ringleaders, including Litster, were rounded up and beheaded. Litster's corpse was chopped in four and sent to Norwich, King's Lynn and Great Yarmouth, with the last part going back 'to the site of his mansion' in Felmingham. It was a classic example of what's known in the bishop game as *sending out a message*.[1]

North Walsham's history was a tad bloody. Even its literary visitors were fans of the dark side. Agatha Christie used to holiday there, writing murder mysteries whilst doing so. Arthur Conan Doyle mentioned the town in two separate Sherlock Holmes stories (both of them heavy with corpses). Even Siegfried Sassoon, the legendary war poet, holidayed nearby (and try thinking of *him* without picturing recently shot teenage boys covered in mud). It was all very death heavy.

So as not to end the chapter on such a dark theme, I'll mention Norfolk boy William Cubitt, who worked in Bacton Wood Mills, on the town's periphery, and there began a life of invention and general usefulness. Amongst his contributions to history were designing the Great Northern Railway, the Shropshire Union Canal, the Museum of Childhood, Crystal Palace (the palace, not the football team) and, less heart-warmingly, prison treadmills.

Oh, dear, I *have* ended on a low after all. What about this, instead: there used to be a café in North Walsham called The Dutch Oven.

Anyway, Coltishall.

---

[1] Although it must be pointed out that one 15th century account of the battle says that very little fighting took place. The historian in question, John Capgrave, wrote, 'By the good management of the Bishop, and of other men who had assembled there, the whole people surrendered, rejoicing that they might withdraw in peace. Jack Litster himself, leaping over a wall, hid himself in a corn-field.' It makes Litster sound like a lovable rogue from an episode of *Heartbeat*. Bishop Despenser, meanwhile, comes across as a kind of Ghandi figure. I'm not sure I believe this account.

Coltishall

Before I began my journey around the county I made reams of notes on each town and village. My research for Coltishall, despite trying very, very hard, was minimal. There wasn't even a Nelson reference I could bung in. Even *he* didn't visit.[1]

There was only one sentence about the village in the hilarious 1949 *Penguin Guide to Norfolk & The Isle of Ely*. Here's what it said: 'Coltishall Church was dedicated in 1284, but retains traces of an earlier Sax. Building.' It then went on to list all of the various ways one could exit the village, as though that would be on the forefront of visitor's thoughts.

Another guide referred to it as, 'Once being more important than Wroxham.' How's that for a glittering review? I went to Wikipedia, God love it, out of desperation. It stated that nearby Horstead watermill had been 'one of the most photographed mills in the country' until a fire took care of it in 1963.

Coltishall wasn't going to be much of a competitor on the 'fascinating history' front.

To get to the real meat of Coltishall's past I had to look at the village website. It was there that I found out about a terrifying spate of vandalism in 2010. Here are the shocking details, in the words of those involved:

---

[1] By the time you've finished this book, you'll realise just how rare a phenomenon this was. Despite spending a good chunk of his relatively short life at sea and abroad, Nelson somehow managed to put in an appearance at nearly every bar, hotel and dance hall in the county. For a one-armed man with the world on his shoulders, he certainly performed more than the average quota of jigs. No wonder he was so slim.

> 8th February 2010
> *This is the second time a bin has been stolen, and there have been bins stolen from Rectory Road and Church Close recently. We have reports the bins have been towed behind cars with youths riding in them – a very dangerous and thoughtless action!!*

> 5th May 2010
> *Less than a week after installation some mindless morons have damaged an important fire exit with disability ramp at the village hall. In addition, the back safety rails have been battered and paint damaged.*

> 21st July 2010
> *Cricket pavilion window vandalised again.*

From then on the vandalism dissipated. Scores of criminology experts and analysts have since had their say on the Coltishall Riots. Several commentators from left-wing broadsheets voiced concern that enough people weren't questioning *why* these troubled youths felt the need to act in such a way. Maybe, they argued, they were simply expressing subconscious dismay at cuts to public services. They called the Coltishall vandals the 'Lost Generation'. The right-wing broadsheets said that the vandals were going to set the economy back £17billion in clean-up costs *and* severely damage the village's chances of hosting the 2023 Commonwealth Games.

The Daily Mail said that Romanians did it.

It's worth mentioning that Coltishall's riots took place a full year before the headline hogging London riots. They were the original trendsetters.

The low blanket of grey cloud had bubbled into a worrying purple. The bus dropped me beside the Sax. church over which the *Penguin Guide* had so heartily enthused. A blossom tree hung over its suggestively ajar gate, snowing pink flakes onto the grass. I love suggestively ajar church gates. They make me think that there may be an attractive young widow in the vicinity, leaving flowers 'pon her lover's grave. (That's where I'd swoop in with my A-Grade chat-up lines: 'So, you're a widow, eh? Why don't we open you up and let the air in.')

There was no widow in Coltishall churchyard. In her stead was an elderly man who looked like he'd won a fair few prizes for oddly shaped root vegetables in his time:

'How yer durn?' he asked.

'I'm doing great, thanks,' I replied. 'I don't like the look of those clouds, though.'

He roared with laughter. The silence was shattered. I wondered whether he'd misheard me. Either that or I was *even funnier* than I already thought. He walked away, still rocking:

'HAHAHAHAHAHA...'

Coltishall was heroically pre-war English. Any minute I expected to see a vicar cycling past, whistling *Jerusalem*. There was an attractive old shop in the heart of the village. It had a Georgian front with tall windows. Size wise, it wouldn't have looked out of place on Oxford Street. Bizarrely, it was being used as a pharmacy. It had to be Britain's grandest establishment from which to buy Complan.

There used to be an RAF base nearby. It closed in 2006. Hero of the skies, and occasional oddball, Douglas Bader had flown from there during World War Two.[1] He was stationed in Coltishall, in part, to improve morale amongst the Canadian pilots who had suffered heavy losses. He achieved at least twenty

---

[1] Norfolk became an RAF hotspot during the war. By 1945, there were 37 operational airfields in the county.

aerial victories during the conflict. The achievement was notable as he had done so after having his legs amputated. He flew whilst legless.[1]

Bader crashed whilst performing aerobatics in 1931. His legs were no more. Some people would be deeply reflective upon such a loss. They'd speak to counsellors and therapists for years before coming to terms with it. Bader, simply, wrote this in his diary: 'Crashed slow-rolling near ground. Bad show.' He had artificial limbs fitted and was flying within a year, having retrained from scratch. Against his wishes, his beloved RAF forced him to retire early in 1933. They simply couldn't countenance having a paraplegic pilot in one of their squadrons. No way. Not a chance. No.

Yet, for some strange reason, during the autumn of 1939, the RAF appeared keen to invite Bader back. They suddenly didn't seem too picky about the number of legs their pilots had. It was almost as if they were in some sort of shit.

Bader accepted the invitation. He got straight into action. He was involved in Dunkirk, the Battle of Britain and numerous other desperately close-run things. From Coltishall he was involved in a scramble that led to him shooting a Dornier Do 17 into the sea at Cromer.

In 1941, after being hit by friendly fire, he was imprisoned by the Nazis. Despite being treated reasonably well, Bader continuously tried to escape. It couldn't have been good for Nazi morale when even a man without legs was routinely slipping past the guards. He was thrown into Colditz where he remained for the duration.

When Bader was first taken prisoner, Goering permitted a small squadron of British planes to fly to Germany unharmed, to deliver the flying ace a new leg. It was dropped off by

[1] A tradition some modern commercial airline pilots are rumoured to occasionally honour.

parachute. It was an incredibly rare gesture of goodwill. The British, never ones to miss an opportunity, didn't just drop off the leg, however. Having been given a clear run through Germany, they also used the trip as a chance to drop off some bombs. The Germans weren't impressed. Even less so when Bader used his new leg to try and run away with the moment it was fitted.

When the war was won, Bader was elevated to national hero status, becoming the subject of numerous films and books. He worked hard for charity but took the occasional dip into murkier political waters. Amongst his recommendations for the improvement of his country, he advocated the reinstatement of the death penalty and suggested that foreigners ought not to live here. He had similar feelings about members of nuclear disarmament groups.

He was known for being brutally forthright. At a dinner in Munich, he entered a room full of ex-Luftwaffe pilots and declared, 'My God, I had no idea we left so many of you bastards alive!'

He died in 1982, as *Sir* Douglas Bader, after what must be described as some fairly stimulating bat-work during his innings.

I initially thought the Coltishall greengrocers was a well-stocked garden. It was adjacent to the mega-pharmacy. It was a small, red brick house with a garden full of flowers and boxed vegetables. The door of the house, a deep green, was shut. Nearby stood two locals, taking it in turns to mock one another. Thinking the coast was clear and the shop shut, I took my camera out.

'Don't let this man's face break the camera,' said the older of the two, pointing at his friend. 'Are we gorn be on the tele?"

'No,' I laughed, before giving them the low-down.

'So my shop's going to be in a famous book!' said the other.

'I hope so!' I said. I didn't have the heart to tell him how many copies my first book had sold.

'Don't let his face break your camera,' his friend said once more, for the record.

The grocer introduced himself as Chris. His older friend made an exit saying 'Goodbye' to us both, whilst warning me not to let Chris' face break my camera.

Chris gave me a potted history of the village. There'd been some Roman pottery discovered in the local soil, but other than that, the *Penguin Guide* was right. But that wasn't a bad thing. Coltishall didn't need reams of historical patter. It didn't need John of Gaunt to have lived there or for Nelson to have danced in one of its halls. It was fine the way it was.

I asked if I could take a photograph of Chris and his shop. I was spurred on by the memory of the old chap in Walsingham whom I hadn't dared ask. I wasn't going to let the moment pass again. He agreed instantly and, without my asking, opened the green door and performed the classic standing-in-the-doorway shopkeeper pose. The kind of pose you see in black & white pictures of butchers from the 1920s. I then took another shot of him waving. It is my favourite ever photograph. His face didn't break my camera.

As I shook his hand, I tried the 'Don't like the look of the clouds' gag again, aware that it tended to go down well in Coltishall. He laughed. Then the rain began to fall. Time to get back on the bus.

Norwich: Part I

'It's one of those places where the locals ask you what you think of it. They do that in Bristol and they do it in San Francisco.'
J.B Priestley, English Journey

I went to meet a girl. It wasn't the wisest plan. She arrived in pristine condition and I arrived from Coltishall looking like Pa Larkin after a hard day with the chickens.

I dumped my bag on the pub table, knocking over an artfully arranged vase of flowers. I was wearing too many layers. I tried to look cool and sophisticated whilst being immensely hot and bothered. Every time I moved I knocked the table again, spilling the drinks and sending the flowers flying.

We were in the Adam & Eve: the oldest pub in Norwich and one of the ten oldest in the country.[1] It was built in the 13th century for the builders of Norwich Cathedral to sup away their aches. Once the cathedral was complete, monks then started to nip in for a quiet pint and a quick go on the quiz machine. The bones of one were discovered during excavation work in the 1970s. His ghost was one of several said to haunt the jaunt.

Talk to anyone about the history of Norwich and the chances are that within two minutes the following fact will be relayed:

'Did you know [Yes!], that in Norwich there used to be a church for every Sunday of the year and a different pub for every day of the week?'

Ideally, I'd like to break it to you that the trivia was a fallacy, therefore allowing you to be condescendingly smug when

---

[1] It is impossible to judge which pub is England's oldest. The Adam & Eve might actually be it.

somebody next brought the subject up ('Actually, I *think* you'll find...' etc). Alas, it was true, with pubs and churches to spare. There used to be 57 churches within the famous city walls. By 1870, there was a peak number of 670 licensed premises. If the churches couldn't cure your ills, the sauce could.

The date wasn't going well. I kept talking about Norfolk. I wouldn't shut up. It didn't help matters that I was making the table vibrate every time I breathed in or out. It shook so much that it appeared as though we were engaged in a particularly energetic séance. I almost wished we were; I wanted to have a chat with the ghost monk about the quiz machine. He probably knew all the answers by now.

The numbers were not quite so dramatic but there was still a hell of a lot of pubs in Norwich. Many were centuries old and had intriguing histories. None more than The Wild Man, named after Peter The Wild *Boy*: a feral child discovered in a German wood by George I on a hunting trip in 1725.

The child was severely disabled. He couldn't read or speak. He walked on all fours. He'd survived by eating wild flora. George I did what any good king would do upon discovering a poor, destitute youth: he sent him to London to be kept as a 'human pet'.[1]

Peter, as the pet was subsequently named, became the talk of the nation. The king tried to domesticate the child by employing teachers and doctors to educate him in the ways of high society. One of the doctors regularly lashed at him with 'a broad leather strap to keep him in awe.' The king even invited Peter to dinner but was repulsed by the boy's table manners:

---

[1] I guess the boy should consider himself lucky he didn't end up with his head on display above the king's log cabin fireplace.

'Good Lord, don't they have dinner tables in the Hanoverian woodlands?... Oh, for goodness sake, child, take that spoon out of your ear... I can't believe this, you try and do something nice and this is the thanks you get... No, boy, no. It's a turkey not a hat!'

And so on.

Once the novelty of his new pet faded (a feral child is for life, not just for Christmas), the king sent the boy to a succession of carers who tried, and failed, to teach him to speak. Not surprisingly, Peter tried to run away and, rather surprisingly, managed to do so. He completely disappeared. It wasn't until a fire broke out at Norwich prison that he was discovered amongst the escaped convicts. People recognised him from the descriptions in the papers and pamphlets that his arrival in England had spawned, most notably by a reliably disgruntled Jonathan Swift.[1] The Norwich people said that the convict acted 'like an orangutan'. Rather than keep him as a pet, they returned him to his carers in Hertfordshire. A lavish collar was locked around his neck, bearing the inscription, *'Peter the Wild Man of Hanover. Whoever will bring him to Mr Fenn at Berkhamsted shall be paid for their trouble.'*

Peter enjoyed his time in Hertfordshire. His carers managed to butter him up - although he preferred Flora - and he lived a life of relative routine and calm. He was said to be a man of 'exceedingly gentle and timid nature.' He remained in Hertfordshire until his death. His gravestone reads, 'PETER the Wild Boy 1785'. He lived to the age of 72 (once you get a nickname, it can be hard to shake). He was certainly the oldest 'Boy' in England. Although the pub had the decency to refer to him as a man.

---

[1] 'His being so young was the occasion of the great disappointment of the ladies [of court], who came to the drawing room in full expectation of some attempt upon their chastity.'

Another notable Norwich watering hole was the long forgotten Samson & Hercules ballroom: a nightly hotspot for both US Servicemen and the Norfolk girls they nightly serviced. The hall had originally been a meeting place for Battle of Britain heroes, among them Douglas Bader, fresh from RAF Coltishall. But when the Yanks swooned in with their supplies of stockings and peculiar chocolate, they overtook the bar. They turned it into, gee, just about the hippest joint in Norwich, England.

Glenn Miller and his band played the Samson in the summer of 1944, weeks before their plane performed one of history's most thorough disappearing acts.[1] The ballroom was now a lobster restaurant.

Our romantic date was dying a slow death. Instead of undertaking my normal routine of dragging it out and hoping for the kiss of life, I left. I'd been inspired by the devil-may-care attitudes of some of the people I'd been finding out about. Would Douglas Bader have persevered with a date that was going nowhere? No chance. He'd have put his artificial foot down. He'd have slammed a hand on the table and declared, 'My God, I had no idea we left so many of you bastards alive!' or words to that effect. In truth, that wouldn't have been the best way to end the evening. So I said Goodbye instead and exited under the Adam & Eve's low doorframe, careful not to knock myself out whilst doing so. It would have undermined my grand gesture if my date had had to call for an ambulance.

I cut across the cathedral grounds. The setting sun had turned the spire a warm pink. Is there anything more magical than sunlight hitting the tops of tall buildings? Building work on the cathedral had started in 1096. The spire remains the second

---

[1] In the 1954 movie, *The Glenn Miller Story*, Miller was played by James Stewart, himself based in Norfolk for large parts of the war.

tallest in England, behind Salisbury. It was completed in 1167 and destroyed by lightning in 1169. It was soon rebuilt. And soon re-struck by lightning. And soon rebuilt. And soon re-struck by lightning. And so on. Using the phrase 'Lightning never strikes twice in the same place' near the cathedral was once a sure-fire way of getting slapped by a monk.

Within the confines of the cathedral walls were offshoot alleyways of old, twisted houses. They covered the cross section of British architectural history. Every era appeared to have a representative house. The gardens burst with colour; birds flitted above the hum of the city. It never fails to amaze me how few people use these pathways. The cathedral grounds offered easy access to the shops, to the train station, to the river, to the, ahem, Court of Justice. Yet visitors, like me, often have the place largely to themselves. Maybe I shouldn't keep on about it. I'd be the first to complain if the place attracted crowds of shoppers or dogging enthusiasts.

I crept past the grave of Edith Cavell, a Norfolk-born nurse of international renown.[1] I always creep past graves. I'm not sure why. It's not as if I'll wake their inhabitants up.

Edith Cavell was in Norwich when the First World War broke out. She headed to the action immediately. She tended both German and British casualties indiscriminately, receiving criticism back home for doing so. They couldn't comprehend her willingness to treat all humans as equals. The monster.

Cavell earned further criticism, this time from the Germans, when they discovered that she'd been helping British Prisoners of War to escape. *Their* criticism was a touch more understandable. Rather than muttering things under their breath

---

[1] To quote the Edith Cavell Trust, by 1912 she was, 'managing one nursing school, three hospitals, three private nursing homes, 24 communal schools for nurses, thirteen private kindergartens, private duty cases, a clinic and was giving four lectures a week to doctors and nurses.'

and writing snooty letters to the press, German criticism took the form of a court marshal. Cavell and a handful of colluders were sentenced, despite international pressure, particularly from the United States, to death by firing squad.

The night before her death, Cavell forgave her killers. They were, she told a reverend, only doing what they had to do: 'I expected my sentence and I believe it was just. Standing as I do in view of God and eternity, I realise that patriotism is not enough, I must have no hatred or bitterness towards anyone.'

Before shooting the friendly nurse, the German army had to weigh up the chances of her surviving the initial round of bullets and mutating into a giant, laser-firing robotic dragon. They clearly felt the chances of this were quite high, judging by the fact they hired sixteen soldiers to kill her. One rifleman allegedly refused to shoot. He was shot in return.

Cavell's body was returned to England. Her death broke the nation's heart. Her previously disgraceful habit of helping both ally and enemy in the treatment room was now, clearly, indicative of saintliness rather than a wanton disregard for what's proper. Her image was quickly used in an array of propaganda posters, which nearly all involved the words 'Hun' and 'Enlist'. It's what she would've wanted.

The consensus was that her body be buried in Westminster Abbey. The family preferred Norfolk. In the cathedral grounds. And there she lay, asleep in the shade created by that great monument to her city's former glories; awaiting reawakening by more suitable footsteps than mine.

I touched the headstone. I'm not sure why.

'Norwich has the most Dickensian atmosphere of any city I know,' wrote J.B Priestley on his tour of England. 'Except, perhaps, Canterbury,' he added, taking the shine off the statement.

There really was a touch of grandeur to the place. To quote Priestley again, 'This is not merely because Norwich has its cathedral and castle and the rest, but also because it has flourished as the big city in the minds of men for generations. It may be minute compared with London, Paris, Rome, but nevertheless it lives its life as a city on the same level of dignity. Norwich really is a capital: the capital of East Anglia.'
At the time of the cathedral's construction, Norwich was second only in size to London. Evolution in trade, and almighty bouts of plague (the Black Death, for instance, reduced the city's population to six thousand from twenty thousand), eventually changed that, but the very name *Norwich* had, as Priestley said, maintained its clout.

At the last count, 26pc of Norwich's population were between the ages of 16 and 39; this was almost 10pc more than the national average and 25pc higher than the Norfolk average.[1] The city's youthfulness can be attributed to the excellent University of East Anglia and the number of smaller, kookier specialist colleges dotted about. Young, intelligent people can have a hell of an effect on a place. Norwich had, and has, a constant buzz. There's always a gig to go to, an exhibition to see, a dance class to join, and a poetry reading to constantly check your watch at.
Nearly everybody I passed was good looking, which I appreciated so long as I didn't catch my own watery reflection in a shop window. Such was the pleasantness of the early summer evening, I almost skipped up the hill to my friend's place, passing the city's second cathedral. This had been built, much like the first, for Catholics. Unlike the first, though, this one

---

[1] Holt, Sheringham and Hunstanton were half-populated by people over the age of sixty. Senokot sales were booming.

still belonged to them. It looked a thousand years old but was actually something of a whippersnapper in cathedral circles. It was completed in 1910, instantly becoming a cause of passive aggressive joviality for people who'd agreed to meet at *the* cathedral.

Norwich had put a bounce in my step. A Shakespearean actor by the name of Will Kemp had also bounced through the city, albeit in the distant past. He danced from London to Norwich during Lent, 1599, in order to raise funds and, bizarrely, his profile. He must have foreseen future tavern conversations going somewhere along these lines:
'Have you heard of Will Kemp?'
'Ah, yes, that marvellous Shakespearean actor. I'll never forget his Benvolio.'
Alas, most conversations about him probably went like this:
'Have you heard of Will Kemp?'
'Ah, yes, that silly twat who clogged up the roads for a fortnight.'
In truth, each town greeted him like a dancing Jesus. Crowds thronged and fought to get a view of him. He attracted the best and worst of Norfolk's Elizabethan society. Some even brought their babies along to see the star in action. He was dressed like a Morris dancer i.e. a complete dick. So packed were the narrow streets that the hem of his garment accidentally became tangled with the dress of a comely wench (for want of a better term) and ripped the wench in question's clothes off, leaving her with nothing to keep her warm but the hollers of the crowd.

Kemp made a modest profit from the endeavour but not as much as he'd been led to believe. As he'd pranced from A to B, people had got caught up in the moment and pledged all sorts of riches. When it came time to collect the money, he found himself knocking on locked doors. As anyone who's ever done a sponsored baked bean dip or ironing marathon will testify, it's considerably easier getting people to part with imaginary money than the real kind.

Kemp's place in history, if we can call it that, was assured. His journey became the stuff of song and legend. Stories about his travels became so preposterous that he ended up having to write his own account of the jaunt to separate fact from fiction. It was called *Nine Daies Wonder Performed in a Daunce from London to Norwich'*. Sales, like my number of successful dates, had tailed off lately.

Wroxham (& Hoveton)

Upon arrival in sunny Wroxham, it struck me that I didn't know what I was going to do. I'd made no plans. With the broads and their day-hire boats a stone's throw away, I headed in that direction.

The Norfolk Broads (which also run through Suffolk) were originally thought to have been natural waterways. The secret of their origins remained for centuries. It wasn't until the 1960s that they were proven to be manmade. The once water-free area had been dug up for peat excavation in the Middle Ages. The then vulnerable land was flooded by rising sea levels.

Right. I daren't say more in case the word *silting* comes into play.

Wroxham was yet another big village. I would call it a town, personally. (Can you think of another 'village' that has a McDonalds?) Wroxham was famous for two things. The first was that it was 'Capital of the Norfolk Broads', where David Bowie claimed you could see the mice in their million hordes. The second was Roys of Wroxham, upon which Mr Bowie has yet to offer an opinion.

Roys of Wroxham was unique in that it was a village shop that seemed to have taken over most of the village. What was even more remarkable was that it had taken over the village of *Hoveton* and not Wroxham, which was actually a little further down the road. Roys bossed the joint. They had a Roys Department Store, a Roys Food Hall, a Roys Toy Shop, a Roys Garden Centre and a Roys clothing store called, I kid you not, RoyZone.

The endeavour started in the late 19th century with two brothers (Alfred and Arnold Roy) selling fruit to holidaymakers from a small store in Coltishall. As the company grew, the brothers moved into the big leagues (in village shop terms, I must stress), setting up a new store on the broads and calling it Roys of Wroxham. They never looked back. They certainly never looked at whether or not they were in Wroxham.

In the 1930s, Roys won a competition that permitted the business to call itself the 'The World's Largest Village Store'. For a time, it possibly was. My copy of *Women's Institute Book of Norfolk Villages*[1] painted a picture of Roys in the middle part of the last century:

'On its long mahogany counters complete with brass scales, tea, coffee and sugar were displayed in lovely decorated containers and weighed to the customers' requirements. Bacon was cut thick or thin by hand and all was personal service and no hurrying.'

Their stores looked American. The food hall in particular had a definite 50s US swagger. There was a touch of *The Last Picture*

[1] There's a line I never thought I'd write.

Show about it. I expected to see a Cadillac roll up with a couple of denim-clad high school jocks in the front and their white-haired sweethearts applying make-up in the back.

The main Roys of Wroxham building, in the centre of the village (of Hoveton), was the star of the show. That's where the hardcore Roys shopping action was. It was the place to go if you wanted owl-shaped pepper pots and Union Jack cushions. Need four place mats bearing a picture of the *Hay Wain*? My dears, you were at the right place. It was Harrods for people that would never go to Harrods. I include myself in that. Roys had the lot. God bless it. As their website proudly proclaimed, 'A visit to Roys is almost a day out in itself.' Almost. You might want to throw in a sky dive to seal the deal.

It wasn't all one big Roys. There were still a good number of touristy shops as well as countless pubs, hotels, restaurants and so on. It had a seaside town feel to it despite not being near the sea. There was more than one shop displaying beach balls and buckets and spades in the window. I didn't know where the sand was kept with which to make these items functional. Maybe there was a Roys Sand Depot.

I continued my journey to the water. It seemed that everywhere I turned I was confronted with a view that you'd expect to see in a crap calendar of regional waterways. The boats were moored and empty, with sunshine bouncing off their clean white exteriors. A gang of seagulls followed me around, perching nonchalantly onto poles and fences, as though trying to supply me with photo opportunities. I wondered if they'd been hired by the council in a bid to increase the quality of photographs people took of the area:

'Hold up. There's someone taking a photo down there,' says Gull A to Gull B.

'Come on, then. Let's go and sit on that bench for him,' replies Gull B.

'*You* can. *I'm* going to perch on that rubber ring and look pensive.'

'Good idea! That will be September sorted for the calendar.'

Gulls are the biggest show offs in the ornithological world. Whenever there's an oil slick, they're first on the scene, hamming it up. I refused to get sucked into their games and headed back towards Roys of Wroxham. In Hoveton.

Wroxham had a moment of celluloid glory to its name. It was used as a location in *I'm Alan Partridge*. In the episode, Alan offends the Norfolk farming community to such extent that they throw a cow on him as he sails under a Wroxham bridge. It's a classic moment from one of *the* classic sitcoms. There will be a commemorative plaque there one day, even if I have to nail the bastard in myself.

Other than *I'm Alan Partridge*, the village's forays into the televisual limelight were generally less celebrated. The place used to feature a lot in Anglia TV daytime documentaries. The sort of thing in which Helen McDermott (East Anglia's devastating answer to Esther Rantzen) went around the region tasting seafood and watching someone I went to school with give glass-blowing tutorials. The shows were called things like *Postcards From Anglia* and *McDermott's Summer*.[1] They used to air at about 2pm, in that much-missed grey area between the lunchtime screening of *Home & Away* and *CITV*. I daresay if you never caught one of her shows, you can imagine what they were like.

---

[1] McDermott got herself into the national press in 2015 after calling her co-presenter a 'See You Next Tuesday' on air. No jokes. Look it up.

*

Wroxham had the wind knocked out of it by the introduction of cheap international holidays in the 1970s. Since then, many of its grander buildings have been demolished or converted into flats. There can often be an underlying sadness to places that have been robbed of former glories, but Wroxham didn't have such complaints. It still drew crowds. The new holiday-lets and daytrip boat rides entertained untold thousands every year.

It is estimated that Norfolk receives an astonishing 31 million visitors a year. A large percentage of that 31 million head straight for the broads. No wonder Wroxham and Hoveton felt the need to team up.

One regular visitor was the ghost of the Roman military commander and Emperor of Britain, Carausius. He was a self-proclaimed emperor, which, if you ask me, is the best kind of emperor (I think *I'll* be emperor of the moon). He allegedly passes through Wroxham every now and then with a train of legionaries and lions bringing up the rear.

Of all the ghosts to see, Carausius and co. would be my preferred choice. Just imagine it. I don't know how the story started. One can excuse a person for thinking they'd briefly seen a ghostly figure standing at their window on a stormy evening, but to see the cast of *Spartacus* is another thing entirely.

From Roman ghost trains to Norfolk miniature trains: all aboard the Bure Valley Railway.

At the miniature station I was given a miniature map of where the miniature train would take me. Aylsham was the destination. It was going to be a long journey; or, rather, a very short journey that was going to take a very long time. Like Walsingham and Wells, the miniature track had replaced a full-sized track once linking the two locations (before our sage overlords decided that, by approximately 1980, we'd all have flying cars and would never need trains again).

The train arrived sounding not too dissimilar to myself after a short jog to the kitchen. It panted and choked. It looked bigger than the Walsingham train. The carriages certainly were.

I'd reached a stage in my journey where I was taking pictures of nearly every single thing I saw. I didn't want anything to be forgotten: Oh, look, a swan; Oh, look, a village hall; Oh, look, a Mazda. I wasn't going to let a miniature train go un-photographed.

I whipped my camera out and tried to get the killer angle of the steaming monster in situ. Whilst doing so, I inadvertently stood in front of a friendly-looking old man who was equally keen to obtain personal photographic evidence of the train's existence.

'Sorry,' I said, with a slight laugh in my voice to show how remarkably affable I was. 'I didn't mean to ruin your photo.'

The old man ignored me and rolled up his cardigan sleeves. He took another shot. He crouched down, tutting.

'I can't get a fahking angle on it,' he said in his finest Alf Garnett voice.

Old people can often be heard dishing out stern criticisms against the younger generation's choice of words. They state how shocking it is to hear such crude language from such young mouths. Well, let me tell you something, hearing a young person swear is nowhere near as alarming as hearing an oldie giving it their best.

'Gina!' he yelled down the platform. 'Gina, love! The fahking thing's too long.'

Never had the Bure Valley Railway received such a blistering critique.

'Fahksake,' he muttered one last time. He walked away and, in a shocking twist, and in a shockingly accurate manner, began singing:

'*Love meee ten-der, love me true-ooh, all my drea-eams ful-fill...*'

I had never been so confused.

I got a perfectly acceptable angle and quickly took a picture. As I walked down the platform I passed the old man. He was in full discourse with Gina. I didn't hear much bar repeated use of the words 'fahking' and 'angle.' It all felt so incongruous. I couldn't visualise any of the other old people I'd met on my trip dishing out cusses so liberally. Imagine that old gentleman who'd given me a lift to the Slipper Chapel ending our conversation by saying, 'I'm fucking ninety!'

I had a miniature carriage all to myself. There was no Earl of Grantham look-alike on board this time. As an added bonus, all of the children were at least two carriages down (getting bollocked, no doubt).

My very own carriage. I felt like royalty. Miniature royalty, but royalty nonetheless. The interior bordered on the plush. The engine peeped. The conductor walked along the platform, shutting doors as he went. I was getting used to this novelty train lark.

As we chugged past hedgerows and farms, I realised that the carriage was small enough (and the train moving slowly enough) for me to sit with my feet sticking out of the window. I slid one open and rested my feet on the ledge. It was divine. The wind blew through my socks and between my toes. I had never been, and expect may never again be, in a situation where I could plonk my feet out of a train window. I had to grab the opportunity. It made me wonder how many people in the history of the world had *ever* performed this rare treat. In the passing fields stood young families on morning strolls. As their children waved energetically at our train, I returned the favour with a lazy swing of the ankles. How different those final scenes from *Brief Encounter* would've been if Trevor Howard had waved Celia Johnson off like this.

The train moved through the most incredible, unseen landscapes. We passed manor houses and villages. We passed sweeping wheat fields and secret churches. I swear at one point we went back in time. We went through Brampton village and Buxton village. Both looked exactly as you would expect villages with such names to look.

Brampton was a noted Roman settlement. When archaeologists visited the parish in the 1970s - those were some wild nights down at the village hostelry, I can tell you - they found endless fascinating things. And some brick kilns. However you dress them up, ancient brick kilns always act as a full stop on one's interest. They could find a brick kiln on Mars and people would still yawn and wonder what was for tea.

The train took me on a Norfolk odyssey.[1] The last stage of the adventure was a jet-black tunnel which seemed to last an eternity; being claustrophobic, I would think that. In reality, you could probably walk through it in four seconds. At the other side was the historic market town of Aylsham.

They say Nelson danced in one of its halls.

Aylsham

The miniature station had three or four tracks and an overly dramatic roof. It resembled King's Cross as seen through the wrong end of a pair of binoculars. As the passengers exited their mini-carriages, they looked like an army of invading giants, hell-bent on destroying Aylsham.

The first view upon leaving the station was of an incredibly arty Tesco. It'd been built from wood and recycled plastic, amongst

---

[1] Norfolk Odyssey is a good name for an Odyssey tribute act. If only it was 1982...

other things.[1] It was 'the Greenest Tesco in the world.' Although, I'd say it looked mostly grey and blue. Regardless, *Green* was the theme here. In 2008, Aylsham became the first town in Norfolk to be plastic bag free. Anyone visiting with a view to checking out the wide variety of carrier bags on offer would leave bitterly disappointed.

Onwards I marched towards the town centre, and what a fine-looking town centre it was. Its only blemish was the car park in the market place. There were considerably more cars than people. Were people just parking up and running away? Aylsham joined the long list of Norfolk beauty spots that looked prettier in the evening, when the cars had gone.
The town sign depicted John of Gaunt sitting on a white horse, looking forlornly into the distance. John of Gaunt all but ruled the country during the reign of his nephew Richard II in the late 14th century. The consensus was that Richard II needed an adviser on account of his being ten-years-old and mostly interested in football stickers. John stepped in, gladly, it must be noted, and ruled the roost until Richard was old enough to get his swagger. (And it was quite a swagger. Richard II was something of a big head. He was the first king to demand to be called 'Your majesty'.)
In Shakespeare's *Richard II*, it's John of Gaunt who delivers the famous lines, 'This happy breed of men, this little world, This precious stone set in the silver sea… This blessed plot, this earth, this realm, this England…'
I've checked Gaunt's famous speech twice over and have yet to see any mention of Aylsham: possibly because he never stepped foot in it. My trusty *Penguin Guide* says Gaunt's money built

---

[1] Next time you're taking the green wheelie bin out in your damp slippers, remember that it's for a good cause: they might make a Tesco out of it.

the church and that he 'used to hold his court' in the area. But neither of those things necessarily proved he visited. He was, however, 'Lord of the Manor', meaning that he had land entitlements. And his links to the town did allow its people to be excused from jury duty and from paying certain taxes. There may be something in it. But I'm not sure I'd make a John of Gaunt town sign on the strength of the evidence.

I was surprised at the amount of fresh-faced pregnant ladies I saw hurrying about. Coupled with the idyllic country town setting, the whole thing had a whiff of *The Midwich Cuckoos*. Good Lord, I thought, I've arrived in the Village Of The Damned - by miniature train!

In moments of such dread realisation, you can only find peace in either prayer or a stiff drink. Unfortunately, the Black Boys pub where Daniel Defoe dined and Nelson, the eternal bopper, danced, was closed. The church it was.

The graveyard had a few notable long-term residents. The most famous was Humphry (without an 'e') Repton, the landscape gardener. Repton had tried his hand at nearly every job going in 18th century society by the time he landed (forgive the pun) on gardening. He made his way in this field (forgive the pun) by drawing up elaborate plans of gardens and presenting his ideas to potential customers in what were called his *Red Books*. He would knock-up picturesque designs, which the owners of the land would then get to work on. He sold a dream rather than the finished product.

Among Repton's achievements were Woburn Park in Bedfordshire, Kensington Gardens (parts of it) and West Wycombe Park, not to mention numerous Norfolk parks, including Gunton and Sheringham. He was even name-checked in Jane Austen's *Mansfield Park*, which goes some way to highlighting his reputation. His lasting legacy, in my humble opinion, was in coining the term 'landscape gardening'.

His grave was lovely. I won't make a habit of quoting epitaphs, but his was worth it:

Not like Egyptian Tyrants consecrate
Unmixed with others shall my dust remain
But mold'ring, blending, melting into Earth.
Mine shall give form and colour to the Rose
And while its vivid colours cheer Mankind,
Its perfumed odours shall ascend to Heaven

There was also the (empty) grave of Bishop Jegan, who died in 1617. He was so unpopular with Aylsham parishioners that they dug his corpse up and tossed his bones about for a laugh.

Another empty casket belonged to Christopher Layer. He worked and lived in the town as an attorney in the 17th century. He plotted the formation of an army to take over the Tower of London and the Bank of England, amongst other things, and restore the House of Stuarts as heads of the monarchy. Or something. Anyway, the plot failed. Although Layer did at least get inside the Tower of London. As a prisoner.

At Layer's trial, one of the pieces of evidence against him was a self-written summary of the plot entitled '*Scheme*'. Talk about dropping yourself in it. He should have given it a dummy name like '*Granny's Secret Recipes*'. Layer was found guilty and given the Tyburn treatment. His bones were auctioned. His head was sold to an antiquarian (the queer chap kept the skull in his house and was buried with it in his right hand). Layer's Aylsham headstone marked his resting place in a purely symbolic manner.

Another of Aylsham's famous sons whose bones couldn't be found in the graveyard was the anaesthetist Joseph Clover. Clover oversaw, among around 13,000 other patients, operations on Napoleon III, Robert Peel and Florence

Nightingale. His self-invented Chloroform Apparatus ensured that he was the safest anaesthetist in the known world, and the go-to man for world leaders and royalty. He died in 1882 and was buried in London. They didn't trust the people of Aylsham with his bones. They'd have been on eBay within a week.

Aylsham also had a famous *daughter* whose inability to produce one of Aylsham's famous sons contributed to her downfall. Her name was Anne 'Six Fingers' Boleyn. You know, from *Wolf Hall*.

Anne 'Six Fingers' Boleyn was born, according to a statue on its grounds, at Blickling Hall, just outside Aylsham, in 1507. 'Anna Bolena hic nata 1507,' it reads. Whether she was actually 'hic nata' is up for debate.

Incredibly, her exact date of birth isn't known, which leads to a certain amount of guesswork when it comes to figuring out her *place* of birth. Some historians say that she was born in Hever Castle in Kent. They argue that the Boleyn family had moved out of Blickling by 1507, so to say she was born there is absolute tommyrot. Yet, other historians say that *of course* she was born in Blickling Hall.

And then a massive fight breaks out.

It's worth pointing out that even if she were born at Blickling Hall, it wasn't the same Blickling Hall that pulled in the modern day punters. The original building fell into ruin and was rebuilt in the 17th century. Anne never stepped foot in the newer version, or its National Trust gift shop.

After a confused childhood in which she went around innocently asking everyone where and when she was born, Anne was sent to Holland and France for her education. She was maid of honour to Claude of France before returning to England to marry her undoubtedly sexy cousin, James Butler. The marriage never took place and Anne soon got herself a nice little earner as maid of honour to Henry VIII's first wife, Catherine of Aragon.

Anne was considered plain looking. It was her wit and feistiness that won admirers.[1] She was a lover of the arts and an intelligent reader of theological arguments, mostly of an anti-Catholic bent.

'That young maid of yours seems rather witty and feisty,' mused Henry one evening at dinner, whilst rubbing his thighs under the table.

'She is,' replied Catherine, sensing the threat. 'But she's got six fingers on one of her hands.'

Catherine broke the ensuing silence by adding that it wasn't all bad news for Anne: she could do a great cat's cradle.

Henry's thighs were rubbed once more.

The rest is GCSE History.

Henry made his move. He began flirting with Anne, sending her gifts and doing crap jokes about hoping that despite being a maid of honour, she wasn't entirely *made* of honour. His ability to wait at least three days before replying to her texts, and added to the fact that he was the most powerful man in the land, ensured that Anne gave in to Henry's charms.

Henry and Anne married. Or, perhaps more importantly, Henry and Catherine *divorced*. The pope smelt something fishy - and it wasn't even a Friday. He excommunicated the king and broke the Church of England's ancient alliance with Rome. There followed centuries of war with European Catholic countries, from the French to the Spanish and their Armadas. Many English commoners, including, you may remember, the people of Sheringham, lived in fear of invasion. Henry's passing lusts subjected his people to hundreds of years of peril. Still, the heart wants what it wants.

---

[1] Her wit and feistiness were later considered, along with her sixth finger, to be indicative of her being a sex-crazed witch.

What Henry primarily wanted, as we all know, was a legitimate son. He had already successfully drilled his royal seed into the fertile young ladies of court and many of the resulting sons shared their father's name (one of them was with Anne's sister, Mary: the *other* Boleyn girl). They were also, like their father, bastards, albeit bastards of a different kind, and therefore couldn't be king. In time, Henry's quest for an heir would drive him from one wife to the next until his number of wives equalled the number that Anne used to get to when counting the fingers on her right hand.[1]

Anne could only produce a daughter. It was a daughter of high calibre, the future Queen Elizabeth, but Henry was not impressed. He was becoming more unpredictable, flying into rages and acts of violence. A nasty fall from a horse contributed to his increasing lunacy. After a failed pregnancy in which Anne gave birth to a 'defective' stillborn, Henry began to think his wife was cursed. Giving birth to deformed babies was seen as a sign of sorcery and illicit sexual acts. The child, predictably, was a boy.

Henry had already started flirting with Anne's maid of honour, Jane Seymour. He soon began the process of waiting three days to reply to *her* texts and wondering if *this* blushing young maid of honour was entirely *made* of honour. He gave Jane a gift of a locket with a miniature sketch of himself inside. Jane would deliberately open it and close it in front of Anne. The combination of the loss of her husband's heart and the annoying clicking noise caused Anne to rip it from Jane's neck in a fury. Things were fast deteriorating into a 16th century episode of *Hollyoaks*.

---

[1] She didn't really have six fingers. There was a slight anomaly on her right hand, nothing more. The sixth finger myth began circulating at around the same time she was deemed to be a witch. I've also used the myth for wicked ends: my rubbish jokes.

Henry had Anne arrested on charges of treason and devilry. She was accused of incest with her brother, George (who also *might* have been born at Blickling). The trial recorded that Anne 'tempted her brother with her tongue in the said George's mouth and the said George's tongue in hers.'[1] One of her acts of treason had been to mention the king's death in passing. To imagine the king dying was simply not acceptable; it was on a par with plotting it.

On the boat ride to the prison, her screams could be heard on both sides of the Thames. She was isolated in the Tower until her sentence was revealed. Not only was Anne sentenced, so too was George and a host of other men with whom she was alleged to have had intimacies. The men were to be hanged, drawn and quartered. Anne, it was decided, would be beheaded by sword, not axe. To be killed by sword was more Arthurian to Henry's eyes. He wanted to add a touch of class to the decapitation.

A large crowd assembled the morning she took her place on the scaffolding. Some worried that, being a witch, she might survive the beheading. Others worried that God would demonstrate his displeasure at the execution of one of His Divine beings. There was no block to rest her head; she was to kneel upright, unsupported. She asked to speak to the crowd. She prayed for God to 'save the king and send him long to reign over you, for a gentler nor a more merciful prince was there never, and to me he was ever a good, a gentle, and sovereign lord…'

It didn't get a laugh.

As she kneeled, she whispered 'Oh, Christ, receive my spirit' to herself as the executioner tried to get a good *fahking angle* on the chop.

---

[1] It's likely that she was sleeping with other men in the royal court. She was desperate to become pregnant. Some have even suggested that she may have slept with her brother to ensure her child looked like a Boleyn, which would mute Henry's suspicions.

Her head hit the ground. A bolt of fear shot through the crowd. The lips and eyes spasmed 'as if in frantic prayer.' She had survived! Terror! Briefly.
She hadn't survived.

I found a fan website devoted to Anne Boleyn. She has almost become a brand name. The website sold t-shirts and books and pretty much anything else a Boleyn fan might reasonably require. It also had a comment thread for fans to leave messages. I have no real business to mention it here other than I thought it was lovely. Here are two of the comments:

'Anne Boleyn is my favourite person in the whole world. I'm only 12 and I'm already addicted. I have seen all of the Tudor shows and I'm longing for more. I plan to research until I know everything I need to know about this time period.'

'She's my favourite person, too! I'm 15 and I've been researching her and the Tudor Dynasty for about 3 years, yet there's always more information to find! I hope to study History at university, and it's all because of Anne Boleyn.
Who knew someone born in the 16th Century could have an effect on someone's life in the 21st? :)'

It's said by some that Anne's headless ghost appears at Blickling Hall on the anniversary of her death. I must point out that it's also said, by many more people, that it doesn't. You decide.
I don't want to end the Aylsham section with talk of beheaded ghosts. So, here are some crap jokes I've written and fully expect to become part of the Henry VIII crap-joke-canon:
Why did Catherine Parr have teeth marks on her arm?

Because Henry Tudor.
Here's another:
Why did Henry take his wife to Specsavers?
To help Jane Seymour.

The bus ride home further highlighted how stunning this part of the county was. It was shot magnificently by Joseph Losey in his 1971 film of *The Go Between*. Never has Norfolk been captured so perfectly. The finest moment in the film is Ted (oh, poor Ted) working the fields outside Melton Constable. If you can put up with Alan Bates' Norfolk accent, it's worth seeing.
The gorgeously peculiar, privately-owned village of Heydon (consisting of almshouses, a manor, a green, and a church) also appeared throughout the film. It looked exactly the same now as it did in 1971, and, most probably, as it did at the beginning of the last century, when the story was set. The last 'new' building to be erected there was the Queen Victoria Memorial Well. That was in 1887. You can give no finer review of the place than to mention that its two business endeavours are a pub and a cake shop.
In my headier moments, I see myself living in the village, pruning roses and listening to cricket on the radio. I don't even like cricket and I've never pruned a rose in my life. But if I lived in Heydon…

Leg Four

Bacton – Happisburgh – Stalham

Bacton & Happisburgh

The day started ominously. I'd woken to the tapping of drizzle against the bedroom window. My first thought, after shaking off the echoes of my obligatory dream about rising water levels, was to save the trip for another day. I turned over and dragged the duvet over my head, creating one of those agreeable little warm waves of bed air. I closed my eyes and fell into a light, dreamy morning sleep (about rising water levels).

The alarm went off. I'd programmed my phone to play *The Littlest Hobo* theme as an alarm in the hope that it would make my mornings chirpier. The effects were dazzling. I was pumped with an early morning zest normally seen only on the faces of kids in Frosties adverts. I got up and dressed. I was alert. I was alive. Seize the day! I opened the front door and stepped out into the spits of funeral rain.

The seize-the-day mentality lasted all of three seconds before being replaced by a sod-the-day mentality. The warm waves of bed air had been replaced by cold waves of wet air; icy fingers slipped down the inside of my collar. I waited at the bus stop in the rain, alone. My trousers were wet. The water levels were rising. Maybe this was a dream!

It wasn't.

The bus arrived, spraying me with expert precision. (Do bus drivers practice this art at Bus Driver Finishing School?) To get to Bacton[1] and Happisburgh, I had to briefly revisit Mundesley – home of Pat Butcher and the smallest maritime museum *in the known universe* - to catch a connecting bus. The rain had dried up by the time I arrived. My trousers hadn't. I looked at the timetable. It told me that my bus was due to leave from this stop in ten minutes. Forty-five minutes later, I sensed something was up.

I walked to the Mundesley Tourist Information Centre (yes, they even had one of those. I tell you, that village had *everything*) and asked where my bus might be. Apparently, it had left half an hour ago from a top secret, stealth bus stop on the other side of the village. But, it wasn't all bad news: there was another one due in two hours.

Weeping bitterly, I staggered around, aimless. Despair occasionally flared into rage as I kicked out at gravel and passing cats. I almost gave up. I considered throwing myself down one of the village's many cliff faces and donating my body to the ages.

What the hell was I going to do in Mundesley for two hours that I hadn't already done on my last visit? I had to take it as a given that the museum was still closed. (It was.) Although there were more shops than the average village, these fitted more into the Amenities category rather than the Things To Look At To Pass The Time category. I couldn't exactly go window-shopping around the pharmacy:

'Do you need any help, Sir?'

'No thanks. I'm just browsing.'

'Ok. Well, if you *do* need any help with those athlete's foot powders, just let me know.'

'Will do.'

---

[1] *I'm Going Bacton My Roots* by Norfolk Odyssey. Available from all good record stores.

Rather than *Kismet Quick*, I wondered if a better name for my book wouldn't be *Loitering Around Mundesley*. The zenith of desperation was reached when I walked into the butchers (not Pat's) to have a butchers (again, not Pat's). I'd been reduced to going into a meat shop to look at meat.

I'll just repeat that, in case it didn't quite register: I was going into a meat shop to look at meat.

Inside, they had the traditional statue of a moustachioed butcher standing proud with his fisted hands on his hips. Unusually, though, next to him stood a replica, one-third of the height. Such was the dourness of the morning, I felt the need to take a photograph of this novelty.

I also took a picture of a wall on which were displayed 'Thank You' cards from children to the butcher. It was a heart-warming sight. Although the inevitable drawings of Peppa Pig were tainted by the fact that her brother's stomach was for sale on the shelf behind me.

I had a Eureka moment. The meat had inspired me.

'I can cure my boredom by eating!' I said, possibly out loud.

I found a great bakery/café and ate a fry up fit for a king. I didn't feel regal for long. The sensation was cut short by the arrival of several youths sitting directly behind me, their performances directed by Mike Leigh. One of them uttered the following line:

'He futtun beat the shit outta me juss cus I ran oover his hamster.'

I imagine the royals seldom overheard such quotes whilst breakfasting. I was dethroned.

I didn't deliver the calculated rant I'd planned for the bus driver. I never do. It's always the same. I plot each line carefully; I even envisage dishing out my monologue to rapturous applause from the passengers. But I'm always so relieved when the bus shows up that my rage fades into meek subservience.

'Hello,' I said to the driver in my chirpiest voice, inwardly hating myself.

I now wasn't going to have time to get off at Bacton *or* Happisburgh. They were lost causes. I'd have to ride through them on the bus and take photographs from my seat. Can you imagine Steinbeck or Hemingway doing that?

The trip was turning into a disaster.

The bus went through, or just past, Paston village, home of the world famous (ish) Paston family, writers of the world famous (ish) *Paston Letters*. The Pastons had acquired their wealth off the back of William Paston's (born 1378) success in the legal profession. He was first to jab the Paston family foot into the ever-closing door of the elite.

You'll be pleased to know that your hero has read a collection of the Paston letters so you don't have to. It wasn't fun. The majority of them were business related, an antiquarian collection of work emails, minus the jokes and flirting. The family (who took their name from Paston village, not the other way around) fortune was spent by the 18th century. The last of the Pastons, another William, died bankrupt in 1732. His three sons had died before him. It was the end of the line.

The Paston's role in Norfolk's history was all but forgotten until the letters were discovered and published in the late 1700s. They've been in print ever since. I wouldn't recommend reading them, though. Unless you're fond of the word 'spake'. However, there was one funny incident involving a servant getting fired after demonstrating a 'knave's lust' and rogering some girl 'in the rabbit warren' (not a euphemism). Other than that, they're a bit of a slog.

*

Bacton was known for two things: the enormous gas works and Bromholm Priory. The priory was founded in 1113, the gasworks in 1969. People rarely confused the two. The bus didn't allow a view of Bromholm's ruins. It was out there somewhere.

The priory's finest hour was in staging the funeral of John Paston in 1466. His body was brought up from London. When the funeral carriage arrived at the Bromholm gates, those at the back of the procession were four miles away in North Walsham. The monks put on a lovely spread, which included one hundred pigs, oxen and calves. Over one thousand eggs and twenty gallons of milk were used. A man was employed to skin animals for three whole days beforehand and a barber stayed on site for five, to ensure that all monks had the tidiest Terry Nutkins hairstyles possible. More than sixty gallons of alcohol were downed. It makes you wonder if the people were celebrating John Paston's death rather than his life:

'I never hath spake ill of the dead, yet surely this man were a complete turd,' spake someone in the *Paston Letters*. 'I'd lyke to hath kicked him up the rabbit warren.'

It was a strange looking place, Bacton. Like many Norfolk villages, it sprawled across a deceptively large area and it was hard to decipher just where the centre was.

Beyond the Eiffel Tower-prototype gasworks were a jumbled assortment of holiday parks and lodges. I'd never seen so much eccentric brickwork in one place. Garden walls at knee height, garden walls at head height, garden walls at waist height. Brickwork, brickwork, brickwork. It was a bewildering place. There were almost no buildings above head height. It was chalet, caravan and bungalow territory. Holidayland. Even the shops were mostly short and squat, like prefabs.

Maybe Bacton's lack of pomp came from the fact that it had never been served by the railways and never had swathes of wealthy Victorians putting up retreats from which to take the North Sea air.[1] Ironically, the village *was* home to a number of train carriages. Many had been converted into holiday chalets or houses. Until recently there was something of a mystery as to how these carriages had arrived in Bacton. The mystery was solved when a photograph (from 1916) was found of a man towing one into the village with his traction engine.

It's true what they say: if you leave something lying around in Norfolk long enough, somebody will tow it with a traction engine.

Happisburgh, for any non-Norfolk readers out there, is pronounced *Haze*-borough. How that pronunciation (or spelling) was decided is anybody's guess. There's no rhyme or reason to any of it. What about if I started to pronounce Great Yarmouth as 'Get Yamff'? And what if everyone else started doing it, too? Would it eventually become so? Would some poor child of the future be chastised by their teacher for idiotically pronouncing it phonetically when it was quite clear that it said 'Get Yamff'?

To get to Happisburgh, the bus had to plough through Walcott, a kind of Diet Bacton, with what must surely be the highest ratio of ground floor abodes per square mile in Europe. Everything was a bungalow or a chalet. A hard wind might wipe it off the map.

Whereas Bacton was famous for its gas towers, Happisburgh was famous for its lighthouse. It had red and white stripes, like a 70s football scarf. Built in 1790, it had stood firm through

---

[1] The North Sea was known as the German Ocean throughout the Victorian age. The name became predictably unfashionable with time.

some of the wildest storms in recorded history. The only time it had really been under threat was when it featured on an episode of *Challenge Anneka*.

Anneka and her specialists decided to repaint the historic landmark. Unfortunately, the BBC supplied the wrong type of paint. The cost to *re-paint* over this failure was around £30,000. It just about survived the ordeal and was still, mercifully, the oldest operational lighthouse in East Anglia.

Happisburgh had been abandoned in its battle against the sea. Each year more houses collapsed into the crumbling ground. The village had been neglected by those with the power to act. I'd naively thought that councils and governments had a duty to do all they could to prevent the loss of people's homes. Far from it. All moves to protect the village have been held back by red tape and bizarre initiatives, one of which being a plan to allow this stretch of coast to erode itself into a bay, losing six villages along the way. It was heartbreaking.

The lighthouse, too, was doomed. It had saved countless people during its own two hundred year life. Maybe, when it finally begins falling, somebody, somewhere, will act. It could be that an initiative to save the lighthouse could, by default, save the village.

It won't be long until we find out.

The lighthouse wasn't the oldest relic in Happisburgh. Compared to recent findings, it was a mere whippersnapper. After the storms of 2013, the tide dragged sand away from the beach, revealing an 800,000-year-old set of footprints.[1] They

---

[1] Happisburgh had already caused an archaeological stir in 2010 when tools from the same era were found.

were the oldest ever found outside of Africa. Archaeologists now believe Norfolk to be the first settlement in Britain, possibly as long ago as 1.2 million years.

The footprints belonged to a race known as Homo antecessor, who stemmed from southern Europe (before being hounded out by UKIP). Back then, Britain was still connected to mainland Europe. The Thames ran into Norfolk, converging with another river to form a large estuary where Happisburgh now stood. It was impossible to comprehend, especially whilst riding over it on a bus. Mind you, if those in power have their way, give it a few years and it might look like an estuary again.

Just what the devil else was hiding beneath those ploughed fields and mown lawns? The Norfolk estuary was once home to rhinos, lions, wolves, hippos, hyenas, bison. Also there, scavenging for shellfish and crabs, were the makers of the footprints. The tallest of them, based on shoe size (not that they had shoes), was 5ft 7inches. He, or she, was accompanied by children. One of the sets of footprints might have belonged to the young Cher. This hasn't been proved, though, and she's yet to reply to my email on the subject.

A British Museum scientist declared it 'one of the most important discoveries, if not *the* most important discovery that has been made on [Britain's] shores... It will rewrite our understanding of the early human occupation of Britain and indeed of Europe.' But then, he would say that, because *he* discovered them.

The BBC had considered hiring Anneka Rice to come and hose the footsteps away with a pressure washer but the returning tide beat her to it. The artefacts were on show for just a matter of days before nature pulled the curtains shut. After one million years, the footprints finally went walkabouts.

Try as I may, I couldn't see St Mary's from the bus. I had my camera primed. I must have been blind: it was said to stand at such a height that you could see thirty other spires from the top. Incredibly, you could even see Norwich Cathedral, sixteen miles away. Somehow, I managed to not even see the *one* spire that was right in front of me.

St Mary's churchyard told of the perils of the sea. It held the bones of the 32 men who died on the HMS Peggy in 1770 and the hundred-plus sailors who died when their inappropriately named HMS Invincible sank in 1801. (Their bones were discovered by chance when a drainage trench was made in 1988.) Many more men and ships had washed up on the sands.[1] Happisburgh, for all its charms, had a cruel history. 'God moves in mysterious ways,' wrote William Cowper after watching a Happisburgh storm in full swing.

The church and the lighthouse: the story of the village in two buildings.

How such a place could be left to the sea's appetite was a mystery. It had real cultural pedigree. It had been visited and adored by Turner (who liked the beach sufficiently to paint a picture of it), Henry Moore (who liked the ironstone pebbles on the beach so much he carved a figure out of them), Sir Arthur Conan Doyle (who wrote a Holmes story from a hotel room overlooking the bowling green), Sir John Betjeman (who visited the church as part of a BBC documentary) and, ahem, Rolf Harris.

No sooner had I seen Happisburgh than it was gone. The bus rode onward. *Can yer tell what it is yet?*

It had passed me by in a Happis.

*

[1] The sands at Happisburgh are called, and spelt, *Haisborough* Sands! I don't make this stuff up. Next stop, Get Yamff.

The question of whether or not one could travel leisurely between the key towns and villages of Norfolk via public transport had been answered with typical country life candour: No. No, you couldn't.

Stalham

Ah, freedom. Fresh air. Stalham was my playground. I planned to make up for missing out on Bacton and Happisburgh. I was going to go to town on Stalham. Oh boy. Stalham was going to get the crap visited out of it.

Due to the bus stop being at the end of the high street, my first view was a Lowry-esque panorama. Stalham looked like a town that you might pass through on your way to Manchester. The high street had a distinctly non-Norfolk appearance. The shops were like little houses. They pressed closely to the street, thinning the pavements. Lots of them had the flag of St George swaying from the rafters. (England flags remind me of two things: firstly, racists waving poorly worded placards and, secondly, losing on penalties. As it was almost World Cup season, this, I assumed, was the reason for the flag abundance.)

Stalham barely garnered a mention in the *Penguin Guide*. The *Rough Guide* said the town centre had 'seen better days'. The *Women's Institute Book* refused to even acknowledge its existence.

The high street consisted of the usual assortment of takeaways, charity shops, pubs and hairdressers. Lots and lots of hairdressers: I counted eight. I found myself checking if the locals all had immaculate hair. I couldn't hold a conversation with any of the shopkeepers without staring at their heads:

'Yes, we've been running the shop for five years now. It's going very well.'
'Great.'
'We thought we might have a problem with Tesco but… Are you alright?'
'Yes. Sorry. No. Maybe. What?'
'Were you staring at my hair?'
'Yes.'
'Could you leave the premises, Sir?'
Amidst it all were a couple of novelties, including a Baptist hall masquerading as a gymnasium. I *had* to go in.

On the wall, as in every church hall ever made, was a multicoloured, 1970s felt display saying 'JESUS'. There were notice boards, onto which were pinned bereavement support posters[1] and coffee mornings in aid of Kenya.[2] Around the perimeter was dark brown Baptist church wainscoting and the occasional dark brown Baptist church wooden rail, into which brass Baptist church coat hooks had been nailed. The walls were a warm, yellowy white from which you could almost hear rebounded shouts of former youth clubs and nursery mornings. Aged windows filtered the sunlight. It was *the* archetypal church hall. Except for the fact that it housed some of the snazziest gym equipment on the market.

I had a conversation with the chap in charge. It was a non-profit community project. The poor guy had to put all of the equipment away himself every night.
'Keeps you fit, I guess,' I said.
'Yep.'

---

[1] Generally consisting of a black & white photograph of a middle-aged woman accompanied by red text: 'I JUST CAN'T DO THIS ANYMORE'.

[2] 'Kenco For Kenya – Tuesdays 11am.'

His tone suggested that he had perhaps heard the joke before and possibly didn't find it as gut-crampingly hilarious as he ought to have done.

I didn't dare do the one about *exer*cising demons.

You can do whatever you like to a church hall and it will always smell the same. Stalham's was no different. This was a place where people came to purposefully work themselves into a gluey sweat on a daily basis, yet it still smelt of gas heaters and varnished wood.

I didn't intend to spend the whole afternoon sniffing church halls, however. I hit the high street again. I saw another church hall. I didn't go in. I could only begin to imagine what was in *this* one: maybe a petting zoo or an amateur wrestling federation. On the notice board outside was a poster saying, '0% Interest? Come in and raise your *expectations*'. Another one read, 'Life: Handle With *Prayer*'. I loved them. Had anyone ever seen one of those posters and decided to convert?[1]

Across the road I spotted a small building claiming to be a firehouse. I initially thought I'd performed a *Quantum Leap*-style waltz back in time, but, on closer inspection, realised it was a firehouse *museum*. It was no bigger, in fact I'm tempted to say it was *smaller*, than the maritime museum in Mundesley, the W.I's supposed 'smallest museum in the world'.

The museum was run by nine volunteers, as the original fire station had been when it was built in 1833. Now, as in the 1800s, the nine volunteers met regularly at the Swan Inn to discuss business. The first firehouse meeting took place in 1832 and was led by a reverend. I hoped he was involved in making posters for the recruitment drive:

---

[1] Outside a Methodist chapel in West Runton, I once saw a poster saying 'Experienced Carpenter Seeks *Joiners*: Apply Within!' I was tempted to burst into their next service wearing overalls and saying, 'I heard there's a carpentry vacancy going?'

'Got A *Fire* In Your Belly? Join Our Brigade.'

'Experienced Carpenter Seeks Fireman - To Put Out The Massive Wood Fire In His Workshop.'

I asked the on-duty volunteer for a picture. Having missed taking a picture of the Walsingham man, I was overcompensating by taking photographs of every other human I spoke to. He agreed, but warned me that he didn't know how to smile. He wasn't wrong.[1] I asked him to say cheese. He said 'sexy' instead. I cracked up. I was definitely going to use that line from now on. What a shame I'd missed the opportunity to say 'sexy' instead of 'cheese' for so many school photographs.

'It shouldn't be just me in this picture really,' he said. 'All the volunteers should be in it.'

And with that, he smiled.

But I'd already taken the photograph.

Walking back to the bus stop, I thought about all the unique business endeavours I'd seen so far and wondered what type of business I'd run if forced into such a move. In the end, I plumped for a local dating service called Norfolk Broads.

In the shelter, an old man told me how he'd worked at an airport in his youth. One night a plane landed, unannounced. Out walked Nikita Khrushchev. I've since tried to find evidence of this but all I can find is one state visit to the UK, in 1956, in which Khrushchev arrived ceremoniously by battleship. I wished I'd paid more attention to the old boy instead of worrying about whether the bus was going to turn up. I may have had an international scoop. An international scoop from the mid-1950s.

The bus took me to North Walsham where I planned to catch the train home. The train was always more reliable. I'd be back in no time.

---

[1] If you want proof, visit my online collection of photos. Details at the back of the book.

'Replacement Bus Service In Operation' read the electronic board. I fell to my knees and sobbed.

Leg Five

Cromer – Burnham Thorpe – Burnham Market – Heacham – Hunstanton – King's Lynn – Downham Market

Cromer

My trip to Cromer had originally been planned for three days previous. Alas, a nasty cold had other ideas. I spent three miserable days indoors whilst the sun blazed through the bedroom curtains.
  It was a stinker. My throat felt as though someone had been at it with a Brillo pad. I was sneezing drawing pins. My nose had been filled with cement. I didn't think to try some of the old Norfolk remedies I'd read about: hot onion gruel or a whole, boiled onion floating in butter. Nor did I try the technique of dipping brown paper in vinegar and resting it on my forehead. I made do with brand name drugs. The effects were no more spectacular. I might as well have slapped vinegar paper on my noggin.
  After three days of moping around the flat, I needed escape. If I didn't leave the house soon, the neighbours would think I was doing a Miss Havisham. I downed some cough mixture. More than the recommended dose. Enough, in fact, to subdue a mountain gorilla. I unlocked the front door for the first time that week. The sunlight made my skin crack. The fresh, sea air tickled itself about my person.
  Oh, the great outdoors. You couldn't knock it.

*

'You should have gone to Cromer, my dear,' wrote Jane Austen in *Emma*. 'Perry was a week at Cromer once, and he holds it to be the best of all the sea bathing places. A fine open sea, he says, and very pure air.'

But Perry would say that, wouldn't he? The twat.

I'd never read *Emma*, but I didn't like the sound of this Perry chap. I could see him already: white flannelette shirt and a bad moustache. Maybe a straw hat.

Still, the advice held true. The virus entered its death rattle the moment I arrived. One day previous I'd been hacking away on the couch and now here I was, invigorated by Cromer's *very pure air*.

'There was no Spain for Margaret that autumn,' Elizabeth Gaskell wrote in *North & South*, 'although to the last she hoped that some fortunate occasion would call Frederick to Paris. She had to content herself with Cromer... Perhaps Cromer was, in one sense of the expression, the best for her. She needed bodily strengthening and bracing as well as rest.'

I'd never read *North & South*, either, but I didn't like the sound of this Frederick chap. I could see him already: white flannelette shirt and a bad moustache. Maybe a straw hat.

As you can probably tell, Cromer used to pull in a noteworthy clientele. Among its visitors were Oscar Wilde (who found it 'excellent for writing'), Alfred Lord Tennyson, and a young Winston Churchill (who wrote, 'I am not enjoying myself very much' there, whilst not enjoying himself very much there).

In later years, Churchill would regularly return to the adjacent village of Overstrand and build sandcastles with children on the beach. One of his favourite games was to get the children to build defences and fortifications. Little did they know he'd be making them do it for real when they were older. It was whilst on holiday in Overstrand that Churchill received information that the Great War had started.[1] He hightailed it to the village's spectacular Sea Marge hotel and used the telephone – the only one in the area – to mobilise the Royal Navy.

It's thought that Churchill's trips to Overstrand were the inspiration behind the novel *The Eagle Has Landed*, which was set in north Norfolk. I'd never read *The Eagle Has Landed*, but I didn't like the sound of this Winston chap. I could see him already: white flannelette shirt... etc.

Not content with merely *attracting* Britain's finest, Cromer had also tried its damnedest to *kill* one of them. Whilst staying in the town, the Victorian writer Amelia Opie caught *the cold that started the coughing that put her in the coffin they carried her off in*. No amount of vinegar paper could save her.

With the sea air's kiss of life on my lips, I headed to the beach via a dramatic set of steps. They were reminiscent of the ones that poor fella gets chucked down at the end of *The Exorcist*. It was rather apt as my fragile voice was on a par with somebody in the midst of possession. At the bottom of the steps I passed an elderly couple. My friendly, though croaky, 'Hello' was enough to convince them that Professor Dawkins had been wrong all along - there *was* a devil. And it was walking around Cromer with a digital camera.

The seafront had taken a battering in the 2013 storm. Reparation work was in place. This was nothing out of the ordinary. Cromer seafront was forever recovering from storms. I can't remember a time when it wasn't undergoing some sort of desperate rebuild. Cromer regularly received more of a meteorological tonking than most because it simply had more

---

[1] Just how many celebrated people were in Norfolk on that fateful day? We've already had Rupert Brooke and Edith Cavell.

to meteorologically tonk. The sea walls were yards away from the arcades, fun fairs and ice cream stalls. Not to mention the pier. It was all perfect fodder for fame-hungry storms.

Poor old Cromer Pier. It always cops it. Every five years or so a super-storm blows in, does its thing and then buggers off, taking most of the pier with it. The pier then slowly gets rebuilt, at a cost of hundreds of thousands of pounds. Then, by the time it's ready, so is the next super-storm. And people act shocked, stunned, that the pier has been damaged, as though it has never happened before: 'Not *the pier*!' they cry.

Yes, my dears, *the pier*. Always.

There had been piers and jetties in Cromer for around 800 years. The jetties were used to aid the import and export of wheat, barley, malt and plague. The current pier, built in 1902, originally had a bandstand where there now stood a theatre. In 1907, the bandstand made way for a roller-skating rink, such was the demand for that exciting new craze. I'd always thought roller-skating had been a 1950s thing. I couldn't picture Edwardians zipping around the pier on them, in white flannelette shirts…

With the pier's illustrious roller-skating days over, it was now geared towards on-stage entertainment (although it remained a hotspot for fishers and crabbers). Cromer Pier was now the type of place where Wheat, Barley & Malt was the name of visiting trio of comedians, rather than departing cargo. Motorised carts replaced the roller skates. It was possibly the same people in them, though.

From the end of the busy pier I looked back. It was, and is, my favourite view of Cromer. The seafront was enclosed by towering hotels and guesthouses. They were painted bright colours: yellows, pinks, blues. To the right, amusements and the helter skelter. To the left, tearooms and fishing boats. It was a scene that hadn't changed much over the years, except for the proliferation of motorised carts. I really had never seen so many in one place. I thought I'd accidentally wandered onto the dodgems.

Beyond the pier, out at sea, lay a drowned world: Shipden. It was a village from the days of plagues and revolting peasants. When the tide was low, Shipden Church still popped its head out of the water, occasionally causing damage to boats. On stormy nights it's said you can hear the Shipden bells rocking in their watery grave, if the destruction of the pier isn't making too much noise.

Cromer Pier was no stranger to the screen. It had been used as a location in movies (most recently Alan Partridge's *Alpha Papa*) and numerous, nay, countless, TV series including ITV's gentle drama, *September Song*, starring Russ Abbott, which is still awaiting its *South Bank Special* – and could do for quite a while.[1] Another show routinely avoided when the South Bank team sit around the table to discuss future specials, is *Most Haunted*. In 2009, Sky's paranormal superstars brought their shaky cameras to Cromer in the vain hope of obtaining footage of the pier's plethora of roller-skating ghosts.

I should give a cursory description of what *Most Haunted* is. It's a programme in which a team of paranormal investigators and an ex-*Blue Peter* presenter stand around in the dark listening for ghosts. Among the *Most Haunted* posse will always be at least one 'professional' medium whose job it is to interpret the ghosts' otherwise secret messages. The team's late night vigils are often filmed in lime green night-vision and inadvertently look like adverts for the army. Any illusion that these people *are* advertising the army is shattered when they hear a mouse fart

---

[1] If even ITV3, a channel that's more than happy to broadcast *Wycliffe* six times a day, won't repeat *September Song*, you know it has to be pretty weak stuff.

and all start screaming. They all look at each other and ask, 'Did you *hear* that?' or, if they're really scared, 'Oh my God, did you hear *that?*'

Most Haunted is a live-action version of *Scooby Doo* in which nobody ever admits to being the ghost.

If, by some cruel twist of fate, you happened to have had prior arrangements the night the episode about Cromer Pier aired, or have yet to find a sufficient window of time to look it up on YouTube, I shall give you a short summary.

It begins with the host, Yvette Fielding, who was last seen lighting the fourth candle on the *Blue Peter* coat-hanger advent calendar, sauntering up and down the seafront. She describes Cromer as, 'A place where phantoms, poltergeists and the dead wander in abundance.' It's a cheap shot. The people of Cromer may be old, but they are still alive. Mostly.

Cromer, Yvette adds, 'is now famed for the many supernatural visitors it receives.'

This isn't true.

'Medieval men in rags have been seen wandering the area,' she purrs.

This isn't true, either.

'Cries of lost sailors can be heard at night as they emerge from the sea and their watery grave.'

Again, not true.

'A man in a tall black hat and an ashen-faced man with jet-black hair have all been seen [all two of them] in the theatre,' she says, as a full-colour shot of the pier fades to a haunted black & white.

What Yvette doesn't mention is that the man in the tall black hat was spotted by the backstage door during a performance of *Oliver*. Or that the ashen-faced man with jet-black hair was seen the night of a Celine Dion tribute act. That's two mysteries solved right there.

Yvette then refers to Cromer Pier as 'Croner Pier'. Are there ghosts on Croner pier? 'We have just 24 hours to find out!' she says.

The big question here is, why? Why *just 24 hours*? What kind of crazy self-imposed rule is that? Why not stay a bit longer and do a thorough job? Surely if there are ghosts wandering in such abundance it might be worth hanging around long enough to catch the sneaky bastards mid-jaunt. Imagine Sir Isaac Newton giving himself a maximum of 24 hours after the apple fell on his head to formulate his ideas on gravity.

Most Haunted is insane. How it gets re-commissioned is a testament to human idiocy.

'There are more things in Heaven and Earth, Horatio, than are dreamt of in your philosophy.' Yes, but none of these 'things' have ever dropped their standards to such a degree that they'd put in an appearance on *Most Haunted*. Ghosts literally wouldn't be seen dead on it.

'We've had glasses that just for no reason break,' reports a member of the pier bar staff, whilst Yvette nods.

I know how that feels. That's why I stopped shopping at Wilko's.

The professional medium in this particular episode is an American called Patrick Matthews.[1] He bullshits his way through the show, giving the distinct impression that he can't believe that people are buying this nonsense. He's dressed like the last passenger on the night bus: a cross between Ian Botham and some bloke who works in the car radio section of an electrical superstore. On his income, you'd expect at least a little pizzazz.

---

[1] I've had a look on his website. You can arrange to have an over-the-phone reading from him. It only costs $600 an hour. A notice on the site says that 'Patrick does not give readings by email', giving up the whole ruse in one fell swoop.

Patrick stands on the pier's theatre stage and says that he can see the ghost of a woman. There was a murder on the stage, he says, and 'people thought it was part of the performance.' The play, he adds, was *Macbeth*. The question I want to ask isn't about the murder or the ghost; I want to know who the hell went to watch *Macbeth* on Cromer Pier. Was there a panto version that I didn't know about?

The resident *Most Haunted* historian probes Patrick further. She asks which character the ghost was playing. The ghost replies, via Patrick, that it was playing multiple characters. The historian nods approvingly and says that this is nothing unusual for Shakespeare. 'Of both sexes they would play,' she smiles.

Of both sexes they would play? What kind of language is that? Is she talking about *Macbeth* or *in it*? In hindsight, the bar staff's earlier comment, 'We've had glasses that just for no reason break,' also sounds as though it was penned by the bard. Maybe these people *are* the ghosts. Like in *The Sixth Sense*.

There's a scene in a backstage corridor in which Yvette asks a ghost to sing to her. Surprisingly, the ghost refuses. There then follows a period of about five minutes in which Yvette repeatedly asks the ghost to sing and waits in silence. It's at this point that you realise that Yvette is the scariest spectre you'll ever see on the programme. She looks like the ghost of David Bowie in *Labyrinth*.

Outside the theatre, Patrick says he can see a castle out to sea: 'I don't know the correct terminology' he says, covering as many bases as possible.

The historian replies that there was once a church out at sea in that exact-ish location. (Good old Shipden.) This psychic vision proves that Patrick is at one with the ghost realm. Although, all things considered, it's surprising that he didn't know the 'correct terminology' for a church.

The episode ends with a séance in the lifeboat house at the rear of the pier. During the vigil, phrases such as 'Do you feel that cold?' and 'Can you smell oil?' are bandied about as though such phenomena are unexpected in a lifeboat house at 2am. By its own terrible standards, this episode is a low for *Most Haunted*.

Yvette Fielding wasn't the first visitor to Cromer, or even Croner, to detect a ghostly chill in the air. Sir Arthur Conan Doyle stayed at Cromer Hall and was told about Black Shuck: a devilish, saucer-eyed black dog who haunted the coast for no apparent reason other than the fact he really liked his walkies. Conan Doyle went on to write *The Hound of the Baskervilles* with this East Anglian legend in mind. I'm yet to see the naughty little mutt myself, but the story goes that if you do see him, you die; it's a threat that has always felt a little thin when you consider the fact that you're also going to die if you don't see him. Another twist on the myth is that if you see Shuck, you die on your next birthday. Why a local artist hasn't got round to making Black Shuck birthday cards is a mystery. They could make a killing.

Satanic dogs notwithstanding, Cromer was a splendidly pleasant seaside town. And if I had to choose anywhere to sweat out a virus, it would be there. As I strolled along the seafront, I felt my immune system rolling up its sleeves. I was getting better.

I decided to climb the church tower. It had been a few years since I'd last paid my pound and ascended its dizzying highs. Back then, whilst living in what F. Scott Fitzgerald termed 'youth's form of chemical madness,' I was altogether more spirited and lithe. The Cream Cheese & Chive Pringles obsession had yet to really kick in. Now, post-Pringles, the world, and, in particular, stone staircases in parish churches, were more formidable foes.

I was walking into a cave. Those of you that have climbed a church before will be familiar with the chill, moist air that accompanies your first few steps. You'll also be familiar with how this air rapidly loses its invigorating qualities and you soon feel as if you're being strangled by invisible angels.

There was no end; the stairs were spiralling further and further, higher and higher. The support rail seemed to have been put into position exclusively for the benefit of NBA stars. At various stages of the climb, I found myself having to reach up desperately to grab at it, stretching my body to its fullest, like testing a smoke alarm without a stepladder. Conversely, at other moments, the railing seemed to be ankle height, forcing me to squat to hold on. All the while, my inner chimp - that's the most recent psychological term for that voice in your head that hates you - began reeling off the many ways that I could die. It also gave me a few potential headlines that could accompany the misfortune: the most tragic being the painfully bland 'Local Man Falls To Death'.

I began to worry that I hadn't passed anyone on the stairs. Was I up there alone? Then I began to worry just what the hell I would do if somebody *did* pass me on the stairs. Surely we'd both slip and fall to our grisly ends: 'Local Men Fall To Deaths'.

The stairs opened up to a respite platform with a large wooden door. I thought I'd reached the top. Through the door's tiny window I saw the bell ropes. It's said that when the church was in a state of disrepair funds were raised by selling Cromer's bells to St Mary's of Bow: the bells which featured in the nursery rhyme *Oranges & Lemons*. People born within earshot of the Bow bells are often classed as *real* Cockneys. Unless they heard them in Cromer.

It was tempting to go into the belfry and give the new, non-celebrity bells a yank. But that required energy. I was close to collapse. I wasn't ready for this. I was ill. I looked up into the darkness. The stairs went up and up, twisting their way towards the heavens.

Then, contact. Human life. Someone was coming down the stairs. Maybe it was God.

It wasn't God. It was a man in Bermuda shorts and a fedora. He had already reached the summit and was pleased with what he'd seen: 'It's worth it!' he said.

'Great,' I said, with the last of my oxygen.

'Great,' he replied.

He then hopped down the stairs with the dexterity of a mountain goat at play.

His glowing review gave me added impetus. *It's worth it*. If he had said anything even remotely negative about the experience, I might have given up. I'd have hanged myself with the belfry ropes, waiting to be discovered by the curate at evensong.

I couldn't stop now: *it was worth it*. I put my foot onto the next step and lifted myself seven inches closer to the sky. *Come on!* I looked out through one of the rare slats at the town below.

The architectural historian Nikolaus Pevsner once said of Cromer that it had 'stylistic elements derived from the Chateaux of the Loire Valley.' I wasn't qualified to confirm or deny this. But I do know that Pevsner made the observation before Cromer got an Iceland.

I somehow made my way to the top. I opened the stiff metallic door, allowing the sun to wash over me. I was done. My adrenalin fell back down the steps.

A middle-aged couple were up there. Smiling.

'Ent it super, eh?' they said, in a nice Nottinghamshire accent.

I didn't know if I could talk. Was there enough air in me?

'Great,' I puffed. It was becoming my catchphrase.

Inwardly, I could speak perfectly. That was no problem at all. Inwardly, I was saying all sorts of things. Outwardly, all I wanted to say was this:

'Heeerrr hee. Fucking hell. Air, please. Heerr. Heeee. Air, now.'

'Are you from round here, then?' they asked.

Please stop making me talk.

'Great,' I puffed.

'Eh?'
'Yes.'
'It's worth it!' they said.
They exited and left me to my quivering, snotty wreck, 160 feet atop Norfolk's tallest church tower. The floor creaked and cracked beneath me. I was too tired to care. So what if the tower collapsed? Falling through the roof would've suited me fine.

The tower was so tall that during the early parts of the Second World War lookouts were stationed on it. Their job was to keep an eye out for Nazis and holidaymakers wearing socks under their sandals (both equally heinous life choices, if you ask me). An absolutely cracking story from around this time involves an official war inspector asking a Cromer man what steps he would take if the Germans invaded:

'Bloody long ones, Sir.'[1]

The view was spectacular. I could see for miles in every direction. I could see East and West Runton (village of my birth), all the way to Sheringham and Weybourne and further yet. I could even see the ghosts of medieval men in rags on the pier. I think.

Somewhere out there, beyond the trees, was Roughton (pronounced, again for no real reason, *rout*-un), the village where Albert Einstein stayed for a month in 1933. He lived there in secret whilst planning to escape to America. Being Jewish, returning to Germany was a non-starter. You didn't

---

[1] In neighbouring Sheringham, mayhem ensued when somebody saw German paratroopers land in fields outside the town. One boy helped his dad dress for battle. One of his tasks was to quickly shine the buttons on his dad's uniform. If ever there was a misuse of time during an emergency: 'Hurry up, Son. We've got to show those Nazi rotters how an *Englishman* polishes buttons.' Needless to say, the reports were false. They weren't paratroopers. They were geese.

need to be Einstein to work that out. But, seeing as he *was* Einstein, he worked it out anyway. He moved Stateside and never saw Europe again. During his brief stint in his hut on Roughton Heath, he formulated ideas and theories that would eventually contribute to the creation of the nuclear bomb and the threat of total human extinction. The signs on the way into the village should say 'Roughton – Spiritual Home of the Nucelar Winter. Please Drove Slowly.'

Despite the exquisite view from the top of the Cromer spire, I wanted to get down. I needed my bed. The virus wasn't done with me. I wondered what the Guinness World Record might be for vomiting from a great height. I was in a position to lean over the side and give it a good run for its money. What an excellent episode of *Record Breakers* that would make.

There's a legend of a boy, Harry Yaxley, who was dangled from the tower to steal bird eggs. He slipped out of his friend's desperate grip and fell. He survived. The idea seemed appealing.[1] It would be better than walking. My inner chimp offered no thoughts on the matter. He was sleeping in his inner tyre.

'It's worth it,' I said to a man on the stairs.

'Great,' he replied, breathlessly.

With my last ounce of energy, I bought a bottle of water from a sweet shop selling the widest range of rock I'd ever seen. Not content with platitudes like 'Welcome To Cromer' buried into them, these sticks of rock were far ranging. They said things like 'Dad's Rock' (a seriously risky phrase) and 'Gran's 80th Birthday'.

---

[1] This story is hard to swallow. No one seems able to put a date to it, or even an approximation. Even a guide to Cromer, published in 1841, reported that it happened 'some years ago.'

It was amazing. I shall shed a tear should rock shops ever cease to be.

I was on the verge of collapse. I kept myself together by coming up with potential phrases for sticks of rock. My two favourites were 'Sorry To Hear About Your Loss' and 'Good Luck With That Application For The Plumbing Apprenticeship'.

The shop fronts were adorned with novelty tea towels and postcards. Many of them used Victorian railway advertisements[1] that referred to Cromer as Poppyland. For years I'd wondered why Cromer was called Poppyland when poppies always appeared to be in such short supply there. I'd only ever seen about two. It might just as well have been called Big Tree Land, as there were probably a couple of big trees somewhere nearby.

Poppyland, I discovered, wasn't strictly referring to Cromer, but, instead, a stretch of coast to the east, around the villages of Overstrand and Sidestrand. The name was coined by Clement Scott, a feared theatre critic of the 1860s.[2] He was also a travel writer and a poet. His adoring articles about the Norfolk coast in the Daily Telegraph made it *the* place to be seen, especially by those in 'the business'.

Scott composed a popular poem entitled *The Garden of Sleep*. Many who have attempted to read it in recent years have accidentally fallen into such a garden, only to be awoken by the telephone.

In the poem, Scott describes waiting for a lover *by the graves in the grass* (always a great location for a date) was a miller's daughter called Louie Jermy. He had visited the Jermy's mill to

---

[1] It was new railway-connected seaside resorts, such as Cromer, that allowed for fresh fish to be sent inland in good time. This led to a sharp proliferation of shops selling our national cuisine, fish and chips.

[2] It was he who started the trend of reviewing productions on their first night.

enquire about accommodation. The family offered him a room. He slipped his feet firmly under the table. Scott spoke about the mill's garden as having 'a blue sky without a cloud across it; a sea sparkling under a haze of heat; wild flowers in profusion around me, poppies pre-dominating everywhere, the hedgerows full of blackberry blossom and fringed with meadow-sweet.'

He was a bit of a dick.

Although already married, and in his forties, he began a relationship with the nineteen-year-old Louie. He introduced her to Victorian society's visiting elite, amongst them, Oscar Wilde, Henry Irving, Dante Rossetti and John Ruskin. She was treated as a curiosity: a bucolic, olde worlde bit on the side. When Scott invited her to live with him in London, it was on the condition that she did so as his servant. The Romantic Age, I feel obliged to point out in Scott's defence, had already ended by this point.

Louie soon moved back to the mill.

Clement Scott's gushing appraisal of the area was so effective that he soon regretted having mentioned it at all. His secret had been revealed. The crowds came.[1] Scott's heaven was tainted and it was all his fault.

If he'd have just a waited a few years before penning *The Garden of Sleep*, he would have found that nobody would have even bothered reading it, let alone act upon his recommendation to visit. After writing an article for a religious magazine in which he claimed that women in theatre were immoral and had all slept their way to the top, he found himself dropped by the Daily Telegraph and nigh on unemployable.

---

[1] The poet Swinburne was seen frolicking up and down the cliffs of Sidestrand singing the local ditty, '*Gimingham, Trimingham, Knapton and Trunch/Northrepps and Southrepps all in a bunch*' whilst laughing hysterically. I can only begin to imagine what the farmhands made of it. I'm sure the word 'wanker' was bandied about a fair bit.

The party was over. Poppyland was eaten by the sea and the man who'd made it famous died a poor man's death. Louie Jermy was buried in those graves in the grass where Scott had once waited for her. She died a recluse and an eccentric. Life is never quite so exciting once Oscar Wilde stops coming round for tea.

Not content with featuring prominently in an absolute rotter of a poem, Cromer had also been immortalised in what has to be the single worst limerick ever committed to paper. As a lifelong hater of comic and nonsense verse it gives me no pleasure to share this limerick with you, but I feel I ought. It's by one of nonsense verse's 'great' pioneers, Edward Lear. Here goes:

There was an Old Person of Cromer
Who stood on one leg to read Homer
When he found he grew stiff
He jumped over the cliff
Which concluded that Person of Cromer

My advice to Lear, pre-writing, would have been to make sure that he had enough rhymes for Cromer to see him through to the bitter end. By enough rhymes, I mean more than two. Who, seriously, in their right mind, would read that limerick and laugh, other than at how dreadful it was?

What I'd give to be able to assemble all nonsense verse and burn it.

There was an ill man from Sheringham
Who got on the bus back to Sheringham
He got on the bus
Yes, he got on the bus
And eventually got back to Sheringham

Burnham Thorpe

Anyone who knows anything about Norfolk will tell you that the tiny little village of Burnham Thorpe is famous for one thing: that no buses run through it.

The lack of a connecting bus, let it be noted, was hot on the heels of the roaring bus failure of Bacton and Happisburgh. It was yet another disappointment. I was going to have to walk. My dreams of an exciting finale in which you, dear reader, were on tenterhooks to see whether or not the challenge could be done, were over. I'd already failed the mission several times over.

So it was that on the summer's hottest morning, with the wind in my face (acting as an industrial fan heater), I made my way, on foot, through the countryside from Burnham Market to Burnham Thorpe. The sign said two miles. I hoped they weren't *holy* miles; I'd be jackal food.

Unusually for me, I'd had the foresight to make a list of provisions the night before. Water was at the top of it. I had never been so organised.

I forgot the water. I'd left the list on my couch. It wasn't all bad news, though, I *did* have a straw hat atop my crown to keep the rays off and make me look a total arse.

The jackals circled.

I may not have packed fluids, but I had somehow managed to squeeze every other item I'd ever owned into my bag. The weight of it made me sweat so much that I realised I wouldn't need the bottled water after all. If I started to wilt I could just wring my pants and drink that. They contained enough moisture to replenish Qatar.

I wasn't wholly convinced that I was heading in the right direction. I saw a man walking his dog. He told me that there was a slight shortcut down a secret path. I was torn. Was it worth the risk, or should I stick to the lane?

'It's simple enough,' he said. 'You go straight down this path here. Take a right. Carry on for exactly four tenths of a mile. No further, mind. Take the second, the *second*, left. Keep going until you reach a stinging nettle. It will probably have a blackbird near it. If you can see the windmill you've gone too far.'

I love it when direction-givers let you know when you've *gone too far*. 'If you can see the windmill, you've blown it. It's over. Give up.'

Although the shortcut sounded appealing in the energy sapping heat, the idea of seeing the windmill and going *too far* acted as a major deterrent. For some reason, I felt bad for not taking the man's advice. So, as he walked away, I made out as though I *was* taking his advice and going via his suggested route. Sure enough, he checked to see which way I was going. I waved at him, whilst pointing down his preferred pathway. He smiled. As soon as his back was turned, I carried on as before. I'm going to make a stonking case study for junior psychologists one day.

During World War Two, Norfolk road signs were repainted, taken down, or fixed facing alternative directions. I'm still not sure they've been properly corrected.[1] This walk couldn't be two miles. I'd been walking for ages. My beard had grown.

I stopped to take in the view between hedgerows. I was on the corner of the county. I could almost detect a curve in the sea's horizon. It's not surprising that the area had produced so many seafarers. The sea spoke to you here. In other parts of the county you could hear the sea, in Burnham you could feel it.

There was an incredible silence; people from Burnham Thorpe must be able to walk five miles from home and still be able to

---

[1] I also love that the people of Great Britain hoped that the Germans would orchestrate a mass invasion and forget to bring compasses and maps.

hear whether or not they'd left the immersion heater on. Even the birds flitted quietly. The only sound was the click of the crickets, darting about the grass (they never did fully recover from Buddy Holly's death). In the fields, dry crops performed a hypnotic sway. This, too, was done mutely. They weren't swishing. Perhaps I needed my ears syringed. 'All is hush at high noon as at midnight,' a rector of this parish had written, many years ago.

One fact about Burnham Thorpe that I hadn't come across was that getting to it required an uphill walk. It was the kind of fact that would barely raise an eyebrow when mentioned in passing conversation, yet, on the year's hottest day, it was a fact that seemed somehow more important than any fact ever recorded in the history of facts.

I saw signs of human life in the distance: a church tower above the trees, a smattering of houses. I reached the signpost I had been waiting to see: 'Burnham Thorpe – Nelson's Village'.

Ah, yes, I forgot to mention. Another interesting fact about this tiny little village – population 168 - was that it was the birthplace of Horatio Nelson. He was born in either the rectory, or, if the local legend was true (and bear in mind, when you make this call, the legend of the ghost-dog Black Shuck) in a barn around the corner.

It's hard to imagine a time when Horace (Horatio) Nelson was simply the name of a little boy from Burnham Thorpe. A time when the name Nelson stood for nothing, had no connotations, no anything. Walking through the village - a homely stretch of silent cottages - I became acutely aware how little it would have changed since Nelson played there as a boy in the mid-1700s. Telegraph poles and tarmac were the only visible additions.

There were *seven* Norfolk Burnhams in all: Deepdale, Norton, Overy, Sutton, Ulph, Westgate and, of course, Thorpe. A nursery rhyme from the Middle Ages told of 'London, York and Coventry - and seven Burnhams by the sea.' Young Horatio[1] would have been familiar with all seven, sailing their various creeks and hidden waters.

The church of which Nelson's father was rector (the rector who, in the above quote, noted that Burnham was rather quiet at high noon) was now a shrine to the village hero. It was a painfully sweet building with lovingly maintained displays. All around were the graves of other Nelsons, including that of his father and his mother, Catherine, who died when Horatio was nine. She was said by Nelson's sister, Susannah, to have 'bred herself to death.' Horatio was one of eleven.

Little is known of his mother.[2] Of his father, what we do know paints a peculiar picture. He was forceful and strict. One of his queerest demands was forbidding his children to let their own backs touch the back of their chairs at dinner. It's no wonder his kids were keen to get out more.

Horatio was a tough child, a good scrapper (despite his unspectacular size) and a risk taker. When asked by his grandmother why he hadn't been scared after going missing on the water one evening, he replied, 'I never saw fear. What is it?' Similarly, when caught stealing pears from a teacher's garden, he stated, 'I only took them because every other boy was afraid.'

It was his uncle who introduced Nelson to a career at sea. At fourteen he was sent on an expedition to the Arctic. He went out one night in search of polar bear skin. Unfortunately for him, a polar bear had also decided to nip out in search of human skin. The two extraordinary creatures collided. Nelson's gun failed him. It wouldn't shoot.

---

[1] He later changed his name to Horatio in an effort to sound more dashing. I'm going to change mine to Ryatio.

[2] Her side of the family were related to Robert Walpole, the Norfolk landowner and first Prime Minister of England.

'Never mind,' he shouted to another member of his party, as though merely finding out that his watch had stopped, 'do but let me get a blow at this devil with the butt end of my musket and we shall have him.'

Not massively enamoured with Nelson's idea of poking the angry beast with a butt end, one of the men fired a blank instead. The bear ran off. Nelson, let it be noted, genuinely thought he could take him. You'd be hard pressed to find a fourteen-year-old willing to go and buy milk now, let alone pick a fight with a polar bear; they'd try and order the stuff off Amazon.

On a different expedition, necessity forced Nelson to dine on turtles, iguanas and rats. One evening he returned to camp to see monkeys cooking in the pots. Even he wasn't brave enough to tuck into that particular feast. He politely declined, wondering if there was a Londis on the island.

After just six years at sea, Nelson became a captain. He excelled as leader. He made a point of caring for his shipmates, many of whom would have been new to life at sea:

'The timid he never rebuked but always wished to show them he desired nothing of them he would not instantly do himself,' noted one shipmate.

He was a man of the people. He would ask a novice to go to the masthead whilst declaring that he would also be going up and 'beg I may meet you there.' When they reached the top 'he would speak in the most cheerful manner' by way of comforting and making light of the task.[1] He maintained this camaraderie despite suffering from both 'dreadful seasickness' and recurring bouts of malaria caught whilst in Nicaragua.

---

[1] In later battles, he would further enhance his standing with the sailors by queuing to get his wounds seen to, when he could easily have demanded to be first in line.

Nelson always informed men of his plans and the dangers they faced. There were no secrets. He taught them the importance of personal hygiene and regularly introduced them to other captains and men of rank, lest they get bored of looking up only to *their* captain. In return, the men adored him.[1] His popularity was helped by the fact that wherever, or whomever, they attacked - American ships, French ships, Spanish ships - Nelson always seemed to smash the blighters up. If he was handed an assignment, it was a given that the job would get done.

During a lull in international tensions (with the American War of Independence all but over), Nelson returned to Burnham Thorpe. He lived with his wife, Fanny, and near his father, Edmund. Whilst at sea, he had always dreamt of the simple life back in Burnham. He envisaged a quiet and uneventful second career as a farmer. The dream came true; he worked the very fields I'd just walked past. Although he was only thirty-years-old, he didn't think he'd go back to sea again.

As the years ticked by, Horatio started to feel the call of the waves. Life at home hadn't been as idyllic as he'd hoped. If they had made sitcoms in the late 18th century, Nelson's Burnham homes would have made the ideal set-up. Everyone was getting under everyone else's feet. Nelson was frustrated. Fanny was miserable. His father was practically blind but refused to wear glasses on the grounds that his eyesight was a judgement from God; he stumbled around the house, knocking things over like a six-year-old playing Blind Man's Bluff at a birthday party. Nelson had to read everything aloud to his father, from personal

---

[1] He was instrumental in saving a deserter who was to be hanged. Nelson had allowed the man a chance to escape into Antigua rather than be caught by the Navy. He made no apologies for his actions, stating, 'I was near, if not cutting the thread of life, at least shortening a fellow creature's days. The law might not have supposed me guilty of murder, but my feelings would nearly have been the same.'

letters to the Norfolk Chronicle newspaper. In terms of excitement, it ranked just below barehanded fights with polar bears.

Although not necessarily the most pulsating endeavour, reading the Norfolk Chronicle *was* becoming something of an eye-opener. Each edition brought further disconcerting news from abroad. France was in turmoil. A glorious uprising was occurring from the nation's streets. More and more members of French high society were finding themselves without a use for their marvellous collections of hats. This was due to a new fad known as the Beheading Machine:

'Oh, right. And what's that used for?' asked a curious landowner.

'Ah, I'm glad you asked, Monsieur,' replied his footman.

Calling the invention a Beheading *Machine* suggested that there'd been a degree of ingenuity and technical innovation involved. The truth was, the machine, also known as the guillotine, basically consisted of a razor sharp blade being dropped onto necks from a great height. There wasn't much to it. It wouldn't have got past the *Dragon's Den*. (The guillotine was used by French authorities as late as 1977. The 'distant past' isn't as distant as we sometimes like to think.[1] Nowadays, thank goodness, guillotines are really only used for cutting paper in GCSE Art classes. Although I do wish they were still called Beheading Machines.)

Week-by-week, French heads and houses fell. Nelson sat back (making sure not to touch the back of the chair) and awaited an official invitation to sea. In the meantime, he spent his days

---

[1] Britain's last judicial decapitation came in 1885. It happened in Norfolk. A murderer by the name of Robert Goodale was hanged outside Norwich Castle. As he dropped to his death, the noose accidentally took his head clean off. The crowd were most disgusted - they'd hoped to see a more tasteful execution.

farming and picking up the things his father had knocked over. (In order to read the paper in peace, Nelson would take it to Burnham Overy-Staithe, where Fanny couldn't accidentally throw it out and his father couldn't accidentally eat it.)

Uprisings are infectious. The establishment had to act. The British war machine clicked into gear. The message arrived at Burnham Thorpe. Nelson's new ship was to be the Agamemnon. Word went out that Nelson needed Norfolk boys to man it.

He didn't have to ask twice. Men from Wells, Blakeney, the seven Burnhams by the sea, Hunstanton, and more, went down to Chatham to board the ship.

Before leaving Burnham Thorpe, Nelson had a farewell party at The Plough (built in 1637 and still standing). I stood outside that very building in the blazing heat. It was now called The Lord Nelson. It was closed. Due to open in half an hour. I walked up the lane, each step taking its toll. Summer was on the offensive. Flies and ladybirds flew at my face. A wasp tried to get *inside* my ear. I was so irritated that I actually told the wasp to 'piss off'. I must have looked insane.

Half an hour passed. I plodded back towards the pub. Sweat was running into my eyes. My straw-hat was stuck to my head like a lolly to a jumper. However, it wasn't sufficiently stuck for it to not be whipped off in the opposite direction by a random hot gust of wind. It somehow landed on its side and began rolling away with the speed of an Olympic cyclist.

It pains me to even recall the moment now. I ran after it, my wheeling hat, on what was surely my last reserve of energy. I was furious. When I finally caught the bloody thing up, I lambasted it as I had the wasp:

'Nice one, you prick,' I said. To my hat.

Across from the pub was a bowling green. In the days before pool and Sunday League football, pubs would compete against each other at bowls. Go to any country pub and chances are there'll be a bowling green, or former bowling green, nearby. Whether or not Nelson ever played on the green, I don't know. But I do know that the pub did nice double-cooked chips. Use this information however you see fit.

Chipped-up and sufficiently hydrated, I left the pub, passing a sign above the door: 'Admiral Lord Nelson passed through this doorway – you who follow in his footsteps remember his glory.'

On that last night in Burnham Thorpe, he left the pub to find youngsters fighting in what was now the car park. (Some things never change.) One of the boys had been teased because he hadn't been invited to Nelson's farewell party. He took a few swings at his detractors. Nelson said the young boy had fought heroically and called him Valiant. Valiant was the boy's name in the village forevermore.

The war with the revolting French had Nelson sailing the world again. He dished out spankings at Copenhagen, Tenerife and the Nile. He also tasted the European high life: from bullfights in Spain[1] to pelvic exercises with various ladies in Italy. How much he actually *saw* of the latter activity is a cause of some debate as just before reaching Italy he had suffered a battle wound to his eye. He initially described it as 'a very slight scratch' but it eventually led to him only being able to see extreme light and dark.[2]

---

[1] At which he was horrified: 'It would not have displeased me to have had some of the Dons tossed by the enraged animal... nothing shall tempt us to see another.'

[2] When he realised that his eye was not aesthetically damaged, he declared, 'So my beauty is saved!'

Some historians have suggested that the eye injury was psychological. It was *fear* of losing his sight, which possibly stemmed from having to watch his father tripping over the dog twelve times a day, which made him think he was partially blinded. He almost certainly never wore the famous eye-patch. Except in films and on the front cover of shoddy books about Norfolk.[1]

One thing on which medical minds can agree was that Nelson may not have lost an eye, but he definitely lost an arm. A musket ball shot through him in a naval scuffle on the shores of Tenerife. His arm had to be amputated immediately, a cold knife tearing the tissue and then sawing through the bone.

Nelson slipped into depression. He wrote to a friend that, 'A left handed admiral will never again be considered as useful, therefore the sooner I get to a very humble cottage the better and make room for a better man to serve the state.' The injury also cast further doubt into the possibility of him ever having played bowls on Burnham Thorpe green.

One arm or not, Horatio was gaining a reputation as something of a catch. After a resounding obliteration of the French fleet at the Nile, his stock rose further. Around Britain the people celebrated. Norwich did so by roasting an ox in the market place - although the ox had suggested that maybe a few simple fireworks would suffice.

None cheered Nelson's successes more than Emma, the young wife of sixty-seven-year-old diplomat and vase collector, Sir

---

[1] His most famous eye-related anecdote took place at the Battle of Copenhagen, during which he refused to follow an order to retreat against the superior number of Danish ships. Instead he said, in what sounds like pure Norfolk, 'Now damn me if I do!' He pulled the telescope to his blind eye and declared, 'I have the right to be blind sometimes... I really do not see the signal.' The attack continued and the outnumbered Navy won. One of the fleet's colonels later reported, 'I never passed so interesting a day in my life or one that so much called for my admiration of any officer.'

William Hamilton. Emma, daughter of a Cheshire blacksmith, had spent the majority of her young adulthood moving from partner to partner until she reached Sir William at society's top end. She had achieved a degree of fame for performing *Attitudes*, a type of dramatic art in which the performer changed from one intense pose to another, presumably in a room choked in awkward silence.

The married couple lived in Naples and corresponded with Nelson whilst he was at sea. Had Nelson lost at the 1801 Battle of the Nile,[1] Naples would have likely been invaded by French troops. He had saved the couple from imprisonment or maybe even death.

Emma's correspondents with Nelson had a more suggestive undertone than her husband's, but both were in equal thrall of the British hero. Emma wrote that, 'I walk and tread in the air with pride, feeling I was born in the same land with the victor Nelson… Sir William and I are so impatient to embrace you… we are all *be-nelsoned*.'

When the trio finally met, in Naples, Emma fell into her hero's arms and cried, 'Oh, God! Is it possible!' before pretending to collapse in awe.

It was even more embarrassing than the *Attitudes*.

'I hope one day to have the pleasure of introducing you to Lady Hamilton,' Nelson wrote to his wife all those miles away in England. 'She is a credit to her sex,' he added, as Fanny sat back and smiled, delighted that her husband had found an attractive young woman to spend his time with.

---

[1] After this victory, in which Nelson, and Nelson alone, foresaw and subsequently cut-off Napoleon's trade route to India, he was given the rare title of *Viscount of the Nile and of Burnham Thorpe in the County of Norfolk*. It's doubtful anyone shall ever hold the title again, unless things get really weird.

After a period of flirting - the kind of intensely palpable flirting which can anger those who have to witness it - Nelson became entangled in a bizarre, but open, relationship with Emma. He effectively lived with both her and her husband, Sir William. The trio travelled together and attended functions as though nothing was going on. It was the sort of relationship that is nowadays the focus of Channel 4 documentaries about kooky domestic set-ups in Doncaster. Everywhere they went Nelson was adored. Sir William Hamilton's antique vase collection barely got a mention.

When they returned to England, the trio attended theatre performances and events (and, naturally, the occasional Norfolk hall dance). A matter of yards behind them would walk Fanny Nelson, in a sad public pretence that she and Horatio were still happily married.

There was only so much she could take. Fanny demanded Nelson to separate from Emma. Rather than bow to his wife's wishes, he cast her off. They didn't divorce but they never saw one another again. Nelson was racked with guilt. He took to aimlessly roaming the London streets at night. To make matters worse, Emma was pregnant (Fanny had guessed as much after witnessing her faint and vomit more than the required amount. She initially mistook it for one of her *Attitudes*). Nelson knew that the scandal could shatter his reputation and was keen to keep his fathering of the child secret. The best way to do this, arguably, wasn't to call the baby girl Horatia, but that was the name they opted for.

Nelson might have been good at attack, but he was lousy with deception.

The game was up. Nelson and Emma moved in together, raising more than a few eyebrows and tarnishing the former's reputation within high society (low society, as ever, couldn't give two hoots).

'Just for that,' said high society, 'you can only come to *four* of our hall dances this year. Instead of twenty-six.'

Fanny Nelson moved away to the West Country.[1] William Hamilton went back to the antique day job, resuming his role as a pre-Victorian Lovejoy.

Whilst living in London, Nelson was called to defend a former shipmate charged with treason. He told the court that he had not seen the defendant for 23 years but that he had been an admirable man and that if somebody had asked for an appraisal in passing conversation, he would say, 'If he is alive, he is certainly one of the brightest ornaments of the British Army.' Despite Nelson's glowing review, the accused was found guilty. He was informed that he would 'be hanged by the neck, but not until you are quite dead, then to be cut down and your bowels taken out and cast into the fire before your face; your head to be taken off and your body quartered.' Nelson received a letter from the defendant which stated that whether his days 'were many or few' he would 'have no other inscription on his tomb than the character given by Nelson' at the trial. The man was buried in a hole next to St Paul's.

Nelson's own wish was to be buried in Burnham Thorpe with his family:

'...I shall never see Dear dear Burnham again but I have a satisfaction in thinking that my bones will probably be laid with my father's in the village that gave me birth.'

Death was never far from his mind. He had already thought himself dead numerous times. After losing his arm he'd yelled, 'I

---

[1] Where she died in 1831. She allegedly kept a miniature figure of Nelson and occasionally kissed it. Nelson, not to excuse his actions, of course, continued to pay her a healthy chunk of his considerable income.

am a dead man!' and after a stray piece of debris bloodied him at the Nile, he declared, 'I am killed. Remember me to my wife.'

Back in England, even after his victories at the Nile and Tenerife, his ego was muted by the sense of death's hand on his shoulder. He began taking opium for his anxiety and had been rocked by rheumatic fever, shaking so much 'my rings will hardly keep upon my fingers.' Somewhere in the back of his mind rumbled the words of a West Indian fortune teller who prophesised, many moons ago, during the monkey casserole holiday, that she could not see a future for him past the year 1805. It was with great trepidation that he turned to January on that year's *Goats In Trees* calendar.

Napoleon was on the offensive. Talk was of an invasion of Britain. Nelson didn't believe it possible. How, he argued, could the French get enough men onto the English beaches without them all being massacred the moment their feet touched the sand? It was a valid point. But it didn't stop the population from living in terror at the prospect of waking up to find they'd become a sub-district of France and would have to start eating garlic and cycling everywhere in blue & white stripy jumpers.

Nelson's public bravado, coupled with his track record of handing out drubbings to the French, led to him acquiring a God-like status upon his Royal Navy recall in 1805. One observer, upon seeing Nelson mobbed in Piccadilly, noted that 'it really is quite affecting to see the wonder and admiration and love and respect of the whole world... it is beyond anything represented in a play or a poem of fame.' A visiting American wrote, 'when he enters a shop the door is thronged until he comes out and the air rings with huzzas... he is a great favourite with all descriptions of people.'

He was a living icon. He was a man of the people and a man of the establishment. He was a leader and a team player. He was arrogant and desperately insecure. He was brave and terrified.

The fear within parliament was that Napoleon was merging his warships with those of Spain to create a united navy. If they could rid the waters of the British Navy, then an invasion of England would be unstoppable. The British would have to do the same; they needed to pool as many ships as they could into one force. The Prime Minister, William Pitt, asked Nelson who could command this new, united British fleet. Nelson suggested, humbly, that the man currently in charge, a Mr Collingwood, would be more than able to do the job.

'No, that won't do,' said Pitt. '*You* must take command.'

He then asked Nelson whether he might, possibly, be ready to take control of the fleet within three days, no more.

'I am ready *now*,' was the reply.

His new ship was the HMS Victory.

Days later, at five in the morning, an officer arrived at Nelson and Emma's London home. Nelson was already awake.

'I am sure,' he said to the officer, 'you bring me news of the French and Spanish fleets and that I shall have to beat them yet.'

The news was indeed that the enemy had been seen making moves and that Nelson was needed at sea. Earlier, on what was to be his last night in England, he had visited the room of his sleeping daughter, Horatia. Before leaving the room, he stopped to look at her four times. He chose not to wake her. In the dark blue of dawn he asked his stable boy to 'be a good boy till I come back again.' The coach then carried him away.

In Portsmouth, word had got out. Things were moving. Nelson was in town. Crowds packed onto Portsmouth beach. Nelson looked at them and said to his flag-captain, Hardy, 'I had their huzzas before. I have their hearts now.'

Meanwhile, British ships stationed in Cadiz awaited their saviour. They were in a precarious situation. If spotted by the enemy, they would be massacred. One of the sailors made a note: 'For charity's sake, send us Lord Nelson!' Things were getting desperate.

'The reception I met with on joining the fleet caused the sweetest sensation in my life,' wrote Nelson on arrival.

The sailors had cheered his coming as though it were a victory.

Whilst laying out his tactics, he was asked how many ships the British fleet would contain:

'Oh,' he replied, 'I do not count *our* ships.'

Nelson knew that the British had the advantage of experience over the French and Spanish. The British had been at sea whilst much of the enemy fleet had been in port. Vitally, the British could fire at a quicker rate. Nelson informed the captains of his ships to, as a last resort, get close to an enemy ship, jump on board, and fight their sailors hand-to-hand. He then showed them all of his combat tips. Even with one arm he looked a deadly opponent.

Information arrived: enemy ships were nearby. Nelson gave orders for his fleet to catch up with their opponents and sail parallel, at a distance far enough to not be spotted. If they were seen, he warned, it would scare the enemy back to the safety of the coast.

The French and Spanish sailed at a leisurely rate, unaware that the British were tracking them. Whilst awaiting the opportune moment to attack, Nelson went below deck and composed a will. In it he asked for little more than for Emma and Horatia to be looked after by the state in the event of his death. He returned to the deck and paced about. He gave orders for decks to be cleared of non-essential items, for muskets to be cleaned and knives sharpened. Such was the confidence of those on board, songs were played and the sailors danced. Nelson visited each of his men, joking with them, telling them exactly how they would bring the enemy down. Whilst walking the deck he stopped and looked out to sea. He remembered something. It was the 21st of October. He turned to one of his officers. Today, he said, was the day of the Burnham Thorpe autumn fair.

The enemy fleet was growing. It was now four miles long. Four miles of warships. The best of France and Spain combined. The British were still creeping. They were close enough to see French and Spanish flags and, remarkably, to even note the colour of the black fixings on their ships. Nelson had ordered his own fleet's fixings be painted yellow, so as to be seen through smoke.

He returned below deck. On the floor of his cabin room he prayed. He wrote the prayer down. In it, he asked God to 'grant to my country and for the benefit of Europe in general, a great and glorious victory: and may no misconduct, in any one, tarnish it: and may humanity after victory be the predominant feature in the British fleet.'

On deck, he asked for a signal to be sent to all of his fleet saying, 'England confides that every man will do his duty'. The man in charge of giving the signal asked to change one word: 'confides' for 'expects'. Expects, the man said, was a simpler word to convey in flag signals.

'That will do,' said Nelson.[1]

It was time to show the British hand.

The Royal Navy fleet began to divide itself, as planned, into two formations, both arrow-like, as they drove with increasing speed towards the unsuspecting straight line of French and Spanish ships. At one arrow's point was Nelson's Victory, at the other The Royal Sovereign, led by Cuthbert Collingwood. Both ships were likely to see the worst of it, being, as they were, at the front of the queue.

---

[1] His favourite flag signal was 'Engage the enemy more closely'. It's almost philosophical.

The Royal Sovereign saw the first action. Nelson watched as his friend's ship drove into the enemy's view and took hits, before violently returning the favour: 'See how that noble fellow Collingwood takes his ship into action! How I envy him!'

On board the Sovereign, Collingwood shouted to one of his officers, 'What would Nelson give to be here!'

Men, dear readers, of a different cloth.

The Victory then swooped within range. Nelson had his wish for action fulfilled. Mayhem. Cannonballs and bullets flew, smashing the ship and shooting deadly splinters through the air. 'This is too warm work to last long,' Nelson cried. He was wearing his full Navy regalia, complete with medals. He was a sitting target. Nobody dared ask him to change. Hardy, Nelson's closest ally, had subtly mentioned the possibility of it. The reply was that, yes, it would probably be wise to change but wasn't it a bit late in the day for such a thing? The last thing the Admiral of the Royal Navy should be doing at a time like this was rummaging through his autumn collection for frothier apparel.

In the madness of the smoke and bullets, one thing was clear: the battle was going the way of the underdog. The plan had worked perfectly. The enemy couldn't cope. It was going to be Nelson's greatest victory yet. Captain Hardy knew the battle was won; it was just a question of time. He looked around in the chaos to see Nelson on his knees. He then saw him fall to the floor. A sniper had caught him. Hardy ran.

'They have done for me at last, Hardy. My backbone is shot through.'

For once, his self-diagnosis was right.

As they carried the admiral below deck, Nelson issued further demands to his shipmates. He covered his own face with a cloth so nobody could see that it was he who had been shot.

On the surgeon's deck, lit by lanterns and filled with the sound of screams and explosions, Nelson told the doctor there was nothing that could be done. A young sailor was carried through, his leg blown off.

'Mind, Hardy,' he said, 'that youngster is not forgotten.'

The doctor noted that Nelson had been shot through the shoulder and that the bullet had ended up in his spine.

'I felt it break my back,' he said. 'Fan, fan… drink, drink.'

Hardy returned to deck. There was still a job to do.

Nelson asked to be 'remembered' to Emma Hamilton, to Horatia, to all of his friends. When a passing midshipman saw him, Nelson recognised the young man's voice. He had sailed with his father many years previous: 'It is *his* voice! Remember me to your father.'

As ever, a crowd formed around him.

'Unhappily for our country,' the surgeon said, 'nothing can be done for you.' He turned away to hide his tears.

Outside, one by one, enemy ships were sinking or surrendering.

'God be praised,' said Nelson, 'I have done my duty.'

Hardy returned below deck, declaring the battle all but won. He shook Nelson's limp hand, telling him that they had taken fourteen or fifteen ships.

'That's all very well,' Nelson gasped, 'but I had bargained for twenty.'

There wasn't long left.

'Take care of my dear Lady Hamilton, Hardy. Take care of poor Lady Hamilton. Kiss me, Hardy.'[1]

Hardy kissed his cheek.

---

[1] It's often argued whether he said 'Kiss me' or 'Kismet' (meaning fate), hence the *hilarious* name of this book. However, I am one of the people who leans towards 'Kiss me' on the evidence that, although it is an unusual thing to say, it was not an unusual thing for *Nelson* to say. He might just have easily asked Hardy to kiss him at a party as he would in the throes of death. Nelson was a kisser, regardless of gender, social standing, or anything else for that matter.

'Now I am satisfied. Thank God I have done my duty.'
Hardy kissed him once more, on the forehead.
'Who is it?'
'It is Hardy.'
'God bless you, Hardy.'
He was turned onto his side. The blood rushed out of him. Death was seconds away.
'I have not been a great sinner, Doctor... Never forget Horatia... Thank God I have done my duty... Drink, drink... Fan, fan... Rub, *rub*...'
The battle was over.
He had danced his last hall.

It says something about the man that despite masterminding a victory that halted an invasion and sealed Britain's domination of the waves for the next century, it was Lord Nelson's death that was *the* leading news story back home. The opening dispatch from the battle mentioned, first, the tragic news of a hero's passing, and, second, the phenomenal victory. A nation wept when it could have danced for joy. One of Nelson's shipmates lamented that he had wished the bullet had taken his own head off instead of planting itself in Nelson's shoulder. Another said he would have rather lost his brother, father, grandfather and Lord knows what else instead of his beloved Horatio Nelson.

Nelson's body was buried not in the village church, as he had wished, but in the vaults of St Paul's cathedral, on the other side of the wall from the convicted shipmate whose life he had once tried to save. He was said to have preferred St Paul's to Westminster Abbey as there was a rumour that the Abbey was built on marshland and wouldn't be around much longer; two centuries later, it still does a fairly good wedding.

*

In any other circumstances, I'd have written about the fact that Captain Woodget of the Cutty Sark was also from one of the Burnhams. But, somehow, that feels a little underwhelming by comparison. And anyway, as a letter to Viz rightly pointed out, the Cutty Sark was a tea carrying ship and no more than an antiquated PG Tips van.

Nor does it seem especially worth mentioning that Burnham Deepdale was used to depict North Korean paddy fields in the ghastly James Bond adventure, *Die Another Day*. Norfolk, whilst we're on the subject, had a rich cinematic history of doubling up as alternative locations: Castle Rising played Denmark *in Out of Africa*; Walpole St Andrew gave an unforgettable turn as Dunkirk in *Atonement*; and much of the county had cameos as war-torn France in *Allo Allo*.[1]

After Nelson's death, Emma Hamilton's life cascaded into ruin. She made an attempt at keeping the family home as a museum and shrine to her husband but racked up debts of hundred of thousands of pounds. If you can believe such a thing, both she and Horatia wound up in debtor's prison. It had been Nelson's solitary dying wish, expressed verbally and in writing, that his family be looked after by the state. Prison couldn't have been what he had in mind.

Emma Hamilton died bankrupt in Calais at the age of 49, once more on the run from creditors. Horatia returned to Norfolk and raised a large family, actively avoiding the public eye. It is a tantalising thought. The Nelson bloodline still runs through the county, in secret, unseen, creeping along the horizon. Waiting.

---

[1] Hmm, maybe it wasn't such a rich cinematic history after all.

Burnham Market

I'm not going to lie to you. The whole seven Burnhams thing was quite confusing.
There was a local mnemonic: *Nelson Of Thorpe Died Well Under Sail*. It didn't really help. (I've always found that mnemonics make things *harder* to remember. I don't understand how adding an extra poem or phrase is supposed to lighten the memory's load.) Luckily I only had to go to two of the buggers. Or was it four? Technically, Burnham Market was three Burnhams rolled into one: Sutton, Ulph and Westgate. It was a Burnham cocktail, a Super Burnham, knocked up by a railway company who, quite correctly, thought that visitors might get confused by the vast amount of Burnhams that Norfolk had to offer. What the railway company failed to take into consideration were poor schmucks like me who would have to conduct research into all of this nonsense in years to come. I was staring at maps prior to my visit and wondering where Sutton, Ulph and Westgate were hiding.
Anyway, there I was, in Burnham Market, or Super Burnham, if you will. I'd made it. The last stretch of the walk had been a little hairy, but the Nelson spirit saw me through. That, and the fact that as I approached the village I saw a poster advertising breakdance lessons in the village hall. If ever a village was unlikely to offer breakdance lessons, it was Burnham Market.

The Burnham Market website proclaimed that this was 'Norfolk's loveliest village.' Aesthetically, it possibly was, with its fancy shops and leafy green. It was close enough to the sea to taste it in the air and the sky was invitingly open. Yet, and it's a big yet, there was something clinical about it. It was like an English village as designed by a Hollywood studio (for a film about Jane Austen: starring Gwyneth Paltrow and Damian Lewis - with Jim Broadbent playing a wacky-jumper-wearing dad).

If I were to tell you that the village was recently used as the backdrop to a collection of modelling shots for the *Next Directory*, maybe that will paint more of a picture than anything else I could say. Or, maybe, that Johnny Depp had regularly been spotted cycling there (he'd never been spotted cycling around Stalham, for instance). Or that there were posters advertising an upcoming afternoon of light jazz at the tennis club. It was *that* kind of place.[1]

Chelsea-on-Sea they called it. The tone of voice in which this was said depended entirely on who was saying it. Some said it with delirium, others with disdain. It certainly resembled Chelsea in one way: nowhere this side of Holt could you see so many parked cars. It was almost impressive.

I sat on the shaded village green. There was an absolute ringer for Forrest Gump on one of the benches. He wore a white suit and red baseball cap. He was talking to an elderly woman, presumably about his hilarious experiences in Vietnam.

I got my *Characters of North Norfolk* book out. It turns out a door-to-door saleswoman had once knocked on the doors of Burnham houses and asked if anyone wanted to come and stare at her recently deceased donkey. For a small fee, of course. Such was the lack of action in the village that night, many did. Burnham Market hadn't always been the home of jazz afternoons down the tennis club.

---

[1] '[It's] possibly the only place in rural England so smart that its fishmonger is an Old Etonian,' wrote the Daily Mail in a gushing, hideous 2014 article about Norfolk's thriving socialite scene entitled *The Turnip Toffs!*.

*

One of my favourite Norfolk stories features a Burnham man called Jimmy. He was a World War Two soldier sent to Singapore. It was the first time he'd ever left Norfolk. He was taken prisoner by the Japanese. The conditions were appalling.
Jimmy survived, he says, because he was used to living on meagre supplies. The Norfolk life was hard back then; the land was unreliable. He knew what it felt like to starve. The bigger lads, he said, couldn't deal with the shock.
After the Japanese surrender, Jimmy was taken, by the Americans, to Okinawa. From there he was sent to Manila, then Canada, then Portsmouth, before taking the train from London to King's Lynn. Home.
He arrived late at night to find the front door unlocked. When he asked his mum why, she told him that she hadn't locked it in all the time he was away; in case he came home in the night.

An old boy was cutting the churchyard grass. He was doing the job with a mower that looked both ancient and terrifyingly futuristic. He paid me absolutely no heed as I walked into the church.
On a table at the back of the building I saw a book about race relations by a guy called Jim Davidson. It wasn't *the* Jim Davidson but I felt for the poor soul who wrote with such honourable intentions with a name like that. It was like being called Jack Theripper and wanting to write a potted history of prostitution.
I made my way to the bus stop to double check what time my carriage to Heacham would arrive. As I left the churchyard, I passed a litterbin so big that it actually made me jump. It could have been a holiday home. It probably would be within a couple of years.

The situation with the buses, as I saw it, was this: there was one bus a day that went from Burnham Market to Heacham. I'd seen it online. All other buses stopped at Hunstanton and would require a changeover, which I wasn't keen to perform. I needed to get the *direct* bus. The village timetable, to my consternation, made no mention of it.

I asked a girl sitting on a nearby bench if she was any the wiser.

'There isn't one to Heacham. You have to go to Hunstanton.'

I explained the situation regarding the once-a-day magical bus that did indeed go direct to Heacham.

She said she'd heard a rumour about it but never seen it herself.

It was as though I'd asked her about Black Shuck.

I enquired in the shops. They didn't know. Some of them didn't even know that buses still existed. I was done for. The bus to Hunstanton was due in thirty minutes, three minutes before the mythical bus to Heacham. I'd return then to receive my fate.

I passed the time by walking the side-streets, wondering if I'd bump into Johnny Depp and whether he'd have a spare copy of the timetable to hand. I saw a white building called The Gospel Hall. It looked like a terraced house. It had homes at either end. I walked down the garden path to the blue front door. Maybe it *was* a house. Maybe it was a house which *used* to be a gospel hall and had simply kept the name to give it an olde worlde charm.

I turned the knob.

Once that was over with, I tried the door. It was open.

It was the kookiest, strangest building. It had all the village hall trimmings plus a few extras. It was defiantly un-caressed by the cold hand of the privileged. Rows of wooden chairs faced a tiny wooden altar. Old electric heating contraptions were nailed to wall up high: heaters that only warm the sphere of air five inches around them, yet sizzle flesh off if accidentally touched.

In the foyer was a table of neatly arranged hymn books with radical names such as *Mission Passion* and *Praise Today!*. The clock on the wall had stopped at ten-past-ten. On what date it had stopped, I couldn't tell. If I had to guess a year, I would have said 1998.

I made a vow to check upon the status of the Gospel Hall every time I visited Burnham Market. If it ever went under, converted into a holiday home or a shop selling designer candles, the village was lost.

The girl was still at the bus stop. We gave each other a half-smile.

Across the road stood The Hoste pub. It was named after a local protégé of Nelson's, William Hoste. Nelson sent him away from action at Trafalgar. He gave him an errand that ensured he wouldn't be killed. He was said to have viewed young William as the son he never had. Nelson had visited The Hoste when it was called the Pitt Arms (the name Arm Pitts was vetoed) many times in the late 1700s. He would visit to get his weekly dispatches and possibly dance in its halls.

The Hoste had had many guises and transformations. It was a brothel in Victorian times. It was now a hotel/restaurant/bar, often frequented by celebrities. Around the back, where most pubs had fights, there was a health and beauty spa:

'Oi, you! Yeah, *you*! D'ya wanna take this round the back?'

'Yes, please. My skin is just unbearable at the moment. It really is the living end.'

The girl broke my reverie with a devastating prophecy:

'That bus won't come. You'll need to get *my* bus to Hunstanton.'

I told her my predicament. I said that despite being in an almighty mess if my bus didn't show up, I *had* to get to

Heacham quickly or I was going to have to postpone it for another day. She told me it was risky.

'I like to take risks,' I replied. It was the single biggest, and most poorly executed, lie I had ever told. With my straw hat, comfortable hiking shoes, brown polo shirt and rucksack crammed with pharmaceuticals, never had a man looked so unlikely to be fond of risk.

It wasn't often on this journey that I'd felt St Christopher, patron saint of travellers, cheering me on from the sidelines, but as a double-decker rode into view, with 'Heacham' lit up in letters of gold, I felt I'd had a brush with the divine.

'This is it!' I yelped, further belying my love of risk. I waved it down.

The bus hit the brakes, making the obligatory end-of-the-world-volume whooshing sound as it did so. I looked through the windows. It was full of children in school uniform.

'Oh, *that* bus,' said the girl. 'That's a *school* bus.'

I could almost hear St Christopher laughing: 'That'll teach you to fuck about in my Gospel Hall.'

The doors opened. The driver looked angry. I had no option but to try my luck. As a desperation tactic, I told him that I needed to get to Heacham as I was writing a book, as though that kind of thing usually pricked up the ears of bus drivers. ('Oh, you're a *writer*? Why didn't you say so? Hop on!')

'Hold on,' he said, eyeing me with suspicion. 'I'll have to ask the Big Man.' He motioned towards his mobile phone. He dialled, keeping his eyes on me.

The Big Man, whoever he was, gave me the green light.

'One thing though, mate,' said the driver. 'Make sure you sit there.' He pointed to the seat closest to him.

I sat down. The doors closed and we pulled away. I waved at the girl through the window. She wasn't looking. A more cynical soul might suggest that she hadn't found the whole escapade as fascinating as I had.

Despite feeling like a convicted paedophile for simply wanting to get to Heacham on one bus rather than two, I was ridiculously happy. I'd done it. I was going to Heacham. Everything had worked out. Operation Pughtree was off and running. Big Man, whoever you were, thank you.

Heacham

It didn't matter what I did on that school bus, it all looked suspicious. If I checked my phone, it looked like I was taking pictures. If I made notes in my book, it looked like I was penning detailed descriptions of the kids. If I crossed my legs, it looked like I was hiding an erection. Ten minutes in, I looked down, mortified to see that I'd placed my straw hat on my lap i.e. over my manhood. It was the oldest trick in the sex offenders' book.[1] I deftly removed the offending item and rested it on the seat next to me. All I could do to keep my respectability in check was sit bolt upright and stare directly forward. Occasionally, the driver would look over his shoulder to make sure that my hands weren't burrowed into the sexy depths of my pockets.
On the upper deck, two deep-voiced high school boys shouted to one another from minimal distance:
'Argh, yur well gay!'
'No I ent! *Yur* the one thass well gay, mate!'
'Futt off! Yur hossun well gayer!'
It was quite a ride.

*

---

[1] Which is a delightful read, if ever you get the chance.

We went through a village called Docking: the birthplace of George Smith. An absolute beast of a man, Smith came in at just under seven foot. He weighed eighteen stone and sported a mighty red beard. He was on missionary work in South Africa in the latter half of the 19th century when he found himself stationed at the scenic Rorke's Drift.

Had George Smith been at Rorke's Drift at any other time in human history, he would have had a splendid time of it. He could have brought a picnic and maybe even stopped to rustle up a tasteful watercolour for above the mantelpiece. As it was, however, Smith arrived at the mission post just in time to see it kitted out for some sort of defensive action.

It had transpired that the Zulu community weren't too keen on the British setting up shop in one of their most cherished drifts. They made their displeasure known by getting a sizeable clique together and making their way towards the mission post en masse. Their numbers totalled four thousand. The British, on the other hand, barely had enough men to stage a decent sized musical.

The obvious solution was to run. As with most obvious solutions, there was a snag. Along with the hundred or so troops stationed in the drift, there were also around three hundred civilians, many of whom were patients in the on-site hospital. The thought of running away whilst trying to carry people on stretchers was a little too *Chucklevision*-esque for the army's liking. They decided to stay and defend their keep.

When the Zulus arrived, Docking's own George Smith walked up and down the rows of British artillerymen handing out bullets. He became known as George 'Ammunition' Smith: mainly because time was too pressing to come up with something wittier. Other suggestions for his nickname were George 'Bullet Handing Man' Smith and George 'Oi, you, get me some fucking bullets! The fuckers are ten feet away!' Smith. Neither of which caught on.

Not forgetting his religious duty, Smith shouted motivational quotes from the bible throughout.[1] He was also heard to shout, 'Don't swear boys, just shoot.' To which the soldiers muttered under their breath that it was 'easy for that prick to say.'

In all, eleven Victoria Crosses were awarded to the men who famously defended Rorke's Drift. Smith was denied one on the grounds that he was an assistant chaplain and therefore a civilian, not a soldier. Instead, he was awarded a full-time job as an army chaplain (which was clearly just as good). Nor was he represented in the 1964 masterpiece, *Zulu*. The casting director might have been unable to find an actor large enough to portray him, what with Brian Blessed being, at the time of filming, only half complete.

The afternoon sun was at its peak. The pavements gave off waves of warm air, like storage heaters. I felt largely unprepared for Heacham. My focal point for the day had always been Nelson's stomping ground. I didn't know where to go and what to see anymore. My brain had overheated. It needed switching off at the wall. The place was famous for its lavender fields. I'd seen some from the bus. That was enough for me. Other than frolicking through them, there wasn't much else to do except stare at them and say, 'Oh, look, some lavender fields.'

My first view of the village centre had been of rows and rows of houses. There was also a quite stupendously sized social club. From the outside it looked like Balmoral. In a more carefree world I would have had time to go and investigate. But the world is cruel. Cruel. As if to hammer this point home, the driver had dropped me off outside the funeral directors. The last thing anyone wants to see when they've been on a bus is an acute

---

[1] Presumably avoiding the 'Thou Shalt Not Kill' part, which can dampen the mood at such events.

reminder of just how precious every minute is.[1] I took a photograph of it. Mainly because I thought the sight of me doing so would look funny to passers by.

Heacham had an above average amount of celebrity connections. Brendan Cole, of *Downton Abbey* fame, was born there (he probably thought the abbey was small compared to the social club). Trisha (no second name needed) went to primary school in the village, making a name by resolving playground disputes. It was also the birthplace, unbelievably, of NBA star James Donaldson. Donaldson played for the hilariously named Utah Jazz. The British equivalent would be the North Yorkshire Swing Quartet. Hardly likely to strike fear into the opposition.

By far Heacham's biggest celebrity, though, was Pocahontas, star of the 1995 Disney film, *Pocahontas*. She married a Heacham man by the name of John Rolfe. Popular history forever ties the name of Pocahontas to John Smith but it's difficult to gauge just what kind of relationship 'Captain Smith and Pocahontas' had. The Disney film shows the pair falling in love and generally larking about in meadows.[2] It's considered by some experts to be unreliable. Not least because Pocahontas would have been about ten when the pair met. Including this in their film would have made for a considerably darker entry into the otherwise jovial Disney canon.

Captain Smith and Pocahontas
Had a very mad affair
When her daddy tried to kill him
She said 'Daddy, oh, don't you dare!
He gives me fever...'

---

[1] Some poor lass at my school did her work experience at a funeral directors. Imagine that. 'Right, love. We just want you to make the tea and brush their hair.' Funnily enough, she didn't end up in the trade.

[2] I prefer frolicking about in lavender fields.

So sang Peggy Lee and countless others. There's no truth in it. Apart from the bit about her catching a fever. That was accurate.

Pocahontas was born in Virginia, into the Powhatan tribe, circa 1595. She had 26 brothers and sisters: a figure at which even Nelson's mother would have winced. She was a confident and charismatic child, establishing a playful relationship with English settlers, among them John Smith.[1] She supplied the English with life-saving food supplies and, according to reports, performed naked cartwheels to the boys of her own age. Despite this unique method of breaking the ice at Anglo-Indian social functions, tensions between the peoples grew and Pocahontas was held captive by the English. During captivity she changed her name to Rebecca and converted to Christianity. It was around this time that she met John Rolfe.

Rolfe had recently sailed to the New World, losing his wife and child to illness en route. He settled in Virginia and contributed to the successful cultivation of tobacco for which that state is still famous today. He was smitten by Rebecca, now a beautiful young woman. They married and had a child, Thomas. The marriage cooled tensions between the rival communities. The two peoples had much to share and teach other. For example, the couple's wedding was the first time any member of the Powhatan tribe had ever had cheese & pineapple on a stick or danced the *Macarena*.

Rolfe was anxious about the marriage; taking a second wife didn't sit easy with his strict Christian beliefs. He wrote a letter

---

[1] The friendship between Smith and Pocahontas ended when Smith was injured by an explosion and sent home to England. The Powhatans were told that Smith was dead.

maintaining that his marriage to the hot young princess was 'motivated *not* by the unbridled desire of carnal affection.'

But that's what they all say. Am I right, sisters?

Rolfe brought Pocahontas to England where she was introduced to London society.

'Shall I do one of my cartwheels for them?' she asked.

'Best not,' suggested her husband.

The idea behind the trip was to present the young woman as an example of a civilised savage (whether she was aware of this plan, I don't know - she may have just assumed she was going on a nice holiday). London's elite took to her. She was a success. The couple then visited Rolfe's home village of Heacham. He was eager to show her the enormity of the social club. A mulberry tree was planted in her honour during the visit.

Back in London there was a chance encounter with a familiar face. Pocahontas saw John Smith at one of the many social events that dominated her new and irreversibly altered life. They talked. It was noted (by Smith, I must add) that when she saw him, 'she turned about, obscured her face, as not seeming well contented.' When they talked, she suggested Smith call her 'child'. Smith said that the term was inappropriate. The conversation ended abruptly. And that was that.

Although keen to stay in England, it was our country's world-renowned climate that proved Pocahontas' killer. She caught every illness going. Experts still can't decide whether it was smallpox, tuberculosis or pneumonia that carried her off. What most definitely *didn't* carry her off was the ship to America. She boarded but only survived as far as the appropriately named Gravesend. She was buried in a London churchyard. She was just twenty-two. Heacham Church had a commemorative plaque erected in 1933. All else that remained was the stump of the mulberry tree.

John Rolfe returned to Virginia and married for a third time. (He must have been feeling *really* guilty about getting married for a third time! I daresay this, too, was motivated *not* by the unbridled desire of carnal affection...) His tobacco plantation was attacked by Natives in 1622 and there ended his story. The manner of his death is debated. He may have died of an illness or he may have died in the attack. Either way, by 1622, Heacham's most famous son, and its most famous daughter-in-law, had had their turn on the stage.

It's true what they say: you can own the earth and still all you'll own is earth until you can paint with all the colours of the wind.

Am I right, sisters?

After Pocahontas, things went relatively quiet on the Heacham celebrity front. It would be more than three hundred years before Trisha got the ball rolling again.

I took a stroll around the shops, taking a particular interest in a bookshop that appeared to specialise in texts exclusively about people called Christian.

I walked to the park. I walked to the edge of the beach. Norfolk was blessed with a plethora of golden beaches: Heacham's wasn't one of them. It was a mixture of orangey pebbles and crushed shells, littered with the occasional snap of driftwood or black rag.[1] The beach looked messy even though it wasn't. Pebbles can have that effect. I was surprised to see so many people there.

If you want to see humans at their most primitive, stand on the edge of a pebbled beach and observe. They don't know how to behave. Their movements become indecisive and confused. Every action is taken with great trepidation, like a dog that's caught its reflection for the first time in a patio door. They don't trust themselves anymore. Shoes are taken off and then

---

[1] What are those thick knots of black rag that are always so prevalent on beaches? I never dare touch one to check.

put back on again. Blankets are laid down and then picked back up again. They crouch down, as though about to sit, and then remember that to do so would be jaggedly uncomfortable, so instead they spend a couple of minutes half sitting, half standing, as their feet slip slyly from under them. Lovers on romantic walks are forced to shuffle along at a rate of two metres per minute. They pick stones to skim along the water, but they're all too small and die soundlessly upon hitting the water. Dogs become equally flustered. The sharp gravel forces them to adopt a camp, leg-flicking walk, like a drag queen who's caught his reflection for the first time in a patio door.

I didn't like to see my fellow beings suffer alone. I felt like I should be out there with them. Maybe I could walk to Hunstanton along the pebbles? I'd already failed the public transport experiment at Bacton, Happisburgh and, now, Burnham Thorpe. What difference would one more omission make?

I asked an old lady how long it would take to get to Hunstanton on foot. She had just got out of a car. Her husband stayed at the wheel, staring sleepily at the windscreen.

'On *foot*!' she replied, her tone of voice answering my question.

'Yes.'

'On... *foot*?' She leaned into her husband's open window. 'Clive, how long do you think it would take to get to Hunstanton on foot?'

'On *foot*!' he yelped, suddenly wide-awake, as though hearing a midnight fire alarm.

After a lengthy discussion in which the words 'on' and 'foot' were used at least seventeen times apiece, they informed me that such self-inflicted misery wouldn't be necessary; there was a direct bus to Hunstanton that went from just across the road.

'A *bus*!' I yelped, assuming that this was how people talked around here.

I pottered around for a bit. I tried to take some photographs. The batteries in my camera had run out of energy. I knew how they felt. Sod the walk.

During the war, a Heacham man discovered an unexploded Nazi bomb. Thinking himself doing an almighty good deed, and possibly envisaging the receipt of some sort of medal or, at the very least, a favourable column or two about his bravery in the nationals, he picked the bomb up, plonked it in a wheelbarrow and walked it to the nearby barracks. The look on staff faces can only be imagined.

It just goes to show, if you leave something alone in Norfolk for long enough, someone will walk around with it in a wheelbarrow.

Hunstanton

After a hearty dinner and an extremely satisfying change of underwear, I took to the evening streets.

Hunstanton was a new town. It had been developed almost as a business venture by Henry Le Strange.[1] It was he who foresaw its potential as a tourist hotspot and encouraged the development of a railway line in the 1840s. The trains brought holidaymakers in their thousands. The town was fit to burst. New buildings were erected, all using yellowy Carrstone, or 'Honeystone', bricks taken from local cliffs. Nearly every

---

[1] The Le Strange family were the big guns around here, as will be made clear.

building looked the same. Hunstanton had a satisfying unification of architecture usually only found in Sylvanian Family collections.

Le Strange's *new* town was originally called New Hunstanton, as there was already another, ancient Hunstanton just around the corner. As New Hunstanton expanded, it became known simply as Hunstanton and the poor old, old Hunstanton became known as Old Hunstanton.

Are you still with me?

The track to Hunstanton was removed in the late 1960s when, as already noted, it was decided that *everybody* wanted to drive *everywhere*. The result of such action, usually, was that towns lost their swagger. Not so Hunstanton. Much is made of the artistic qualities of the forgotten seaside town, with their cheap tea and revolting toilets, but those in search of faded glory in 'Sunny Hunny' would be disappointed. It was very much alive. I saw no derelict shop fronts, no empty arcades. The cafés and chip shops were packed. It had such an air of Victoriana that I half-expected to be thrown onto a boat and sent to fight in the Crimea.

Due to its location on England's rump, Hunstanton had the unusual claim of being an eastern town that faced west. It was also one of the few English towns where the sun set over the sea. The beach overlooked the Wash. On the horizon rested a dark green line between the water and the sky: Lincolnshire and the roads north. The sea was like a bay. It was beautiful. I only wish I'd spent more time looking at that and not trying to get a picture of a seagull I'd seen that looked like Ross Kemp (it flew away before I got a shot of the evidence).

On a clear day they say you can see the Boston Stump, which, despite sounding like a 1970s dance craze, was actually a church way over in Lincolnshire. That said, it *was* a clear day and *I* couldn't see it. Mind you, I did still have half an eye out for the Ross Kemp seagull.

*

There used to be a Victorian 'pleasure pier' in Hunstanton. The town had experimented with a Victorian 'world of pain pier' too, but it never caught on. The pleasure pier *did* catch on, though; fire, normally. It was first aflame in 1939, then once more in the 50s. It was Mother Nature who had the final say. She spanked it across her stormy knee in 1978 and the ol' pleasure pier was never seen again. Remains of the 1978 storm, a fifteen-foot protrusion, served the town well, until 2002, when it was noted that it hadn't had a fire in good while and the situation was promptly corrected.

Added to the long list things I never knew about Hunstanton was the fact that the cliffs were stripy. The bottom half was ruddy and the top half was white, like a wide glass of real ale. A sign at the bottom warned that 'These Cliffs Can Be Dangerous', unlike those child-friendly cliffs one so often saw.

Perhaps Hunstanton's darkest hour was the terrible train crash of 1863. A fittingly terrible poem was written and published that same year. It contained the following lines:

The news soon spread throughout the town
Physicians soon were there
And quick a good Samaritan
Did oil and wine prepare

You can imagine the rest of it. The crash had been caused by a bullock walking onto the track.

I've composed a few extra lines for the poem:

A bullock on the track did walk
And fixed the train a stare
The driver did omit this squawk
'Fucking hell! A bullock!'

*

I saw an alluring poster in a chip shop window:
'*Battered Cadbury Crème Eggs Only £1!*'

I had to. What sort of explorer would pass up that opportunity? Not me. I'd heard the stories about battered Mars Bars and battered pizzas, but never battered Crème Eggs. And for *Only £1!* I'd have expected a battered Cadbury's Crème Egg to cost at least £458.

It was served on a polystyrene chip tray. It had the freedom to roll around (a free-range Cadbury's Crème Egg). It looked like a chicken ball from a Chinese restaurant. I used a wooden fork to jab into it. Hot yellow lava erupted like melted Carrstone. It almost singed its way through the tray. Before bringing it to my mouth I checked the vicinity for the nearest bin. When you're trying risky new foods it's vital to have a vomit depository nearby. I spotted one within retching distance. I was ready. Deep breath. Fork to mouth.

Well now.

It was good. The batter made it sweeter. It was the profiterole's embarrassingly brash cousin. I liked it.

But never again.

Away from the beach, the high street consisted predominantly of independent stores, save for the occasional bookmakers. There was bunting hanging off nearly every building. The party never ended.

Just off the immensely chirpy thoroughfare were various kooky little stores, including the Norfolk Gun Trading Company, which occupied the premises next to the bank. How convenient. Alas, there wasn't a Getaway Car Hire outlet across the street.

*

Remember that P.G Wodehouse biography I bought in Blakeney? Well, it turns out he was a regular visitor to the town. He was a friend of Charles Le Strange,[1] staying at his home, Hunstanton Hall. Wodehouse would sit in a boat on the hall's moat on summer afternoons and bash away at the typewriter (not a euphemism). He wrote the novel *Money For Nothing*, as well as many other pieces, from that idyllic spot in his 'beloved Hunstanton':

'I spend most of my time on the moat, which is really a sizeable lake,' he wrote to a friend. 'I'm writing this in a punt with my typewriter on a bed-table wobbling on one of the seats. There is a duck close by which utters occasional quacks that sound like a man with an unpleasant voice saying nasty things in an undertone.'

He used the blueprint of the hall as a setting for countless short stories and novels, changing only the name, sometimes dumping it in a different county altogether. Jeeves, Wooster, Mr Mulliner, Uncle Fred, Aunt Agatha, Pongo Twistleton, Lord Emsworth and the Empress (his prize pig) had all walked/trotted the grounds of Hunstanton Hall.

'It's one of those enormous houses, about two thirds of which are derelict,' he wrote. 'There is a whole wing which has not been lived in for half a century. You know the sort of thing - it's happening all over the country now - thousands of acres, parks, gardens, moat etc, and priceless heirlooms, but precious little ready money.'

Despite his love for the house, Wodehouse was quick to try and escape when the duties of the social life arose. Not one for meeting new people or talking to socialites, Wodehouse would perform what his close family called 'the Wodehouse glide' and disappear for a walk along the stripy cliffs.

---

[1] There's that surname again. Wodehouse described this Le Strange as 'between ourselves – a weird bird.'

Other literary visitors to the area included the Posh & Becks of early 20th century literature, H.G Wells and Rebecca West. They were alleged to have had a secret 'love-nest' on Victoria Avenue. Whereas H.G Wells is still revered (P.G Wodehouse, hot on the heels of calling Charles Le Strange a 'weird bird', called H.G. Wells an 'odd bird'), Rebecca West's name has faded somewhat. In her prime, she was a respected, authoritative voice on world events, most notably the Nazi trials at Nuremburg, which she reported from the front row. Wells first became aware of West when she referred to him in print as 'the Old Maid among novelists'. Wells was incensed. He whipped off his pinney and gave her a slap with his marigolds. Just like a modern day Rom-Com, the two bickered like crazy when they first met. But it didn't take long for them to get together, have an affair in Hunstanton and then give birth to a secret baby.

Actually, maybe it wasn't like a Rom-Com.

One member of the Le Strange dynasty had also dipped their toe into literary waters. Roger Le Strange (born 1688) was one of the first English journalists, writing anything from supportive Royalist tracts to pamphlets slagging off John Milton for, among other things, being blind. He also translated *Aesop's Fables* and the works of Flavius Josephus, which dealt with one of the rare historical accounts of Jesus.

The Le Strange family were once said to 'Own everything in the sea as far as a man on a horse can throw a javelin at low tide.' They didn't mention which man was throwing the javelin. If it was me, they wouldn't own much. My javelin skills once prompted a supply teacher to call me a dickhead. The comment, and resulting laughter from the other pupils, still stings.

A seabird with a wingspan of seven feet was shot near the town in 1835. Within seconds a horse and carriage drew up and a Le Strange got out, javelin in hand:
'Ahem. I think you'll find that's mine.'
Hunstanton had weird birds, odd birds and enormous birds.

King's Lynn

It was pouring. Bus stations are far from handsome beasts even during clement weather, but in the rain they really excel themselves. Hunstanton station, which had passed me by in the balm of the evening previous, now appeared to be a post-apocalyptic vision of tomorrow. A post-apocalyptic vision of tomorrow with lots of old people standing in it. They were all tourists. The locals were staying indoors, watching the morning rain from the comfort of the sofa. Only a tourist would go out in this - or an idiot who was trying to visit forty towns and villages by public transport.
Buses to every single *other* destination in England splashed past us as we waited. Nobody got on or off. Time stood still. Eventually our bus began spraying its way towards us, drawing muffled sounds of high-pitched approval from behind zipped-up-to-the-very-top jackets. The bullets of rain were more pronounced in the bus' full beams. I was the last to board. (I have a knack of positioning myself in such a way that I always wind-up last in the queue to board any bus. I'm equally skilled at being the last to be served at the bar.)
I fudged around for the wet wallet in my wet pocket. I handed over a soggy ten-pound note. The driver looked at me as if I'd given him a stool sample. They don't like ten-pound notes. In

the past this was understandable. When the bus used to cost 45p, of course handing over a tenner was an inconvenience. But, now, all Norfolk bus rides cost between £2.50 and £6. Who regularly has that kind of loose change?

I took the back seat. I didn't have much choice. The air was oppressive. Rather than stepping onto a bus in Hunstanton, I felt like I'd stepped off a plane in Ghana. I couldn't breathe. The windows were steamed up.

I was penned in at the back by a family I was sure I'd seen on a recent Channel 4 benefits expose. A mother and three sons. The youngest had the exact same voice as Crazy Frog. The eldest kept doing hot, spicy farts that genuinely made me worry for both his health and mine. The mum told him off in what I could only guess was some form of forgotten Gaelic:

'Grrr. Tek a turrlet an wurp yer bum wrren we grrett hurm.'

She sharply slapped his thigh with her fingers to give the suggestion added clout.

I leaned against the window and waited to die.

I wiped some of the steamed grey away. Through the hand-shaped gap I saw the forming of a new river where the road used to be. The hand-shaped window closed up. Headlights shone through. Little else. Rain pounded on the roof.

'Grrr. Armmma gorn mekk yer crapppon a turrlet aht hurm!'

When King's Lynn was attacked by a zeppelin in 1915, some people claimed to have seen the aircraft being guided by a mysterious pair of car headlights. The car drove along, flashing its beams as though showing the zeppelin where it needed to go. An MP conducted a report and even posed questions in Parliament. The mystery was never solved. The mystery of wherever the hell I was *was* solved by the bus stopping and everybody shuffling off. We were in King's Lynn. Never had I wanted to leave a bus more quickly. The farts had almost killed me.

The rain lashed down.

'I think it's clearing up,' I heard somebody say, without a hint of irony. Maybe they were talking about a motorised road sweeper they'd just seen.

My research may have been slightly askew on this point, but it's my belief that King's Lynn bus station had never been put forward for any major architectural awards. And if it had, I can only deduce that the nomination was made without those involved having seen it in the wet. It wasn't pretty. But it was vast. And confusing. And vastly confusing.

My first job, before sampling the town's high life, was to find my departure point for the journey to Downham Market. Ideally, considering the enormity of the bus station, there would have been a poster listing where each bus departed. I couldn't find one. I bit the bullet and asked an attendant in a bright orange high-vis jacket. Only in desperate time does one want to speak to high-vis attendants. They're usually surly brutes with a decorated background in taking the piss out of people who don't know everything about the bus station they work at.

This fella didn't let me down.

'You want what?' he said.

'A bus to Downham Market.'

'Dave?' he yelled. 'Dave?'

Dave, also wearing an XXL bright orange high-visibility number, walked out of the Men's toilets, rubbing his hands on his waist.

'What?' said Dave.

'This one wants to get to Downham Market?'

'Downham what?'

'Market.'

The rain smashed against their jackets.

'We don't know, mate. We're not from here normally. We do Lincoln,' said Dave.

'They'll be knocking this place down soon, anyway,' added the other, ignoring the fact that this information was only going to be of use to me if they planned to knock it down and rebuild it within the next couple of hours.

'Ok,' I said. 'Thank you.'

I decided to hit the town and deal with the Downham bus when the moment arrived. I entered the high street via a shopping complex. The rain *was* beginning to clear up. The man at the station had been right.

There was an Iceland, an HMV, a TKMaxx and, God's my witness, a Wimpy. I'd thought Wimpy had folded at around the time ITV cancelled *New Faces*, but there it was, in King's Lynn, going strong. If I hadn't had breakfast already I would have been in there like a shot. There was something heartening about the fact that a restaurant named after a minor character from *Popeye* (seriously) had survived the 21st century's swinging axe. Whereas Woolworths and many others had folded like wet blankets, Wimpy was making a fist of it. Popeye would have been proud.

I headed away from Lynn's non-historic three-quarters and into its celebrated historic quarter. It was a shock to the system after standing outside Wimpy.

King's Lynn was a government selected overflow town for London communities in the 1960s. In a tragically short-sighted attempt to move with the times, historic buildings were knocked down and replaced with less-easy-on-the-eye alternatives until just the quarter remained. The buildings that *had* survived were astoundingly well preserved. The quarter was set by the water and comprised of trade buildings from, in some cases, more than 500 years ago.[1]

---

[1] It was in 1537, during the reign of Henry VIII, that Bishop's Lynn became Lynn Regis, or King's Lynn. (Lynn Regis would be a good name for a dinnerlady.)

I couldn't think of a larger area of historic buildings in the county (maybe the cathedral grounds in Norwich?). It had been tastefully revamped in recent years, which, on one hand, made everything more accessible and, on the other, created a wall between now and the past. It was hard to visualise the halcyon days of the restored 17th century Custom House, for example, when there was a Vauxhall Astra parked beside it.[1]

The historic quarter was used as the backdrop to the 1985 movie *Revolution*, which starred Al Pacino as a soldier in the American War of Independence. It won a host of awards, including Worst Film, Worst Director, Worst Actor and Worst Musical Score. It received such a trouncing from the critics that Al Pacino thought it best to wait four years before making another film. It has since been edited and re-released by the BFI, who, predictably, didn't think it was all that bad. They described it as a 'powerfully unsentimental film' and 'a tour-de-force of epic filmmaking.' (Their poor old marketing team have had to dress-up some real dross over the years. I'm yet to see a BFI DVD that hasn't been accompanied by a booklet crammed with kindly essays. They don't understand that we'd much rather read honest essays detailing the many differing ways in which the main feature is utter tripe.)[2]

Although panned for being filmed in Norfolk, *Revolution's* choice of location was apt. Norfolk men played a vital role in the story of the New World. When not busy sleeping with princesses and bringing them back to plant mulberry bushes in

---

[1] A poem by R.N Curry tantalizingly said of the Custom House that it was *'So feasibly attributed to Wren.'* I could find no other information on this. The design is usually attributed to Henry Bell, a contemporary of Wren.

[2] I later caught *Revolution* on Movies4Men, between screenings of *The Man With Three Ears* and *Dr Quinn: Medicine Hussy*. The film also starred Annie Lennox and a young Sid Owen (*Eastenders'* Ricky Butcher). They weren't the worst performers in it. Nor were they any good.

Heacham, many locals performed more admirable, though possibly less pleasurable, duties. For example, John Mason, the King's Lynn-born founder of New Hampshire and the first vice-admiral of the *New* England; it was he who drew the first English map of Newfoundland, releasing an accompanying essay entitled '*A Briefe Discourse of the New-Found-Land with the situation, temperature, and commodities thereof, inciting our nation to go forward in the hopefull plantation begunne*'. The BFI recently called it one of the most interesting, unsentimental essays ever written, despite it not being fully appreciated at the time.

Another transatlantic hero from the area, commemorated in statue form in the historic quarter, was George Vancouver. Vancouver was a seafarer from childhood. He accompanied James Cook on explorations of the Pacific and the Antarctic at the age of fourteen. The mission lasted four years and devoured the period of Vancouver's youth that you or I would have spent revising for maths exams and listening to *Now* albums. He was part of that fateful Hawaiian voyage in which Cook was walloped on the back of the head and stabbed by a native. It was a good few years before the King's Lynn man could hear the sound of slack-key guitars without getting flashbacks.

Vancouver later sailed up the North Pacific coast of the Americas, mapping areas for the first time (Oregon, Washington and Hawaii among them). He planned to call Alaska 'New Norfolk' but the idea was dismissed. The city of Vancouver was named after him. He is so revered there that in 2007 the Mayor declared 22nd June to be George Day. It was the 250th anniversary of his birth. There was even a commemorative stamp produced, in which Vancouver, the man, was depicted looking at Vancouver, the place.

Ironically, it was these exciting voyages of discovery to America that halted King's Lynn's rise as a port of importance. The growth of the USA suited ports on the west coast of England, rather than the east. Thus the rise of King's Lynn was checked. Sources claim that prior to that, King's Lynn was England's biggest port.

One day I hope to find a port that wasn't once England's biggest/most important. I'll probably have to leave the country to do so.

I found a misshapen little building known as the Exorcist's House. Until recently it was available on a housing website. It was listed at £190,000. It dated back to 1635 and, according to the website, 'gained its rather curious name from an earlier house on the site, which was occupied by a well known exorcist.' I'm not sure whether its spooky history raised or lowered the value. It would certainly add an edge to those 3am visits to the lav.

The Exorcist's House backed onto the church of St Nicholas, inside of which were a number of slabs commemorating the name Robinson Cruso (minus the 'e'), all of which pre-dated Daniel Defoe's novel. (Had he seen the name whilst visiting there?[1]) There was no grave, however, for Margery Kempe, author of the first autobiography written in English.

Born in King's Lynn in the 1370s, Kempe was said, mainly by herself, to see Christian visions. The visions often compelled her to roll around in the streets. She was also said, again, largely by herself, to be able to smell strange odours and see Christ-like figures walking around (maybe she'd just wandered into the bus station). She claimed to have witnessed the crucifixion firsthand. She also said that she'd been present at Christ's birth (possibly holding up Mary's leg). She later went through a spell of

---

[1] Defoe said of King's Lynn that there was 'more gaiety in this town than in Yarmouth or even in Norwich.' I wasn't aware Yarmouth and Norwich were considered such gaiety hotspots.

madness during which she was attacked by demons who tried to convince her to commit suicide. The scamps. The cause of her death has remained a mystery, as, clearly, has much her life.

Her autobiography is regularly ignored by the selection panel of Richard & Judy's *Summer Reads*.

I cut towards the Tuesday Marketplace via the freshly sodden high street. In 1987, King's Lynn town centre became the first in Britain to use CCTV. Aside from the occasional set-to involving gangs of boys called Darren, the most regular crime it recorded was people weeing where they oughtn't. George Orwell had missed an open goal by failing to include the Urine Police in *Nineteen-Eighty-Four*.

Beautiful, antiquated buildings surrounded the Tuesday Marketplace. I was taken aback by its grandness. 'King's Lynn,' wrote Paul Theroux in his grumpy *Kingdom By The Sea*, 'was dignified and dull, its stately centre so finely preserved it looked embalmed.'

Well, I liked it.

It had been the site of a witch burning in 1590. During the event, the heart of the witch in question, Margaret Read, exploded from her chest. It then leapt across the street, hitting a house opposite, before bouncing all the way into the river Ouse. Above the window of one of Tuesday Marketplace's old buildings could still be seen the heart-shaped stain left by Margaret's well-travelled blood-pumper. A cynical mind, or any mind scoring 'Borderline' and above on an Intelligence Quotient percentile chart, might cast doubt on the story. Nevertheless, it has at least ensured that Margaret Read is remembered. Many more supposed witches in Norfolk were murdered and forgotten.

Between the years 1575 and 1679, around forty Norfolk women (and the occasional man) were killed for their presumed allegiance with the devil. They were either hanged or, less frequently, burnt. One poor woman, killed in 1610, went by the name Christiana *Weech*. She didn't stand a chance.

In the Duke's Head hotel in Tuesday Marketplace, a mummified cat had recently been discovered. It had been put there as a deterrent to witches and evil spirits over 300 years ago. This was common practice. Bodies of cats line the walls of buildings up and down the country. You might be sitting next to one right now. Maybe Theroux was right about the marketplace being embalmed.

Such was the fear of witches in King's Lynn, the infamous Witchfinder General, Matthew Hopkins, was paid £15, a stupendous sum, to rid the town of their evil.

'Just stuffe a dead cat betweene yer brickeworke,' he said, pocketing the dough.

Sadly, that wasn't what he really said. He more than earned his money.

Hopkins operated as Witchfinder General for only a couple of years (retiring from the position in 1647) yet oversaw the deaths of around 300 people in Norfolk, Suffolk, Essex and Cambridgeshire. He was drawn to the role after overhearing a group of women talking about their meetings with the devil. Maybe he'd been watching that performance of *Macbeth* on Cromer Pier.

What were the clues as to whether or not someone was a witch? Hopkins and his two glamorous assistants, John Sterne and Mary Phillips, considered the growth of boils, birthmarks, third nipples, moles, and blemishes to be strong indicators. They would stick pins into all of the above and if they didn't bleed the case was as good as done:

'They are most commonly insensible, and feele neither pin, needle, aule, &c. thrust through them.'

If a neighbour owned a cat, this, too, raised eyebrows (the situation, not the cat. Cat's don't raise eyebrows at anything; the best you'll get from them is a contemptuous flick of the head, with expert comic timing). Cats were animals of the night, a sure-fire pointer to an allegiance with the dark side. It was common knowledge that witches fed blood to cats from their third nipples, whereas normal people just killed them and stuffed them between the brickwork.[1]

Wherever Hopkins went he brought misery. He hurried trials to convict as many people as possible. His personal best was nineteen hangings in one day. He was responsible for around forty percent of the total number of witch murders in England from the 1400s through to the 1700s, when the practice was largely abolished. He visited King's Lynn and Great Yarmouth whilst in Norfolk. Whether or not he did so by public transport whilst writing a jovial book is anybody's guess. Aside from his actions during his brief stint as Witchfinder General, precious little is known of him. He was born in Suffolk and was frighteningly young at the time of his Witchfinder role (approximately twenty-five). When it comes to trying to piece his life story together, there's only hearsay and legend for historians to go by. It's otherwise difficult to prove that he ever even existed.

He was much like a witch in that respect.

I'd considered visiting the controversial Seahenge but time was against me. Not that I was too disappointed. I've never been

---

[1] It's important to remember that killing those in league with the devil was, to most people, seen as the sensible thing to do. To quote C.S Lewis on the subject: 'It may be a great advance in knowledge not to believe in witches, but there is no moral advance in not executing them when you do not think they are there. You would not call a man humane for ceasing to set mousetraps if he did so because he believed there were no mice in the house.'

fond of 'henges'. Stick that particular suffix on the end of anything and I lose interest. They're second only to recently excavated brick-kilns in my list of The World's Most Boring Things.

Seahenge was a timbre circle with a tree root in the middle of it. It had formed part of the seashore for the best part of forty centuries: until somebody decided it would be better off in a museum. It was officially discovered in 1998, although locals had known about it for years and respectfully left it alone.

The press were the ones to dub it Seahenge. It took all of three seconds to think up the name. It was retrieved from the shore, in the words of the Norfolk Museums Service, 'Because of the perceived threat of damage and erosion.' Others argued, with sound logic, that it had survived the last 4,000 years pretty effectively.

Another reason not to go to the Seahenge museum was that I already knew the best sea-related story that King's Lynn had to offer: that a fisherman once kept a seal as a pet and used to take it to the pub.

The bus to Downham Market wasn't due for another *forty* minutes. Balls. I'd rushed for no reason.

The seats at the station were metallic and carried enough surface rainwater to bathe a small hippo. A man with a tattooed face asked if I had a pound I could lend him, as he needed to get to Thetford. Then another man with a tattooed face asked if I had two pounds I could lend him as he needed to get to Peterborough.

A headache started to form.

A one-man-band walked around the corner and I admitted defeat.

A woman shouted to nobody: 'You can piss off, you liar. Holding my hair. I've got seven of these. Seven!'

The one-man-band clattered about, awaiting a round of applause that never came. Even toddlers in pushchairs didn't bother looking at him. It wasn't a one-man-band sort of day. He walked off, sounding like a tambourine falling down an endless flight of stairs, until the noise faded.

The bus exited King's Lynn via a different route. It was a grand old place. I'd never seen such a spectacular library in all my life. It looked like a castle. A castle you could rent DVDs from. We rode past the town's iconic South Gates (if I lived here I'd call them the 'Gareths'), an imposing 14th century gateway.

It was outside the Gareths that many criminals were executed (if the marketplace was busy). Two of these no good, disregarders of the law included a seven-year-old boy and his eleven-year-old sister. They stole a loaf of bread and were duly hanged. The punks.[1]

Colossal shopping complexes surrounded the town. I mean, really, stunningly, enormous. Aircraft carriers. King's Lynn was *the* shopping district for the huge and sparse area of west Norfolk. It was clearly more convenient for people to drive to these megastores than it was to go through the Gareths and get things from the high street. Plus, there probably weren't any one-man-bands around. There were effectively two King's Lynns: the historic, hypnotic town centre (witches, Wimpy, castles, statues, Gareths) and this international airport disguised as a retail park.

*

---

[1] The theft of 'a loaf of bread' must be history's most recorded, and harshly punished, crime. Why did criminals always want to steal bread? I'd have tried to steal money.

A 2008 report about the area didn't make pretty reading. The town's workforce was considered 'low value' with a 'low skills base'. Earnings were significantly below the national rate and work was often seasonal. Also below national average were education and work-related qualifications. The town was reported to offer a 'poor lifestyle' whilst also being 'unattractive to investors and professionals with higher disposable incomes.' But King's Lynn was evolving. Changes were being made. New trades and industries were coming to fruition.

Norfolk coastal towns were built on business generated from the sea. When the sea dried up, if you will, a thousand years of industry went with it. It's natural that some of these towns needed time to adapt. Imagine if the banking sector suddenly decided to pack up and leave London. There'd be a required adjustment period there, too, after the initial street parties.

King's Lynn used to be the home of Campbell's soup. A huge, isolated tower once overlooked the town. It had 'Campbell's' emblazoned across it; it would have looked dystopian if it weren't for the fact it was promoting tinned soup. The company moved in 2007, taking hundreds of jobs with it. The tower stayed until 2012 when it was gleefully blown up in a controlled explosion by a woman who'd lost her father there in an industrial accident. That's catharsis for you. How satisfying. This should become a regular thing. Imagine being allowed to blow up, for example, the site of a horrible job or a school where you were bullied. I jotted the following note in my pad:

'Check whether can put name forward to blow up bus station.'

Downham Market

When I set about planning this madcap trip, it was the thought of a day in Downham Market that made me grimace the most. It was a vague, distant place. I had never been there. I had never spoken to anyone who had been there. I had never heard of anyone going there. Even Daniel Defoe, in his otherwise glowing review of Norfolk, said of the area that he 'saw nothing that way to tempt curiosity but deep roads, innumerable drains and dykes of water [with] a base unwholesome air.'

Those drains and dykes of water were the Fens. I'd hoped to see something of them on my travels but as this bus route was as close as I was going to get, it seemed unlikely. I once saw a comedian who said of Norfolk that it was a place where you could watch your dog run away for three days. He must have had the Fens in mind when he said it. They're not the prettiest of Norfolk's natural attractions. Few could warm to their endless miles of flat, drained marshland. Their value, however, is incalculable. They alone make up half of England's finest grade agricultural land. They're a farming goldmine.

The bus dropped me off in the car park of Morrisons, next to a brick wall onto which was nailed the legend 'Downham Bus Shelter'. Adjacent to that was an empty black frame where a bus timetable ought to have been. As far as getting the return bus was concerned, this was all I had to go by. I didn't know *where* the bus back to King's Lynn would depart from. Was it there, in the lovingly restored 'Downham Bus Shelter', or elsewhere?

Near the car park exit was a decorative continental road sign pointing to Civray, France: Downham's twin town (possibly not its identical twin). It said 628 miles. So I wasn't entirely without guidance:

'Hmm, let me see. So, Civray is 628 miles in *that* direction. That means the bus to King's Lynn must go from...'

I had to find the Tourist Information Centre. The signs to it led me through litter-strewn alleyways and back gardens. Surely this wasn't really the route? It couldn't be. The way things were going I was going to be printing off timetables in somebody's lounge.

Just as I began to lose faith, it appeared. It was a modern build: a community centre and a library rolled into one. It was the sort of place recently retired people spent Wednesday afternoons learning about websites. In the foyer I found the door I needed. It said 'Tourist Information'. Great.

It also said 'Closed'.

Do Tourist Information Centres think these things through? This particular one was open Monday to Friday. Were these really the peak visiting times to a town known, and promoted, as the 'Gateway to the Fens'? Maybe it would be better to be closed on, say, Mondays, and open on, say, *Saturdays*. Go through your memory bank. How many times have Tourist Information Centres been open when you've needed them compared to the times they've been shut? They seem to operate solely for the purposes of people who don't work. Bloody things.

Downham had comfortably the oldest looking population I'd seen so far. For a trip of Norfolk, that was saying something. I walked through a car park, past the obligatory group of youths playing techno at each other from their freshly pimped rides. Even *they* looked old. They didn't look like real youths. They looked like those baby-faced men who get cast as teenagers in BBC sitcoms. They were all about 35. They were the only disaffected youths I'd ever seen who could remember *Live Aid*. Where were all the kids? Honestly, it would have looked like a scene from the film *Children of Men* had it not all been so thoroughly fucking pleasant.

I wanted to be angry but the town was so inoffensive I couldn't get the juices flowing. I went to kick a stray can but ended up just putting it in a recycling bin.

In the *good old days* of the 19th century, much of the surrounding fenland population took opium to cope with the sheer misery of life on that unreliable, flood-prone land. It was added to beer and tea. It was even given to children. When people left the Fens to come to Downham (to bring their goods to market, naturally), it was often the chemists that they'd head to first. People dozed around the town in a stupor, tripping over nothing and leaning on walls that weren't there. It wasn't until the Fens were properly drained, and subsequently became more profitable, that the opium use died down. Although it did still feel as though there was a touch of some sort of sedative in the air.

I went into the church: home of the alternative opiate of the Fenland people. It housed a bizarre 250-year-old wax effigy of a lady. It had been her dying wish to be captured in wax. (My dying wish, for the record, is to *not* be captured in wax.) She was a cross between Grotbags and Russell Grant. It was super creepy. Would've made a great candle, though.

It's believed that Charles I hid in Downham after his defeat to Cromwell at Naseby. He dressed as a member of the clergy, which, as disguises go, was pretty lazy.[1] Amazingly, it worked. Or, rather, nobody grassed him up. He hid at the Swan Inn before making a getaway to Scotland, where he probably dressed up as that bloke from the Quaker's Oats box. He was

---

[1] He was no better than those droids who go to a fancy dress parties as James Bond.

eventually captured and charged with treason. (He wore two jackets on the day of his beheading. He didn't want to shiver and give the impression he was scared. Isn't that sad?) His dying wish, too, was that he *not* be captured in wax form. In an act of mercy, Oliver Cromwell[1] decided that, rather than be displayed on a spike, Charles' head should be sewn back on.

The sentimental old fool.

After the event, Bridge Street in Downham Market became known to locals as King Charles Way.

Not too far from Bridge Street, down past the town's striking (literally) white town clock, was the alluringly named Paradise Road. It was so-named not for how heavenly it was, but because it was where criminals were hanged. The idea being that this was as close to paradise as they were ever going to get.

Paradise Road, ladies and gentlemen, now leads to 'Downham Bus Shelter'.

I needed to get to the bottom of the mystery of where my bus would depart. If I missed the next one I was done for. I asked around. Nobody knew:

'I think one bus go from there,' said an old fella, pointing at a random lamppost. 'It used to.'

Whenever an old man says something 'used to' happen, he could either mean it used to happen three months ago or that it used to happen in 1926. The sense of longing in his voice suggested he was talking about the latter. I went into a shop.

'They sometimes go from Morrisons' car park,' said the woman on the till.

I toyed with asking if she had any opium under the counter.

---

[1] Who was also from the Fens (the palpably rubbish, obviously-nowhere-near-as-good-as-Norfolk, Cambridgeshire wing).

I headed back onto the street. I walked Paradise Road back onto King Charles Way; ironically, my afternoon was going the Way of King Charles.

Nothing made sense. Nobody knew anything. The town clock tolled. I felt a long way from home. Mainly because I was. If all went well, which it undoubtedly wouldn't, it would still be a *five hour* journey back home to Sheringham: a distance of approximately forty miles as the crow flies. To put this into context, a flight from Heathrow to Moscow takes only four and a half hours - and *their* terminals are always clearly marked. The historian Bernard E. Dorman wrote, 'In the Middle Ages and well on into the eighteenth century it was easier to travel by sea from Norfolk to the continent of Europe than to penetrate the Midlands or to visit London.' Things hadn't changed much.

After several equally unenlightening discussions with locals regarding the location of the bus stop, I decided the best thing to do was to set up camp in a café overlooking 'Downham Bus Shelter'. That way, if a bus came, I could rush out and catch it.

The waiter was wonderfully nice and told me that *all* buses went from the shelter. Wow. Release. Heaven. It was like being told that not only had I won the National Lottery, but also that Liv Tyler was coming to my house to slip me the cheque.

With fresh confidence I sat back and enjoyed my tea. My seat faced out onto the road, scanning the vista. I spent a few minutes reading about a chap by the name of George William Manby. He'd been born in the village of Denver, five minutes down the road from Downham (or six weeks by bus). Manby claimed to have gone to school with Horatio Nelson and watched him sail paper boats down the sewage stream that once ran through Downham high street. Nelson was seven years older than Manby and, as you may recall, was at sea by his early teens, so there might be an element of fibbing going on. (We only have Manby's word as evidence for Nelson ever having gone to Downham Market school at all.)

As well as lying about Nelson, Manby did some truly great things. He invented the first pressurised fire extinguisher, named the 'Extinctuer'. He devised a lifesaving apparatus for those who had run into trouble near the shore. This entailed firing a line from a mortar to the ship, which the men would winch themselves along to safety, like linen on a washing line.[1] The apparatus saved thousands of lives. He also invented various means of saving people who had fallen through ice, as well as an unsinkable lifeboat (which later proved to be surprisingly sinkable). He was one of the advocates for a national fire brigade and one of the founders of the RNLI.

As the years passed, Manby became more and more obsessed with Nelson. He filled his house with so much Nelson memorabilia that he ended up having to live in the basement.

There had certainly been less interesting lives lived than his.

Whilst looking out of the window at the grey Saturday sky, I reflected, too, on the story of a Norfolk Titanic survivor, a Downham Market man by the name of Frank Prentice. It was a corker.

As one of the ship's staff, he'd helped put the famous LA socialite Virginia Clarke into a lifeboat, telling her it was a 'precaution' but one worth following through. Hours later - after much following through from all concerned – Virginia Clarke's lifeboat returned to the site of the sinking and fished bodies from the water. One of them was Frank Prentice. The beautiful Miss Clarke threw her coat around him and rubbed his limbs. Just like with Buttercup Joe's massage by nurses after the 1953 storm, Virginia's hands had the desired effect. Frank

---

[1] He worked on the invention after witnessing a terrible sinking off the shore at Great Yarmouth. The people on the beach could only watch as the ship and its crew went under.

regained consciousness. He had saved her life and she had returned the favour.[1]

Despite the friendly waiter's assurances that *all* buses went from the shelter, doubts began to creep in. This wasn't helped by the radio station, KLFM (you work it out), playing hits written exclusively to unnerve me. They all seemed to suggest impending bus doom. Maybe I was reading too much into them:

'I ain't missing you at all, since you've been gone, away...'
'Come back. Baby, come back. Come back. Baby, come back...'
'Baby, when you're gone. Days go on and on...'

My *Penguin Guide* said that a dwarf called Boots drank himself to death in Downham Market. If I missed my bus I planned to join him.
I looked up from my book and saw a bus fly past!
Argh!
I grabbed my things into a confused bundle and zipped out of the open door, leaving my cup of tea to fend for itself.
The bus had stopped fifty yards up the high street. It had bypassed 'Downham Bus Shelter'. I thought about running. Then I twigged: the town had a one-way system. The roads went round in a circle. If I waited, instead of running like a sweaty fool, the bus would come back around. The waiter had been right all along. Easy. I didn't need to run after it; I could

---

[1] Earlier in the evening, as a good illustration of the warped sense of priority the Titanic placed on its staff, Prentice had, in his own words, gone 'down to the storeroom with a gang of men and collected all the biscuits.'

just wait for it to disappear around the corner and then reappear at the trusty 'Downham Bus Shelter'.

We all have those moments when a gentle voice dishes out a little erudite advice, a small suggestion from an altogether better sphere. I received one there and then. Maybe it was the ghost of a long-deceased family member, a guardian spirit sent to nudge me towards predestination. Maybe it was good old Boots himself, half-pissed and teary-eyed, egging me on. Whoever or whatever it was, the advice was clear:

'Don't risk it, boyo. Get on that bus now.'

So I ran. I was holding my coat over my arms; I had a book about George Manby in one hand, and a book of Norfolk Titanic survivors in the other. I could hear coins falling out of the coat pockets. Then something heavier. My wallet. I stopped to pick it up. The bus whooshed. I saw the doors close. I ran harder. My gallops rumbled like the 2.40 at Exeter.

The bus started rolling away. I went turbo. I hadn't even known I had the potential to *go* turbo. I was defying logic and gravity. And possibly medical advice.

I arrived in time to bang on the doors as it pulled into the road. I'd always wanted to do that.

The driver opened the doors. He didn't ask to see my ticket. He knew it wasn't worth the wait. Breathing like a beached whale, I clamoured towards the back seat, knocking treasured memories out of old people's heads with my bag as I went.

And was I right? Was the friendly waiter right? Did the bus then follow the one-way system and go back round to 'Downham Bus Shelter' where *all buses went from*?

Did it fuck.

From the window I saw flashes of the Ouse, into which Virgina Woolfe had drowned (near Cambridge) in 1941. The New York Times reported that her hat and cane had been found on the riverbank. She had done it through fear of mental illness. 'The river's life is one long holiday' wrote the poet Jean Ingelow of the nearby Waveney. One long holiday full of heartbroken corpses.

The bus from King's Lynn cut a satisfying route across the heart of the county. It raced through villages and houses of historical note neglected by the tour. Near the village of Harpley was a turning that led towards Houghton Hall, originally owned by Robert Walpole, the first Prime Minister of Great Britain.[1]

Houghton Hall was once home to a valuable art collection. It was sold to Russia's Catherine The Great to help clear the gambling debts amassed by Walpole's grandson, George. After collecting £40,000 from Catherine, he celebrated by buying a greyhound and naming it Tzarina in her honour, whilst promising, of course, that his gambling days were over and that he'd only bought Tzarina as a really fast pet.[2]

One eye-catching fact about the hall was that it housed a library book taken from the Sidney Sussex College library in the 1660s. It was discovered in the mid-1950s and duly returned, 288 years overdue. They kindly waived the fine.

The parkland surrounding the hall still contained oak and chestnut trees planted during Robert Walpole's time. Tiptoeing around its grounds were over 600 deer, including, in Houghton's website's words, 'rare species from around the world, such as Pere David, Sambar and Chital.' Not being much up on deer

---

[1] Technically. The title of Prime Minister didn't exist at that time. People called him 'Prime' Minister as a form of mockery. I guess that's still largely how the term is used.

[2] George is thought to have started the first ever greyhound-racing club in 1776 (and he is sometimes credited, incorrectly, with founding the sport). His racing club regularly met at a pub in Swaffham, now called The Greyhound Inn.

species, I'll have to take their word for it on the subject of their rarity.

When Houghton Hall *desperately* needed expanding, Robert Walpole knocked down the village of Houghton and turfed its villagers out to buildings outside the grounds. The poet William Goldsmith was less than impressed and his verse *The Deserted Village* was considered a direct swipe:

> *The man of wealth and pride*
> *Takes up a space that many poor supplied;*
> *Space for his lake, his park's extended bounds,*
> *Space for his horses, equipage, and hounds:*
> *The robe that wraps his limbs in silken sloth*
> *Has robbed the neighbouring fields of half their growth*

Demolition of communities was not an unusual occurrence in Norfolk. The village of Euston was torn down and rebuilt in the 1700s because the owner of Euston Hall felt that the village 'spoiled the view from his bedroom.'

Sitting in one of Houghton's *neighbouring fields*, was Raynham Hall, the 400-year-old home of the Townshend family. The most famous Townshend being, of course, Charles 'Turnip' Townshend, one time leader in the House of Lords and general turnip enthusiast.

It's easy, with historical figures, to focus on one aspect of their life and forevermore associate them with it. For example, it's hard to think of Queen Victoria without thinking of her in a dark shawl, alone, reminiscing about Albert. It's equally difficult to think of Nero without picturing him knocking out a ditty on the fiddle whilst Rome combusts in the background. In the case of 'Turnip' Townshend, however, it's really not too unfair to link him with that dour vegetable. He was obsessed with them. Alexander Pope despaired that whenever he sat down to dinner with Townshend, the conversation soon turned to 'that kind of rural improvement which arises from turnips.'[1]

Townshend had a deep fascination with agricultural improvement (don't we all?). His major contribution to British farming was the introduction of a system that rotated four crops annually: wheat, barley, clover, and, of course, turnips. General practice at the time was to rotate three crops (although the four crop idea was originally Flemish). Each field would perform a different function each year. Instead of letting fallow fields go unused, as was usual procedure, Townshend's system encouraged the growing of clover in them, on which animals could graze. This added nitrates to the soil and increased its effectiveness for the next year's crop.

Are you still awake?

In that simpler, pre-internet dating age, Townshend didn't need to search far and wide for a wife. He married Robert Walpole's sister, Dorothy, said by many to be something of a rare beauty. Although there was one flaw: she possessed little interest in turnips. Had she had an online dating profile, she could have listed turnips as one of her dislikes. As it was, Townshend entered the marriage ignorant of his wife's shortcomings. Their marriage bed soon resembled the groom's fourth field: fallow. Dorothy began looking elsewhere for a good seed drill. This came in the form of a twatty-haired flouncer by the name of

---

[1] A quick word on turnips, if I may? Although unlikely to set dinner party conversations ablaze as a subject, that humble, hardy, purplish Brassica contributed to the doubling of the British population after its introduction during the Agricultural Revolution. The turnip's ability to survive frosts meant that it could be picked and fed to cattle throughout winter, thus supplying communities with fresh meat (and fresh, meaty cow turds for the fields) in even the harshest months.

Lord Wharton. He charmed Dorothy into a secret tryst that would have a world famous ending.[1]

Townshend and Walpole may have been neighbours and brothers-in-law, but they were anything but friends. They shared political and professional differences and Walpole's expansion of Houghton was seen by Townshend as a personal affront.[2]

Townshend's infamous temper flared upon discovering that his wife had been employing a crotch rotation system to rival that of his own beloved crop rotation system. The game was up between Dorothy and Lord Wharton. One version of events claims that Dorothy's affair was revealed by the wife of Lord Wharton, who herself had failed to see the lighter side of the matter. Townshend violently threw Dorothy into one of Raynham Hall's bedrooms and locked the door. She didn't leave the building much after that. She died there in 1726. Some say she died of smallpox (after a suspiciously nasty fall down the stairs), others that she contracted syphilis from Lord Wharton's well-used trouser sword.

Despite not being seen much in later life, a great number of people claim to have seen Dorothy in her afterlife. Her ghost was first spotted at Raynham Hall after a Christmas party in 1835. Guests reported a mysterious brown apparition on the main staircase: a woman of an 'aristocratic look'. Her eye-sockets, according to one witness, were empty and glowing.[3]

---

[1] Actually, it's more of a world famous *epilogue*. You'll see what I mean when I get to it.

[2] A contemporary wrote, 'Lord Townshend looked upon his own seat at Raynham as the metropolis of Norfolk, and considered every stone that augmented the splendour of Houghton, as a diminution of the grandeur of Raynham.' They were a right couple of characters.

[3] Ah, that unmistakable empty eye-socket aristocratic look.

The next person to spot the brown sugar was the spectacularly named author Captain Marryat (real name: Fred), writer of *Children of the New Forrest*. He stood behind a door and watched through the chink as the brown lady glided silently down the dark, midnight corridor towards him. She stopped outside his door, turned slowly to look at him and 'grinned in a malicious and diabolical manner.'

Victorians were made of sterner stuff. Rather than run away or freeze to the spot, dripping urine from his undercarriage, Captain Marryat threw the door open and shot the Lady in the face, putting a hole in the wooden panelling and startling the rare deer over at Houghton Hall.

Marryat's daughter later said that it was the ghost's sheer nerve to grin at him that had 'infuriated' her father so. How much better *Most Haunted* would be if Captain Marryat replaced Yvette Fielding:

'Oh my G-G-God, did you hear that?' says a spooked cameraman.

BANG!

'Hear what, dear fellow?' replies the Captain, blowing smoke away from his pistol.

With a fresh bullet in her orifice, the ghost of Dorothy became the ghost of the ghost of Dorothy. She was often spotted by children. A vicar wrote in 1918, 'I have heard that children of people in the Hall asked who the brown lady was who came into their room frequently.' In 1926, she was spotted again on the stairs, again by children. They said that the ghost looked just like the portrait of Dorothy that hung on the wall, except slightly more brown. Lady Townshend (not Dorothy, a much later edition) later wrote to a friend that the sighting had scared and puzzled the children because 'they could see the stairs *through* her.'

In 1936, two photographers from *Country Life* magazine (nothing to do with butter) arrived to take snaps of the house.

Whilst taking pictures near the staircase, one of them saw 'an ethereal veiled form coming slowly down the stairs.' He quickly took a picture. There hadn't been a better shot of the brown lady since the one Captain Marryat put through her face.

The *Country Life* image of the blurry phantom floating down the Raynham Hall staircase became the most famous ghost photograph in the short history of that bizarre medium. Not only was the picture famous, it was also difficult to disprove. In fact, it has never been definitively debunked. There are theories about how it could have been done using models and lighting effects, but these remain theories. Roger Clarke, in his excellent *A Natural History of Ghosts*, in which many other ghost stories are picked apart, conceded that one of the theories must be that 'it could really be a ghost.'[1]

Only after we reached Fakenham did the importance of my decision to run for the bus, rather than wait for it to go around the Downham one-way system, hit home. Had I missed it, as I so easily could have, I would have had no way of getting back. I would've had to have stayed in a travel tavern.[2] It was a thought that put more wind up me than any story involving a brown lady dicking about on a staircase.

---

[1] It's worth bearing in mind that both Lady Townshend and the photographers benefited financially from the picture. Lady Townshend had just written a book about ghosts (obviously, the added publicity created a spike in sales - from around six copies to 20,000) and the photographers made money from print sales.

[2] There was a train station in the town. But it would have required going all the way to Cambridge and then to Norwich and then home. Estimated travel time (with connections): five hours. Estimated flight time between London and Cairo? Five hours.

Leg Six

Norwich – Hingham – Watton – Swaffham - Dereham

Norwich: Part II

Sleeping on couches isn't the ideal way to spend a night. The hope is that as you grow older you have to do it less. University is generally one's peak couch-sleeping era: being awoken at twenty-past-six by your friend's housemate (whose name you still don't know – is it Gary or Harry?) clanking around the kitchen before his Saturday shift in the M&S café. (You hear him tutting and muttering things to himself like 'This place is a dump' and 'Where's my fucking cup?' whilst you covertly slip *his fucking cup*, the cup you used last night as a vessel from which to drink liebfraumilch, away from his line of vision, before retreating under the grotty blanket and pretending you're innocently mid-slumber.) You shouldn't really need to sleep on too many friends' couches in adulthood. Unless things go pear shaped i.e. you find yourself writing a book about Norfolk.

Luckily, as you grow older, friends' couches become much comfier. They tend to be less springy, and have fewer Tesco Value Digestive crumbs. They're a more attractive proposition all round. Even so, when I'm on one, I still struggle to sleep. The night before my trip to Hingham was no exception.

I watched tele in the dark. *BBC News* on a loop. I got to the stage where I'd seen the same five stories, delivered with identical facial expressions and vocal inflections, three times over. I began to fade. The last thing I remember seeing was the presenter saying it was time for a weekly economics show. This was followed by a masculine woman in a pink suit talking against the backdrop of a stock exchange. The share numbers rolled along the bottom of the screen and I was off. Goodnight.

I love Norwich market. It's brilliant. Where else could you find Hanson's debut album and hoover bags in the same place? The stalls are clean and well maintained, painted in striking primary colours. If you order food, you have to stand to eat. It's like being in New York, except you can hear Take That on the radio (and are usually stood next a surly 58-year-old in a high-vis vest-jacket who thinks you're a flagrant homosexual because you only ordered one all-day-breakfast).
Even more satisfying than the fried food is the cup of market tea. The tea on Norwich market tastes as if it's been brewing since the days of Kinnock's Labour. It's strong enough to make you see dragons soar across the skies. It's hotter than fire.
'Sugar?' asks the person behind the counter, holding a teaspoon suggestively near the industrial-sized sugar bag.
'Yes, one, please,' you say.
'Right you are,' they reply. They put the teaspoon down. An Olympic coxless pairs oar is retrieved from beneath the counter. 'One sugar, coming up,' they say, scooping it onto the oar and shovelling it into the mug.
There's more sugar in one cup of Norwich market tea than the entire city was allotted in rations during any given week in 1943.
I drank my brew and waited for the hallucinations to pass. Once the last dragon had flown, I made my way towards the station. It was early. The city was populated by smartly dressed twenty-somethings on their way to the office. I adore the sounds a city makes in the early morning, especially in summer. The office workers wear shoes and heels which makes for a nice assortment of clopping noises. And they're usually moving

around busily, which sounds even nicer, as though there are lots of packhorses trotting about. There isn't much traffic except for buses and motorised road sweepers. It's still early enough for the birds to be heard. Early enough to hear a stray laugh or sneeze. Early enough to hear plates and coffee cups being washed and chairs being set out on the pavement. Early enough to hear church bells ringing, somewhere.

I walked past a building claiming to have been the site from which the first ever postcode had been rolled out in 1959. Norwich was full of little forays into the quieter side of history. It had recently become one of the few Unesco World Cities of Literature. I can do no better than to quote a statement from the city's Writer's Centre on some of the historical literary developments:

'Norwich has a sensational literary past, from the first battlefield dispatch (1075) to the first woman published in English (Julian of Norwich – C15th), the first recognisable novel (C16th), the first blank verse (C16th), the first printed plan of an English city (C16th), the first published parliamentary debates (Luke Hansard C18th), the largest concentration of published dissenters, revolutionaries and social reformers (C18th/19th); the first provincial library (1608) the first provincial newspaper (1701)...'

I headed to Hingham with added verve, keen to add my own sentence to the story of Norwich and Norfolk's sensationally bookish past.

First, and last, idiot to try and travel to forty Norfolk places on public transport whilst consistently moaning and blabbering on about nothing in particular (C21st)

Hingham

To the much-maligned 'untrained eye', Hingham would appear to be a village. It had a village green, a village signpost, village shops, a village bus stop, and a population with an average age of 102. The number of inhabitants, also, hovered around the village-like 2,000 mark. To eyes that *have* been trained, however, to those well-schooled eyes of the wandering Norfolk investigator, the village was clearly a town. Clearly. As one of the *towns*folk warned me, 'Don't let people hear you call it a village. It's a town.'

High summer was at its highest summeriness as I strolled out to paint the Hingham *town* red. It was one of those glorious English mornings where the air was fresh and the sky a clear, light blue, with occasional frothy clouds floating across in a race to nowhere etc. I walked across the *town* green, taking pictures of the quaint *town*houses encircling it. I studied the *town* signpost. It depicted three Bee Gees standing in a row. (They might have been pilgrims. But they looked like Bee Gees.) They were halfway through a 17th century rendition of *Saturday Night Scarlet Fever*. The sign also depicted a lonely chap looking out to sea at other pilgrims, who possibly hadn't invited him because he smelt, sailing to the New World.

The pilgrims were led from Hingham by one of its former vicars, Robert Peck. Peck had made a name for himself as something of a wild child (in church circles, at least). He was accused of such terrible acts as 'levelling the altar, pulling down the rails and sinking the chancel a foot below the nave.' The mad bastard. On April 8th 1637, he swanned off across the Atlantic with his Hingham peeps (or pilgs). When the Peck massif arrived at their desired location they wasted no time in changing its name from Bare Cove, which sounded a little too nudey for their pilgrim tastes, to Hingham.[1]

The great Hingham emigration continued in the following years. In 1639, a certain Samuel Lincoln decided to move from one Hingham to the other aboard a ship with the alarmingly flimsy name of the John & Dorothy. Amazingly, the John & Dorothy made it across the ocean without sinking.[2] Whilst in the hip *new* Hingham, Sam Lincoln married an Irish gal, had eight children, lived a happy enough life, and died in 1690. As an added nugget of trivia, his great-great-great-great-grandson went by the name of Abraham. He remains somewhat popular in the modern day United States of America.

With the pilgrims leaving Hingham, the town lost so many prominent figures that it had to rebuild itself. Peculiarly, the town transformed into a locale for socialites. In the 1700s it became known as 'Little London'. Its city-slicker visitors were responsible for building the Georgian houses that still surrounded the green. Or, I should say, they bought *Elizabethan* houses surrounding the green and rebuilt them to make them look more fashionably Georgian:

'They were trying to keep up with the Joneses,' said a friendly, purple-haired pensioner I'd met by the bus stop. 'These houses all have Georgian façades and Elizabethan rears,' she added, as I desperately tried to avoid doing a joke about bums.

---

[1] The most famous boat to sail to the New World was, of course, the Mayflower. Of the 107 on board, 32 were from Norfolk.

[2] I wouldn't have got on it. If I ever had to cross an ocean it would have to be in a ship called the Destroyer or the Untouchable. I just wouldn't have faith in the John & Dorothy getting the job done. They sound like the names of two middle-aged people who live next door to your nan and occasionally do her shopping. (When you go round to see her she tells every single thing that's happened in John and Dorothy's lives since you last visited.)

*

Hingham was consistently exquisite. As was my wont, I spied through people's windows and over their garden walls. There was wealth in the town, but there was little of the kooky, pseudo-rustic nonsense that occasionally blighted Norfolk's other upmarket quarters. I didn't see a single string of fairy lights. And, most pleasingly, I had never in my life walked past so many gardens in which people were working on projects. I closed my eyes. Above the distant traffic and the wood pigeons I could hear planks being sawed, grass being cut, hammers hitting nails, hedges being trimmed. I could hear exact phrases of conversations going on fifty yards down the road. A man on a roof was telling a man on the ground about his new bread maker. It had cost him the best part of a hundred quid and was showing precious little wear on the paddle.

Equally fascinating was the selection of shops. There was a convenience store called Harrods of Hingham which, unlike Harrods of Knightsbridge, had smiley-faced toy vegetables in the window. The shop sold homemade jams and sauces. It had been named Harrods after its original owner. You'll have to believe me when I tell you that they were allegedly asked by Harrods of Knightsbridge to add 'of Hingham', lest people confuse the two. It couldn't have been too regular an occurrence:

'I didn't know what to get you for your birthday, darling, so I thought a voucher for Harrods would suffice?'

'Oh, Roger! Now I can stock up on those Happy Shopper tinned tomatoes that you know I so adore.'

Just down the road from Harrods (of Hingham) was a shop of such intrigue that it had the same pull on me that Eve must

have felt when she first saw the apple. A sandwich board outside read:
'Best Quality Hand Painted Russian Christmas Decorations.'
Another read:
'We Accept Rubles, Grivna, Euros, £s, $s, Cars, TVs, Houses etc.'

I wondered if it was a twee business endeavour that had gone too far. I intended to find out.

I expected to walk in and see elaborate decorations hanging from the walls and a pretty lady in a floral dress standing by the till listening to Radio 4. Instead I walked into a room I'd once barged my way through on *Call of Duty*.

Hanging from the walls were occasional decorative Russian flags and tapestries. There were cardboard boxes and faded decorations occupying the dusty shelves. On one shelf sat a row of army boots. The owner sat facing the entrance.

He was *real* Norfolk. Note the use of italics. He had the same raspy accent as my nanny. It was straight from the heartlands. The standard Norfolk accent, like all accents, is enticingly simple to slip into. It's an easier way of talking. The accent that this man had was slower and heavier, it required lifting. It came from the depths.

I asked him what he loved about Russia.

'They got more histry than us, hant tha,' he said, without the question mark. 'I go three months a year. In winter. Go 'n look in there,' he said, motioning towards a back room. I went alone.

The room was stacked with army surplus. One of my many hypocrisies is that I'm a pacifist who loves army clothing. If it hadn't been such a warm day, I would have picked something up. I went back to the front of the shop. The man was still on his chair facing the door. He pointed at some faded photographs pinned to the wall. They were of halls and houses. Each time I asked where the places were, he replied that they were 'garn now.'

I told him about my book and how awful some of my experiences with buses had been. He quickly replied that Hingham's bus service was perfect. I asked if I could take a photograph of the shop. He said, 'Yes, but I don't know what for.'

I don't think he liked me much. I don't blame him.

I knew I'd be disliked the moment we met. Real Norfolk people rarely trust an outsider without giving them approximately twelve years to prove themselves. Unfortunately I only had another hour and I wanted to see the church. He told me Hingham's was the biggest in Norfolk. He pointed towards it, again from his seat. I left and said Goodbye.

'Yeah,' he said.

And off I went, out into the light. I looked back at the shop. The front door was open but the darkness inside had created an alternative black door in its place. I laughed as I imagined the look on the face of the next person to walk in. There should be a camera, like on white-knuckle rides, set-up in the doorway to capture people's reactions. It was so unique that I wanted to go back and keep talking. I wanted to know about his trips to the Russian winters. I wanted to know everything. He was a riddle wrapped in a mystery inside an enigma - who also happened to sell Christmas decorations on the side. His store was defiantly real Norfolk in a town that could easily have slipped into another cartoon world of the upper-middle class. It was an unmissable main attraction. It was Hingham's Kremlin.

Russia might have had more history than us (how this was measured, I don't know), but there was still a hell of a lot of it in Norfolk. The war memorials were testament to that.

Norfolk men, and children, were always quick to enlist. But, for those who couldn't fight abroad, the 1940s offered a novel opportunity to satiate that desire by joining the Home Guard.

Across the county, as across Britain, men and boys volunteered to do their bit for the Allied cause. The training resources were scarce. Some members of the Norfolk Home Guard reportedly threw vegetables at each other in lieu of bombs and, in Hingham, recreated the sound of enemy machine guns by running a stick along a corrugated iron fence. The Nazis must have been shitting themselves.

Not that everyone was keen to get stuck in with some of the Home Guard's more creative drills. One villager was woken in the dead of night by the sound of gravel hitting his window. He opened it up and asked what the devil was going on:

'There's an imaginary bomb crater in the village green and all of us have to go and fill it in,' came a whisper.

'Well, imagine I'm there,' was the shrift response.

Such stories can sometimes cloud over what was, and remains, the bravest thing the people of Britain have ever been called upon to do. Enlisting in Dad's Army didn't just mean wacky training drills and jokes about boys called Pike not telling people their name. Beneath it all was a chilling undertow. It was the members of these voluntary squadrons who were most likely to be the first publicly hanged when the Nazis invaded. And such an invasion was very much considered a *when* not *if* situation. To quote one member of the Norfolk Home Guard:

'We were given three morphine tablets. One to ease the pain if injured, two to knock us out and three to kill ourselves if taken prisoner.'

That's an episode of *Dad's Army* nobody wants to watch.

There was a morning communion going on. As I opened the church door, it made a noise akin to the demolition of the King's Lynn soup tower. Seven parishioners sat in the far corner, encircling the gowned preacher. Nobody flinched at my interruption.

It's surreal to see communion in action, especially on a random weekday morning. Outside, the modern world rollicked on. Inside, a quiet ritual. God become flesh. Flesh become bread. Eternal life. Freedom from fear. Maybe. I decided to wait outside and come back when the service was over. I stalked the graveyard taking crap pictures. Flesh become cack-handed photographer.

I returned to see the takers of communion participating in a coffee morning. Some of the harder skinned social commentators of the day claim that this England doesn't exist anymore. They claim it's gone the way of mental arithmetic and the red squirrel. Well, let me confirm that this England most definitely does still exist: cardigans, yellow cords, green ties, knitted tights, personalised cotton handkerchiefs, mint imperials, glasses cases. It's *all* there, as it was in the beginning, and ever shall be, world without end.

I spoke to the preacher. He was a layman. He was the archetypal village, sorry, *town*, preacher. He was jovial and funny, with energetic body language. He showed me a bust of Abraham Lincoln. He told me that Americans regularly made a pilgrimage to Hingham to see the birthplace of an ancestor of a pilgrim who had left Hingham to go to the new Hingham. It was all very confusing. He asked why I hadn't stayed during communion. I said I hadn't wanted to interrupt.

'Everyone always says that! It's Wednesday morning communion for crying out loud! It's not a funeral,' he laughed.

'But it's a spiritual moment,' I said.

His response was to wave his hand in front of his face dismissively, as though swatting away a fly.

'Stay for coffee,' he said. 'Have some cake. Some tea.'

I said I didn't have time. The truth was I felt self-conscious. Isn't that a silly thing. No question mark needed.

Watton

It was market day. In the distant past, the street would've been crowded with cows and pigs and men shouting 'Hoy', now market days just meant that the pavements would be slightly busier. Watton market was once famous for its hares. With 'Wat' being an old name for hare and 'Ton' being another word for town, my balding head had finally arrived in Hare-Town. Discussions between hare-buying customers and traders must have been quite confusing back then:
'Got any wat?'
'You what?'
'Ewe wat? No, thanks - that sounds horrible. I meant, have you got any *regular* wat?'
'Eh?'
'No, we've got plenty of 'ay in the barn! Any wat?'
'Oh, I see. Yes. We've got lots of wat.'
'Well, *I* don't know what you've got lots of - you're supposed to tell me!'
And that, ladies and gentlemen, is the kind of dynamite material the Two Ronnies would have been doing had they been around in the 1500s.
The modern market at Watton was a typical example of all Norfolk markets. Here are some of the things I saw on sale: flowers, dog toys, fruit, biscuits, imported deodorant, duvets, batteries, lighters (in packs of eighty), double plugs, colouring books, hoover attachments, wind chimes, seafood, diaries, rubber shoes, fleece jackets with Dalmatians on, t-shirts depicting Native Americans looking pensive (whilst, as ever, riding Harley Davidsons), plant pots, Clive Cussler paperbacks, boiled sweets and more besides. But no wat.

*

Watton's most curious curiosity was the belief that the story of the *Babes in the Wood* might have been based on a local legend. The story was first published in 1595 by a Norwich printing firm. It was originally called '*The Norfolk gent, his will and Testament and howe he Commytted the keepinge of his Children to his own brother whoe delte most wickedly with them and howe God plagued him for it.*' With a name like that, nobody ever suspected that it would take off as a panto.

The story goes that a Norfolk man was tasked with looking after two of his brother's children. He decided, instead, to pay a couple of men to take the children to the woods (Wayland Woods, outside Watton) and kill them so he could claim their inheritance. The murderers took the children to the woods. An argument started. One murderer killed the other and told the children that he would look after them. He left to get provisions but never returned (he possibly got sidetracked looking at Dalmatian fleeces on the market). The children were left to wander the woods alone. They eventually died. Their bodies were covered over with leaves by the birds. And that's that. It's an odd one, right? There are no discernable morals to it, other than to always hire professional assassins.

The story has had to be greatly amended for pantomime. It wouldn't go down well to see a former *Emmerdale* star and a retired middleweight successfully concoct the deaths of two kids. The auditorium would be awash with the sound of confused sobbing and parents demanding their money back.[1]

---

[1] The 1932 Disney cartoon version put a more positive spin on the story. Although their adaptation was a mixture of *Babes in the Wood* and *Hansel and Gretel*. It involved a house made out of sweets. There definitely wasn't one of those in Wayland Woods.

It's said that the mysterious wails of the *Babes* can still be heard through the wood's trees. This seems less mysterious when you factor in that one of Her Majesty's finest penal establishments is nearby; the wailing could easily be the sound of distant harmonicas. Regardless, I'd still want the *Most Haunted* team take a trip to the woods, just to clear the issue up once and for all:

'I'm seeing a large brownish thing with a greenish aspect,' says resident medium, Patrick. 'I'm not sure of the technical term for it.'

'Ah, yes,' smiles the historian, 'that's probably a tree. In woodlands they would grow.'

On the edge of the town was the intriguingly named Loch Neaton: the only loch in England. During the building of a railway embankment, large parts of the land were excavated, leaving behind what locals might have called a 'gret oul' hole. The gret oul hole was filled with water and the surrounding area became a leisure park. From the early 1900s onwards, it was *the* place to be seen (in Watton). The Watton train line, I needn't inform you, was ripped up in the 1960s and as a result, I again needn't inform you, the park's flow of visitors buffered.

The loch now looked less like a place where flaxen haired wenches took their wights on Sunday afternoon walks and more like a place where corpses were found floating in grisly Danish crime thrillers on BBC4.

Why was it called a loch and not a lake? Because of the Scotsmen who worked on the embankment and dug the gret oul hole all those years ago.

*

I wandered into a bookshop like a recovering alcoholic sneaking into Oddbins.[1] The interior was enormous. It was the bookshop equivalent of the Tardis. The owners were a friendly couple. They were sitting by the till, talking. I joined in, uninvited. We talked about Watton.
'It's a very Methodist town,' said the husband, proudly, in the crispest of English accents. Reading between the lines, I took this to mean that it was left-leaning. 'Watton has never been fashionable,' he continued. 'It often gets left out and forgotten.'
'Well,' I said. 'I best be off.'

Watton used to have an airbase. I mention this for no other reason than the fact Lord Haw Haw, history's oft-forgotten ballbag, proudly broadcasted to Britain that the mighty Luftwaffe had wiped it out in a stunning night raid. What had actually happened was a German pilot had misjudged the target and bombed seven bells of shit out of a chicken run. Still, the RAF had lovely sandwiches for the next couple of days.

I passed a collector for the Salvation Army. An elderly man donated ten pounds. Without wishing to pre-judge, he didn't look the type to have plenty of ten-pound-notes going spare.
'Oi'm givin yew this,' he said, 'cuss yew were good to me when oi wuss a little boy. Oi hent forgot ut.'
Near the bus stop was a precinct in which were gathered five motorised carts in a row. It was Cromer Pier all over again. Their elderly drivers surveyed the scene. They were like those

---

[1] Wine merchants have gone the way of the video shop. On the face of it, this sounds like a good thing. The grim truth is that almost every corner shop in England now overflows with cheap booze. It's depressing to think about. Luckily, I'm always too pissed to do so.

gangs of riders you saw in Saturday afternoon films about teenage delinquents. At any given moment they could vroom off in unison and hit the open highway: that long, hot highway to Swaffham, where the girls were smoking and the beers were cool. Where danger couldn't get no sleep.

'Swaffham, please,' I said to the bus driver in my best smiley voice.

Swaffham

Long before the arrival of its hilariously named fishing paraphernalia shop, Kev's Tackle, Swaffham was a seasonal retreat of the well-to-do. Swaffham was their party zone; they hosted glittering social events and gatherings. The town held more balls than a General Practitioner. Nelson and Emma Hamilton were frequent visitors. They were said to have danced in its halls, when not busy dancing in other halls.

Not that Swaffham was all foxtrots and suggestively raised eyebrows back then. It had a rough side. One lad, by the name of Jem Mace (affectionately known as 'The Swaffham Gypsy'), was England's bare-knuckle boxing champ in 1861 and 1866. Boxing was illegal at that time and Mace was repeatedly arrested for doing it. He later moved to America where the sport was a popular sensation (and legal). He won titles and prizefights galore. He was the first boxer of note to model boxing gloves and promote their use to audiences around the world. He was also a versatile musician (*without* gloves. With gloves, he was rubbish).

Mace lost his fortune through gambling. His last recorded fight was in 1909. He was 78.[1] A career that had taken him from Swaffham dirt-tracks to packed stadiums in the USA came to an end on the streets of Jarrow, where he busked for pennies. He was buried in an unmarked grave in Liverpool. In 1990 he was inducted into boxing's Hall of Fame as 'a pioneer'. He is often referred to as the 'Father of Modern Boxing'.

Swaffham town centre was an immense, open triangle of space. In the middle was a Butter Cross. Butter Crosses, for those sad-cases *without* a working knowledge of historic market places, were shelters under which dairy traders sold their goods. Swaffham's was pleasantly pompous. It looked like a Roman orator's platform; the kind of place on which you might witness Caligula nominating his hamster to oversee construction of the aqueducts. It had a domed roof propped up by white pillars. Atop the dome stood the Roman goddess Ceres, for no notable reason other than the fact she appeared to take pleasure from being up there.

On a flag outside the town museum flapped the words, 'Swaffham Museum: The Howard Carter Story'. It sounded like one of those films you might see on True Movies at three in the afternoon (just after their screening of Al Pacino's *Revolution* and *Columbo: Murder on the Butter Cross*). Inside, I told the staff that I was writing a book and they generously let me have a cheeky tour of the Howard Carter Story in exchange for putting a quid in the donation box. Ah, the perks of stardom. Was this how The Beatles felt when they'd jetted into JFK airport?

*

---

[1] An extraordinary age. Even Rocky decided to call it a day at 67.

Howard Carter wasn't born in Swaffham, but his parents were Swaffham folk and he visited many times during his youth. Young Howard had inherited his father's artistic genes. He was a precocious talent with an obsession with the past. For his seventeenth birthday his grandma gave him a chisel. He was the only seventeen-year-old to have ever received a chisel for their birthday and not instantly run away from home.

Later that year, Carter was sent to Egypt by the Egypt Exploration Fund. While there, the youngster mastered the art of copying tomb decorations and devised new, efficient methods of excavation. He discovered the tombs of Thutmose I (*Fellowship of the Thutmose*) and Thutmose III (*Return of the Thutmose*), although both had already been discovered by thieves and stripped of their treasures.[1]

In 1907, Carter was financed by Lord Carnarvon to search the Valley of the Kings and find the tomb of Tutankhamun. Fifteen years later, Carter still hadn't done so. Carnarvon began to lose patience; archaeology expeditions didn't come cheap. He told Carter that he had one more season to find the tomb before the mission was cancelled. Carter was desperate; he even considered asking the locals to think back to where they'd had Tutankhamun last.

Then, on the 4th of November 1922, his team discovered a set of steps leading down to a sealed doorway. Carter sent a wire to Lord Carnarvon asking him to come and witness the opening of the door.

As luck would have it, Carnarvon was just the sort of person to attend the opening of a door. He arrived in Egypt, with his family, as soon as possible.

Carter knew that his destiny was on the other side of that closed entrance. It was either a place in history or a place on the

---

[1] Why are thieves so good at finding ancient tombs? If only they'd got chisels for their birthdays, too. They'd be incredible archaeologists.

boat home. He nervously made a breach in the top left hand corner with the very same chisel given to him by his grandmother all those years ago. The door gave way. A little. He cracked it open, felt the wave of cold air wash over him, and entered, candle in hand. In the flickering yellow light he saw it all.

Outside, the tension was unbearable. Brows were being mopped at a frantic rate.

'Can you see anything?' Carnarvon called.

'Yes,' came Carter's echo. 'Wonderful things!'

It took months to catalogue the findings. With one twist of his chisel, Howard Carter had opened the door to 3,000 years of history. It wasn't until early the following year that the burial chamber was opened, unearthing the corpse of the child king. The news was a worldwide smash. The photographs taken at the time are so otherworldly that they still raise goosebumps.

Since Carter's discovery, experts have deduced that King Tut died at nineteen, needed a cane to walk, had a cleft palate, was just under six-foot, had a Mr Burns-style overbite, and was possibly conceived out of wedlock. They even know that he had a wet nurse called Maia. Incredibly, for all of this, scientists don't know *how* he died. Theories range from contracting malaria to being crushed in a chariot race. (There were two mummified foetuses also found in the chamber, believed to have been his.)

Carter retired from archaeology soon after the excavation, preferring instead to give the occasional lecture and generally potter about. He died at the age of 64, long enough to belittle the myth that by opening the tomb he had opened up a curse. He'd lived a rich and happy life. He had seen some wonderful things. And he had a lovely chisel.

*

I had one final jaunt in the now-roaring afternoon heat. In *Bridgewater's Norfolk*, the author called the Swaffham town sign 'one of the most attractive in Norfolk'. As attractive as it was, I don't advise visiting the town on the strength of it. It depicted a 15th century character called the Tinker of Swaffham. His proper name was John Chapman. The legend goes that he had a recurring dream that told him that if he went to London Bridge he would 'hear news greatly to his advantage.' So he walked all the way to the capital from Swaffham, laughing at Kev's Tackle as he passed.

On arrival in London, a shopkeeper told him that it was ludicrous to act upon a message in a dream. Why, the shopkeeper added, he himself had had a dream about a wacky far-off place called Swaffham in which he dug under the apple tree of a man named Chapman and found a pot of gold. And you didn't see *him* walking to Norfolk, did you?

Chapman, being the tinker that he was, bit his tongue and legged it back to Swaffham. He dug under his apple tree and found the pot of gold. On it was an inscription that read:

Under me doth lie – another richer far than I

Not one for the interpreting experimental free verse on a strictly metaphorical level, Chapman got back on his knees and resumed digging.

'Do you see anything?' asked a neighbour.

'Yes,' he replied. 'Wonderful things! Plus an arse-load of soil.'

True enough, there was another, larger pot of gold underneath. The tinker was rich.

Intriguingly, to add a bit of spice to the legend, an inventory of the reparative work on Swaffham Church reveals that a man by the name of John Chapman paid for the rebuilding of the north aisle. There's also a 15th century stained glass window depicting a kindly donor. And a wood carving of a tinker-like figure inside the church, although this is thought to have been made after the legend spread, as much of the church was given a ruinous *60 Minute Makeover* by gun-wielding puritans during the Civil War.

The extent of Oliver Cromwell's hatred for anything with a hint of Catholicism can be neatly gauged by the bullet holes seen in Swaffham Church's rafters. It was there that his grandmother was buried, complete with a creepy, colourful memorial (in which she's depicted holding a skull). If you were willing to rough up the resting place of your gran, there probably weren't many things you'd baulk at. Chopping off a king's head, for example.

Within close proximity of Cromwell's grandmother, was a brass inscription dedicated to the 'Splendid Memory' of a certain Harold Bell, who, according to the plaque, was *'killed by a tiger May 25th 1916 while safeguarding some of the natives of his district.'*

There have been some miraculous, outrageous scientific developments over the last hundred years: we can now send a message from one side of the planet to the other in a second; we can watch live satellite feeds from buggies on Mars; we can take pills to actively kill infections; we can photograph stars that are so far away that their brightness in our night sky is one ten-billionth of the capability of the naked eye. These leaps from the shoulders of giants have all been done, in truth, in the hope that professional brass engravers never again have to sit in the workshop and get to work on carving out sentences like *'killed by a tiger May 25th 1916 while safeguarding some of the natives of his district.'* Nowadays they tend to carve things more along the lines of *'West Norfolk Pool League (Division F) Runners Up 2008'* and *'World's Biggest Pisshead'*. It's a beautiful thing, really.

Dereham

I used to live near Dereham. It was in the wilderness years after university, when the stabilisers came off the bicycle of reality and I was left wobbling in the road in a direction I hadn't planned (even though I'd just had three years of lazy, lecture-free afternoons with which to formulate such a plan, instead of watching *Neighbours,* followed by *Murder, She Wrote*).

Dereham had changed little in the eight years since. Woolworths was gone, of course, replaced by its creepy younger brother, Poundland. Other than this minor re-jigging of the shops, all seemed fair. It had maintained its always unexpected feel, and look, of an outer-London borough.

Up until the early 1700s, Dereham had a reputation for being the 'dirtiest town in the country.' Not county, *country*. It was a renowned stomping ground for brutes. The streets were uneven, lopsided, soaked in sewage. There were pits of stinking water here and there. It was greatly ravaged by plague in 1646, more so than many other places in Norfolk, and was slow to recover.

To be the dirtiest town in the country in the 1600s really took some doing. It took so much doing that something had to be done. The streets were levelled, the sewage drained and town largely rebuilt. Many of the rebuilds were still standing. As were a couple from its less salubrious days. One of which was Bishop Bonner's cottage (now a museum), which was possibly not a cottage (it might have been a guildhall) and possibly didn't belong to Bishop Bonner. Even so, it was an interesting place. It was even more interesting, I daresay, when it was open.[1]

---

[1] It's a good job I *hadn't* made a point of visiting the Norfolk museums. The bloody things were always shut.

Bishop Bonner's tiny thatched cottage was plonked next to the church in which he was Rector from 1534 to 1538 (before becoming Bishop of Queen Mary's London). At that time, Mary was trying her best to undo her father's work in the field of Catholic bashing. She was a staunch Catholic and wanted her country to be so. Bishop Bonner had similar feelings and the two got on like a house on fire. Or, even, a protestant on fire. Of which there were soon many.

The famous *Foxe's Book of Martyrs* (wouldn't that be a great sticker album?), published in 1563, wrote of Bonner:

'This cannibal in three years space three hundred martyrs slew.
They were his food, he loved so blood, he spared none he knew.'

With his habit of personally overseeing the fiery deaths of unrepentant men, women and children, it's said that Bonner was the most hated man in the country. *Country*, not county. It wasn't until Elizabeth replaced her sister on the throne that the Bishop's feet were kicked from under the table. When he was officially presented to the new queen, she refused to let him kiss her hand.

As England swung back from one religious extreme to the other, Catholic mass became illegal. Bonner was caught openly practicing it. In his defence he wrote, 'I possess three things: soul, body, and property. Of the two latter, you can dispose at your pleasure, but as to the soul, God alone can command me.' He was thrown into the prison in which he was to die in 1569.

Bonner's cottage actually consisted of three impossibly small houses that had since been knocked into one. The *Penguin Guide* called them undoubtedly 'the best example of ornamental plaster work in the county.' *County*, not country. It was a colourful building. Looking at it from the correct angle, with the church in the background, was like stepping back in time.

Fortunately a new Wetherspoons pub had been built just around the corner to ease any such destabilising thoughts.

The pub had also bought a 17th century cottage which sat between them and Bonnner's cottage. Their intent was to knock the thing down in the name of decency and shove a beer garden in its stead: 'This will at least bring the area back into use, and deal with an eyesore in the conservation area,' read one of their statements. 'Our aim is to keep some of the cottage walls to make a courtyard and our intention is to build on a successful pub by extending the garden,' read another, thinking on similar lines.

The old building was still standing on my visit. It was in great disrepair, home to an extended family of pigeons. I wouldn't bet on it being there next time. Still, what a lovely idea for a beer garden. A bit of class, right? Maybe in a few years Bonner's cottage could be transformed into a nice external toilet, too. It would bring a more cultured feel to proceedings as one's 'Beer and a Burger' passed through.

Considering its former owner's appreciation of the damaging effects of fire, Bishop Bonner's cottage somehow survived the obligatory town infernos of 1581 and 1670. As did the church of St Nicholas, situated to the rear of the cottage. It had a random bell tower in its yard, standing like a church without the nave. It had been built because the main church spire wasn't considered strong enough to hold bells.

I wouldn't be trying to climb that one in a hurry.

Unlike its pathetically wimpy twin, the lone bell tower not only held bells, it had once held French prisoners during the Napoleonic Wars. One night, one of them made a daring escape. It went perfectly for the first twelve yards. He then found his progress halted by a bullet lodging itself into his neck. Doing what any of us would have done in his situation, the soldier keeled over and died. He was buried in the churchyard. Sixty years later, when relations between the French and English became a lot less fighty, a commemorative headstone was erected in the churchyard as 'a tribute to that brave and generous nation.' (There were plenty of volunteers to re-word that specific part of it circa May 1940.)

Another intriguing Napoleonic War anecdote involved a Dereham lady dressing as a man and enlisting so she could follow her husband to war. Her husband was in the 24th Regiment. She enlisted in the *54th* by accident. I can find no other information about this. I can't tell you if the couple were reunited. Nor if they'd had a blazing argument about *who'd* said *what* regarding regiment numbers.

Buried within shooting distance of the French soldier was the poet William Cowper. Although rather forgotten in the modern era, he was once revered by peers and the public. In his early thirties he was declared insane and institutionalised after finding his job as a London clerk too stressful (which it must have been, in the days before calculators and sneaky Facebook chats). His mania may also have been a result of being refused permission to marry the cousin with whom he had become obsessed.

Whilst in St Albans' funny farm, he attempted suicide three times, making the farm seem distinctly unfunny. He found Christianity his great healer. He began writing hymns. He moved into a rectory in Huntingdon, where he stayed with a rector and his wife, Mary Unwin. The rector died in a horse riding accident and Cowper and Unwin began a relationship. It was during this time that he began to work on his most popular hymns at the behest of John Newton, a former slave trader turned hymnist (writer of *Amazing Grace*). Cowper's most lasting line came from this period, '*God moves in mysterious ways*', which, you may remember, he wrote whilst staying in Happisburgh. Also on his Greatest Hits album was a hymn called *'What Various Hindrances We Meet'*, which is as good a name for a song as any I've ever heard.

Cowper lived a life of confusion, depression, hypochondria, madness and sanity. He dreamt of voices commanding him to kill himself to appease God. Mary Unwin stood by her lover, encouraging him to write his way through his dark periods. It was remarked by a rival for Cowper's heart that Mary loved him 'as well as one human being can love another.'

The couple moved to Norfolk in 1795, staying at Swaffham, Mundesley and, finally, Dereham, where Mary died soon after. She was buried in the chapel. Cowper slipped into depression once more. He wrote possibly his finest, and certainly one of his most famous poems, *The Castaway*, in this period. In the spring of 1800, he died of dropsy. It was a fitting finale. Against both his and Mary's wishes, the couple didn't share a grave. Their relationship had been frowned upon. Mind you, everything was frowned upon back then. Except hanging people and shooting escaped prisoners on sight.

There is a window in Westminster Abbey to commemorate Cowper. There was also one in Dereham Church, above his grave. The stained glass at Dereham depicted him reading to some hares, given to him as a gift to alleviate depression. (It was a long shot.) Elizabeth Barrett Browning[1] visited the church and wrote a poem for Cowper:

'Wild timid hares were drawn from woods to share his home-caresses/Uplooking to his human eyes with sylvan tendernesses'

It was the Victorian equivalent of *Bright Eyes*.

It would have been nice to have gone inside and had a proper look at its famous window, but the unusual red church doors were situated behind an impenetrable iron gate.

---

[1] Owner of English literature's most ludicrous hairstyle.

I feel the same way about locked church doors as I do about locked pianos. Both should be taken to with an axe.

Round the back of the church was a holy well, said to have sprung from the 7th century grave of St Withburga (no relation to Wetherspoon's 'Beer With-Burger') after her body was stolen by monks. Withburga had built the first church in Dereham (with the help of some professional builders). Her well, in keeping with much else in Dereham churchyard, was cordoned off with iron railings. It was grassy and prettily decorated with flowers. I was pleased to see it in such clement weather. On darker days, its crypt-like appearance might have been a little scary. It bore more than a passing resemblance to some of the prised-open resting places in Michael Jackson's *Thriller* video.
During the post-plague regeneration period, it was hoped Dereham might become a spa town. A bathhouse was to be built over the well and people would come from miles around to dip themselves in it. The plan was ultimately vetoed but the well remained. They say that if you drink of its water your wish will come true. Especially if you wish for chronic diarrhoea.

Talking of chronic diarrhoea, Dereham's public toilets were pretty special. Of course, it's pretty pointless to critique public toilets. It's common knowledge that they nearly all act as supporting evidence for the theory of the Fall of Man. Yet Dereham's commodes, nestled up an ominous looking back passage, so to speak, between Natwest and Specsavers, really were rotten and really needed critiquing.
Once I'd crept up said passage, away from the town centre, everything went eerily quiet, as though I'd slipped into a different time continuum. The high street was but yards away, yet all sound was muted. *You're on your own, kid.* The back of

Natwest ran the length of the alley. It had tiny, prison-barred, square windows, creating the impression that I'd entered a 1950s jail yard. I expected to see Tim Robbins walking about, shuffling soil down his trouser leg.

I could smell the toilet block before I could see it. Maybe smell isn't the right word. Smell makes it sound optional (for example, one might bow down to *smell* a rose through choice). The Dereham toilet smell wasn't optional. It attacked. It was mustard gas. One whiff of it would give Sassoon flashbacks to his evenings with Wilfred Owen. It ate at the face. It made the eyes bubble.

There is little on God's green earth as contagious as human waste. If you want to catch a virus, go to a communal toilet. That's where they thrive. Just as evolution has taught us to be wary of spiders and rats, it has also given us a defensive reflex for infected air. It's called gagging. My own reflex was in fine fettle as I took a bold step towards the toilet door:

'Huboorwah, shitting HELL, gurghhahh,' I said, quoting Wilde.

I clamped my thin summer polo shirt over my mouth. As gas mask designs go, this one was unlikely to be snapped up by the MoD anytime soon. For all my desperate clamping, I could still taste the warm, piss-flavoured air seeping through the cotton. I pressed the shirt even harder onto my face. It was practically in my mouth. Still the stench oozed through.

I hadn't even opened the door.

I didn't want to use these toilets but I had to. I was desperate. I couldn't just wee in the alleyway, although, judging by the aroma, other people hadn't felt quite so reserved about the idea. Neither did my tight schedule give me time to go gallivanting around trying to find alternative loos. I had to go there and then.

I put my fisted hand to the door (making sure to touch only the parts of it that people might not usually touch) and pushed it open, slowly.

It was a dungeon. My only guide was a white beam of sun cutting across the gloom from a high window. The door creaked shut behind me. It clicked into place. *You're on your own, kid.* Actually, I wasn't on my own. I was surrounded by a swarm of flies busily recreating the funeral scene from *Ghandi*. They were everywhere: buzzing in sufficient unison to create the sound of a low flying bi-plane. What did I think about western civilisation? I thought it was a good idea.

Not only was I concerned about inhaling the most hip and happening virus strain, there was also the fear that I might find myself joined at the urinal by one of those members of society who take a more liberal approach to the idea of public toilet discretion. Maybe word had got around that a stranger had gone into the 'clubhouse' and was no doubt yearning for someone to go and stare at his penis. It certainly had the feel of a place where such carefree gentlemen might occasionally rendezvous to break the monotony of life.

I forced my wee out. I didn't want to wash my hands. I'd yet to touch any part of the building with my fingers. I couldn't leave without some form of contact with soap, though. I twisted the tap with my elbows and smashed the gel dispenser with my forearm – *Bang!*

The flies made an explosive buzz and retreated. For two seconds. Then they returned where the fly equivalent of Richard Attenborough had directed them to hover:

'*Fly Ghandi.* Scene six. And... action!'

My hands were clean but had never felt dirtier. I elbowed the tap into the off position and hooked the door open with my left foot. I stumbled out into the sun, down the alleyway, knock-kneed like a beggar.

A recent newspaper article revealed that the Dereham toilets were to undergo a 'long awaited' renovation. According to a town councillor, 'This issue seemed to be raised with monotonous regularity at town council meetings by members of the public.' Obviously it hadn't been brought up with sufficient monotonous regularity to get someone in charge to act swiftly.

The renovation will cost the town a startling £168,000. The toilets themselves, design-wise, were no worse than any other. All they needed was a good clean, two light bulbs and regular inspection. Rather than wasting a fortune on new toilets, the council might be better served *employing* somebody to maintain the current ones. It's startling how toilet maintenance seems such a complex thing for councils to organise. Why are there so many horrible public toilets out there? Why were the *monotonous* people of Dereham even having to force the point? What's going on here?

Anyway, that's enough toilet talk. Actually, quickly, while we're on the subject, this part of the county wasn't without form when it came to sanitary inspectors. In 1915, a Swaffham-based sanitary inspector fought for the Norfolk Yeomanry at Gallipoli. He survived the massacre – and mosquito bites - and returned home to join the Royal Flying Corps, thinking it safer in the air, away from all those bullets and bugs. In his case, he was right. He enjoyed flying so much that he began to write heroic stories about a pilot, using the pen name Captain W.E Johns. His fictional pilot was called Biggles.

Maybe Dereham town council could apply to the Arts Council for that £168,000.

As the bus rode through the outskirts, past the regenerated steam railway and between the new and old townhouses, it dawned on me that I'd forgotten to find out more about William Wollaston. He was born in the town in 1766. He discovered palladium and rhodium, worked on theories of electricity[1] and created one of the first camera lenses. There was even a crater on the moon named after him. I knew nothing more of his experiences of Dereham other than that he was born and baptised there. All I'd done was flick through a twenty-page local book called *Dereham's Forgotten Scientist*. Then, true to form, I forgot him.

---

[1] When Faraday published his world famous writings on electricity there was general consternation that he hadn't mentioned Wollaston's founding work.

Leg Seven

Martham – Winterton – Caister – Gorleston – Great Yarmouth

Martham

Smiley-faced Carol dished out the weather on *BBC Breakfast*. Sunshine everywhere, she said, smiling. Except, she noted, this time with a concerned semi-smile, for a 'wee tract of rain' which would make its way down the east coast. I began following that wee tract of rain the moment I opened my door.

The flecks thickened. My socks were wet by the time I reached the bus. To make matters worse, the windows were covered in advertisements. They made the bus unnaturally dark, as though it were wearing a giant pair of those 3D glasses they give you at the Odeon. I felt as though I was being escorted to prison.

I, and the wee tract of rain, arrived in North Walsham with time to spare before the connecting bus. The last time I'd visited Walsham, you may recall, I'd been filled with nostalgia. This had now been erased.

To pass time, I went into a discount store and looked at the goods. It was all the usual stuff: gnomes, picture frames, bean bags, cushions, black & white canvasses of the New York skyline, mugs, odour eaters, value clothes. On a menswear rail hung a child-sized t-shirt bearing the legend, 'I SCORED ON THE REBOUND'. It was white, with a picture of a football on it (in case the joke wasn't clear enough). The women's section had the same t-shirt, this time in black. They were the ideal gift for recently divorced couples.

Considering prior form, there was more than an air of relief when the bus to Martham arrived on time. Unlike earlier, this one had normal windows. I would be able to see the wee tract of rain in all its pomp.

We crossed the broads at Potter Heigham, stopping briefly to allow a flurry of elderly folk off at Lathams department store. If ever there were a rival to Roys of Wroxham's broadland shopping crown, it was Lathams. It was near enough the exact same shop, just in a different place.

When I was twelve I bought series two of *Goodnight Sweetheart* on VHS from Lathams. I hadn't been back since.

'Martham!' shouted the driver on arrival, as though driving a Greyhound in a film from the 1970s. I don't know why he did this. He hadn't shouted the names of any other stops. That he felt the need to shout it out might have been a reflection on the village's inherent clandestineness.

The wee tract of rain was doing a fantastic job of keeping pace. So much so that when I finally stepped onto Martham's hallowed turf, my first action was to dive under the nearest shelter and wait for the bus to Winterton.

A woman with an empty pushchair was sitting there. I felt the need to say something but didn't know what. I could tell she was feeling the same way. The weather, as always, saved the day:

'Raining hard now,' said the woman.

'Yep.'

'They said it wouldn't.'

They. I love our distrust of meteorologists. As though *they* are trying to screw us over by deliberately feeding us misinformation.

'I think they said something about a tract of rain going down the east coast,' I added.

'Typical.'

The rain pounded on the shelter roof. I looked at the empty pushchair and wanted to ask if the baby had also been forewarned of the wee tract and stayed home.

I had ten minutes until the Winterton bus. I couldn't just stand there and not see Martham. I broke free from the shelter and careered around in the flood, taking pictures of anything and everything. They were arguably the most pathetic and pointless images ever captured.

It was a nice place. I just didn't feel in the mood to get soaked. It looked quintessentially Norfolk. There were modern builds around the periphery and an old, handsome village centre with the archetypal, colossal English green. There was also a pond (although it might have been a massive puddle).

The church was gigantic. Probably the biggest in Norfolk: along with Cromer, Happisburgh, Hingham et al. I didn't have time to go in. There's a gravestone there for Alice Burraway, upon which is inscribed:

'In this life my sister, my mistress, my mother and wife.'

The story behind this is so confusing that I don't know if I can do a job of explaining it. Basically, the writer of the epitaph was the offspring of an incestuous affair between his father and sister (that's the mother and sister part dealt with). The boy was not informed of this and when he grew up he worked, unbeknownst to him, for his sister (hence, she was also his mistress). He then had an affair with his mistress and eventually married her. It's the kind of plotline that the producers try to steer clear of when working on script treatments for the latest series of *Lark Rise to Candleford*.

I stood at the bus stop in the rain, getting helplessly soaked by the spray of passing vehicles. I was sad to have not seen Martham in its best light. When I told my mum I was going to Martham she said she went there on a school trip in 1975 and drew a picture of the church. She'd never returned. I wondered if I ever would. Probably not. It was just another simple, pleasant Norfolk village which hid itself away and got on with things in the Norfolk way: slowly, steadily, quietly.

The driver laughed when he saw how wet I was. He was less jollity when I presented him with a twenty-pound-note for a two-pound ticket. It's the small victories that matter.

We headed for Winterton, with the wee tract leading the way.

Winterton-On-Sea

Something miraculous happened on the short journey to Winterton.[1] As I looked out at the rolling countryside from the bus, Carol's wee rain tract faded. The sun broke through and the sky turned light blue. The bus dropped me off by the village green. There was a little boat with flowers growing inside. I

---

[1] The 'On-Sea' bit was added in the 50s to avoid confusion with a town of the same name in Lincolnshire. Again, as though anybody ever confused the two:

'Oh, you meant Winterton *in Lincolnshire*...'

didn't know if this was a piece of local art or a result of the recent floods.

I felt my jeans drying as the air warmed. This was more like it. Winterton was a warren of lanes and lokes, pathways and fishermen's cottages. It was so perfectly picturesque and cute that I wondered if it hadn't been made on a table in God's attic for his model railway.

There was a craft fair going down in the village hall. It was kicking off big time.

The stalls sold mostly jam and tea cosies. There were more people manning stalls than perusing them. A serving hatch had been opened with plates of cakes laid on the counter. The room smelt of squeezed tea bags and Calor gas.

Elderly people sat around small tables, wearing coats of neutral colours and talking about what's-his-name. I didn't want to leave. Some people fear old age. Not me. The idea of pottering around craft fairs and eating biscuits of a weekday morning is much more appealing than sitting in an ill-lit meeting about targets. The elderly have got it sussed.

Between the village and the beach was a sweep of sand dunes and marram grass. The grass was grown deliberately as a sea defence in the 1700s. On the whole, it had worked damned effectively. Maybe someone might think to take a truckload of the stuff to Happisburgh at some point in the not too distant future.

The beach looked strangely exotic. Caught in the right light you could probably film a decent Bounty advert there. In fact, Monty Python had used this part of Winterton as the tropical location for their brilliant *Whicker Island* sketch. (Look it up if you haven't seen it. It's better than a Bounty advert.)

It's hard to look at grassy dunes on a sunny, windy morning without wanting to stalk poetically across them. So I did precisely that. A piece of laminated A4 had been stapled to a post. It read, 'Beware of Adders'. The hasty look of the sign suggested that it had been put there by an irate bite victim who felt people ought to know about this slight twist in the otherwise charming story of the marram grass. By all means stalk poetically across it, it suggested, but bear in mind that you might be going home by air ambulance.

I watched my step. I'd heard that there were Natterjack toads lurking about the place too. They'd formed a colony. There was also a colony of seals nearby. More concerning than colonies of toads and seals was the rumoured colony of nudists. The Winterton dunes were a designated *Area of Outstanding Natural Beauty*. They attracted birdwatchers en masse; within spitting distance of the nudist beach, groups of corned-beef-sandwich-eaters lurked, holding powerful binoculars.

I didn't wander far enough to see any little snakes or blue tits. Luckily. The last thing one ever wishes to see whilst strolling along a beach is a pair of 67-year-old testicles clanking into view. Naturists are never like they are in the films. They're never the young, shapely girls you see flicking their blonde hair and giggling during games of Swingball. They're usually grey-bearded accountants from Tamworth.[1]

In the mid-1800s, a number of Winterton families moved down the coast to Caister. Whilst there, they helped form the Caister Beachmen. The Caister Beachmen might sound like a jazz trio that you'd normally find setting toes tapping down at

---

[1] Talking of blonde, shapely girls: Jane Fonda filmed *Julia* in Winterton in 1977.

Burnham Market Tennis Club, but they were, in fact, the forerunners of the modern lifeboat service.

One of the Beachmen's most popular members was James Haylett. He lost two sons and many friends during the Caister lifeboat disaster of 1901, when a lifeboat was sunk during a stormy midnight rescue. Haylett was 78 at the time and watched the events transpire from the beach. Despite his age, he jumped into the water and pulled bodies from the wreckage. During the inquest, Haylett was asked why the men didn't simply give up the rescue and turn back:

'They would never give up the ship,' he replied. 'If they had to keep at it til now, they would have sailed about until daylight to help her. Going back is against the rules when we see distress signals like that.'

The legend was born: Caister men never go back.

Haylett was rewarded for his years of bravery with a visit to Norfolk's royal residence, Sandringham House. George V chatted with him about the sea and gave him a collection of food hampers to take back to Caister.

Another legend was born: Caister men never go back to Caister from Sandringham without food hampers.

Rather sweetly, when the king had said 'Hello, Mr Haylett,' Haylett had replied 'Hello, Mr King.'

Shipwrecks were common here. The village churchyard was choked with the corpses of sailors. Daniel Defoe called the stretch of coast 'famous for being one of the most dangerous and most fatal to the sailors in all England.' He noted how nearly every house in the area had, at least in part, been built from the wood of wrecked ships. Even his own Robinson Crusoe got himself into trouble on these waters during the early part of his travels:

'...we made slow way towards the shore; nor were we able to reach the shore till, being past the lighthouse at Winterton, the

shore falls off to the westward, towards Cromer, and so the land broke off a little the violence of the wind. Here we got in, and, though not without much difficulty, got all safe on shore, and walked afterwards on foot to Yarmouth.'

The sea was Norfolk's only predator. Enticing and deadly. Norfolk seafarers equipped themselves with an array of puzzling rituals to avoid its perils. They were to never carry money at sea, to never say 'rabbit' (they had to say 'conies' instead) or 'pig' (these were called 'dirty beasts'), and they were to never whistle on board because it could stir up the wind. Cross-eyed women were also considered bad luck. You had to avoid eye contact with them at all times. Which was fairly easy.[1]

Like the Burnhams, there was an open, ethereal feel to the Winterton atmosphere. It was captivating. It made me want to do some additional poetic stalking. Preferably into the waves. How enticing...

The church tower towered (that was the best adjective I could think of) over all. I hadn't noticed it on my way into the village but it really was a whopper. You won't believe me when I tell you a certain claim about the tower: rumour had it, *it was the tallest in Norfolk*. Legend says that it was 'A herring and a half higher' than Cromer, taking our grand total of *tallest* churches in Norfolk to 419.

I wandered past the Fisherman's Return. I was disappointed to see that the sign above the door didn't depict a couple of fishermen hitting tennis returns. The pub had been there for

---

[1] As if the moods of the sea weren't dangerous enough, fishermen and seafarers also had to contend with the risk of being attacked and captured by enemies. Many innocent Norfolk fishermen were taken as Prisoners of War.

three centuries. On Boxing Day each year (I don't know if this still happens. I imagine not) bickering locals would get together and have a truce, sharing drinks and singing songs.

This tradition of belting out shanties led to one Winterton man, Sam Larner, becoming a celebrity in his later years after the BBC Home Service recorded a performance of his for a documentary. He soon became a regular on the wireless. He'd been a sailor since the Victorian era and had an incredible knack of remembering the songs he'd heard at sea, some of them wholesome and hearty, others more risqué. His fame lasted for three years before his death in 1965. Luckily, many of his songs were recorded.

In a stark example of how times have changed in the hundred years since Sam Larner first heard those shanties, you can now hear them being sung, by the man himself, on online streaming services. I recommend doing so. If the sound of his voice doesn't bring a tear to your eye, you're of harder heart than I. A blue plaque marked his home.

I went to get chips. Their holy scent washed through the air. They came fresh out of the fryer, with the fat still jumping off them. I gave them the salt and vinegar treatment and stuck my wooden fork in.

I took them to the bus stop. This was high living. A sea breeze whipped my hood against the back of my head. I had chips in my lap, and Norfolk in my lungs. The sun warmed my neck. Maybe one day there'd be a blue plaque to commemorate this happy moment:

Here Sat Ryan T. Pugh During His Tour Of Norfolk For The Multi-Award Winning, And Financially Rewarding, 'Kismet Quick'. Here He Ate Chips And Fell In Love With Winterton-On-Sea.

For the first time on the trip the bus was early. Into the bin went the chips. The sun only shines for so long.
I looked at the sky. Was that another wee tract of rain?

Caister-On-Sea

I spoke to a local.
'The kiss-me-quick brigade took over,' he said. 'This all used to be lovely.'
He gestured towards what I think was the high street. The road was wide and the buildings and businesses were spaced apart and lacked cohesiveness. Caister looked more suburb than town.
'Got swallowed up whole by Yarmouth,' he said, making even the urbanisation of a quiet settlement sound like a fireside legend. Swallowed up whole and now resting in the belly of a Great Big Yarmouth.
'I hate what the kiss-me-quicks have done,' he sighed.
I told him I was writing a book about the area.
'What's it called?'

At the turn of the 20th century, Caister was visited by a chap called John Fletcher Dodd. He was an active socialist, an original member of the Independent Labour Party. He bought a house in the village[1] and put up tents in his garden. He invited some of his socialist pals round to stay. Rather than looking

---

[1] If you can call it a village. With a population of 9,000, Caister is officially the most populated village in the United Kingdom.

confused as to why their host was making them sleep in the garden instead of one of his many bedrooms, the guests enjoyed the novelty. They came back for more.

As the years passed, the number of visitors increased. Among them were Labour's first ever Member of Parliament, Keir Hardie, and George Bernard Shaw. The camp even held the occasional cabinet meeting. The rules of the camp were strict. There was no drinking, no gambling, no swearing. Although, surprisingly, mass debating *was* encouraged.[1]

Eventually the camp opened to non-socialists. Talks by respected modern thinkers were replaced by knockabout sets from Des O'Connor and a young Ronnie Corbett (imagine how small he was *then*). It was a precursor to the holiday camps we all know and, ahem, love today. It's thought to be the oldest holiday camp in the dang country and is now owned by Haven.

Caister also had one of the oldest moated castles in the dang country, called, naturally, Caister Castle. It was built for Sir John Fastolf, a fighter of renown, and notoriety, during the Hundred Years War. He was a well-travelled fella, visiting Jerusalem as a young man and stopping at many places in between. But it was his holidays to France for which he was best known, in particular his 1429 jaunt to Orleans where he had hoped to have a get together with the local maid. The Maid of Orleans, known to most as Joan of Arc, was equally keen to have a quick word:

'Bastard, bastard, in the name of God I command you that as soon as you hear of Fastolf's coming, you will let me know,' she demanded, using language that would never wash on Caister's socialist campsite.

Joan of Arc's army met with Fastolf's (the Kill Me Quick Brigade) at the Battle of Patay and soundly thrashed it. Sir John

---

[1] Sorry. Couldn't resist. Very childish.

was alleged to have escaped the battle when he saw the game was up and was labelled a coward on his return to England.

He went back to France on numerous occasions afterwards and fought valiantly. Not valiantly enough, however, for an oddly-haired playwright from Stratford to use a variation on Fastolf's name whilst creating his fool, John Falstaff. And that Stratford-born playwright's name was... Jonny Bigglesworth.

Not really. It was William Shakespeare.

The famous saying 'The better part of valour is discretion' is among the many jewels the bard put into his fool's mouth.[1] If ever there's a question about Shakespeare on *University Challenge*, the answer is usually John Falstaff. You can thank Caister-On-Sea for that.

Fastolf's castle had fallen into disrepair at some point in the 1600s. After dying without an heir, nearly every person in Norfolk claimed to be the rightful owner of his castle. None more so than the Duke of Norfolk and the heads of the famous Paston family, who, as we already know, liked to vent their rage in the form of long-winded letters.

Sir John had intended his castle to one day become a place of prayer and devotion. Instead, the Duke of Norfolk sent 30,000 men to overrun it from the inhabiting Pastons. Around thirty men kept the 30,000 at bay for two months. By the time the Duke had captured the battered castle, it looked not too dissimilar to how it did now. It was left to further ruin. Still, it was worth all the killing.

The castle grounds are now a car museum. The first ever Ford Fiesta is in there, as is Christine Keeler's Cadillac.

Isn't the world strange?

*

---

[1] I'm extra fond of the Falstaff line, 'Banish plump Jack, and banish all the world.'

I didn't go to the seafront. I'd seen it from the top deck of the bus on the way in. It was caravanland; I walked among some graves instead. I'd never detected too much of a difference between the two, anyway.

I asked a passer-by if he knew the way back to the village centre. He said he wasn't from around here.

'Oh, ok, never mind,' I said.

'I'm from Yarmouth,' he added.

How Yarmouth didn't classify as being 'around here' was a mystery. Yarmouth was literally *all around* Caister. He couldn't possibly be *more* from 'around here' if he tried. I let it slide. I didn't want to start a debate. After all, this was a graveyard, not the lawn of a socialist holiday camp.

I walked along the main road as car and lorries whipped by noisily. Of all the places I'd visited on this tour, Caister was to leave the smallest imprint on my memory. I don't recall much from my visit at all. Even my photographs did little to stir the memory. The main thing I remembered was a shop with a sandwich board outside stating that you could buy seven sausage rolls for a quid. It was hardly an anecdote likely to get me on the Booker shortlist anytime soon.

Caister men never turn back. But I turned my back on Caister. It was a funny little place. I never did find the heart of it. It seemed to be a sequence of corner shops and salons surrounded by caravans and guesthouses. It truly lived in the belly of Yarmouth. Swallowed whole. Even the rickety racetrack stadium on the outskirts was called Yarmouth Stadium; inside it, greyhounds and stock cars ran round and round in circles. As I paid my fare to Gorleston-On-Sea, I knew the feeling well.

Gorleston-On-Sea

Gorleston used to be in Suffolk. Then, in 1835, for electoral convenience, Great Yarmouth, as it liked to do, swallowed it whole. Caister was to the west of Yarmouth, Gorleston to the east. To get there, the bus had to go through Yarmouth, past its rows upon rows of terraces, through its jam-packed public thoroughfare, and out over the bridge across the surprisingly gaping river Yare and its docklands.
With steely clouds forming slowly overhead, the general view of the docklands was reminiscent of series two of *The Wire*. The area used to be home to a thriving fishing industry. It was now used largely for oilrig supplies, after the discovery of black gold in the North Sea in the 1960s. A wind farm flickered on the horizon.
I never knew that the Yarmouth docks were still so active. Ships and boats towered above their surroundings. Across their sides were names painted in foreign languages and letters. I jotted one down in my notepad: *Malaviya Twenty*.
Gorleston nil.
Whereas some areas of the docks had survived the transitions of the 20th century, others were falling away. There were scores of abandoned buildings and sites left to rust and collapse into themselves. We passed the most awesome heap of scrap I'd ever seen. It stood on the opposite side of the river. I expected to see metallic goats grazing up it. It wasn't pretty. Jason Statham went to school near here. It must have prepared him well; every film he's ever made could have been filmed on these docks.
Yarmouth - and the contents of its belly - really got the treatment during the World Wars. It was the first recipient of a zeppelin aerial bombardment during the First (despite what the

plaque in Sheringham said) and was almost flattened by the Luftwaffe in the sequel. It was often the last notable location the Nazis flew over on their way back to the Fatherland. Any spare bombs they had knocking around were dispatched over the town. Streets of sentimental and historical value were ripped apart.

The bus dropped me outside a modern terrace, on the end of which was a plaque stating that the row had been built on the site of a lodge where the country's longest serving GP had worked: '*Dr Kenneth Hamilton Deane Practiced Here For 62 Years 1923 – 1985.*'

After 62 years of practice, he was damn near perfect.

Terraces everywhere. What a sprawl Yarmouth had. The Gorleston streets were narrow and made to look even more so with cars parked on both sides. How anyone ever got in or out of their parking spaces was a mystery. Strangely, for all its parked cars and infinite houses, I counted only six people on my walk between the bus stop and the high street. No wonder Dr Deane went on for so long. He probably spent most of his time whistling or doing the Times crossword.

Attached to the gate of the public gardens was a disarming sign which occasionally appeared in Norfolk's shadier communal spaces: the Norfolk Constabulary 'Respect Zone' notice. This area, it read, was monitored by patrolling police.

The bobby on the beat must have been on lunch when I visited. I spotted a gentleman sitting on a bench in a Carlsberg Export-induced stupor. He had a couple of cans by his feet. He called out to me:

'Cahsitdanoverheremate.'

I kept on walking, head down, no better than one of those bastards in the parable of the Good Samaritan.

'I shed fahkingcahsitdanoveremate. Neshta me,' he motioned to the space on the bench next to him.

Here was a chap who clearly hadn't read the Respect Zone sign thoroughly.

'Cahmon!' he shouted, thumping the bench like Judge John Deed.

Honestly, you give these people immaculately tended flowerbeds and this is how they repay you.

On the high street was a sandwich board showing a picture of fried egg and beans accompanied by the words, 'Home of the £1.89 Breakfast – by far the best value in town.' And I should think it was, too. £1.89! It must cost them more than that to turn the cooker on.[1] Mind you, not everyone would be impressed by the offer. People from Caister would possibly turn their noses up at such so-called value:

'£1.89?' they'd sneer, 'you can get fourteen sausage rolls for that.'

The high street was a largely uninspiring mixture of charity shops and hairdressers (again with the hairdressers[2]), although it was enlivened by a wonderful social club. It had hanging baskets in full bloom and chalk notice boards. I love a good social club. Through the darkness of the window, between the floral, Caramac coloured curtains, I could make out the flashing of fruit machines and electric beer pumps. In a perfect world I would have had time to go in for a lager-top. As things stood,

---

[1] Gorleston had been something of an upmarket holiday hotspot, back in the days when the Empire coloured the map pink (and when paying £1.89 for a breakfast would've required re-mortgaging the manor).

[2] Maybe I'm more attuned to them because I know I'll never need to go in one again. My haircuts are all done with a pair of clippers in five sombre minutes.

though, I had to get back on the bus to Great Yarmouth to see if it had any plans to swallow any other places whole.

I had a quick look at Gorleston's chimney-like, brick-built lighthouse and made my way back through the town and across the Respect Zone (where the drunkard was now catching up on some sleep).

There was an old local ditty that went like this:

Pakefield for Poverty
Lowestoft for Poor
Gorleston for Pretty Girls
Yarmouth for Whores
Caister for Water Dogs
California for Pluck
Beggar old Winterton
How Black she do look!

Could they really not find a better rhyme for pluck? I can think of at least one – and that's without putting any effort in at all.

The ditty contained a degree of accuracy. I'm not saying that Yarmouth was riddled with whores (it might be though, I intended to find out later), but Gorleston did have a track record at producing Pretty Girls. Both Hannah Spearritt (of S Club 7 fame) and multi-millionaire mansion-tax-hater Myleene Klaas were Gorleston gals. I didn't see either of them tucking into the £1.89 breakfast, though, nor necking a couple of tins in the Respect Zone. Maybe they were busy. Maybe they'd gone to the Venice of East Anglia.

Where's the Venice of East Anglia, I hear you cry. Well, according to the *Penguin Guide to Norfolk*, the Venice of East Anglia is Great Yarmouth.

'It has also,' the book adds, with a touch more solemnity, 'been likened to Blackpool.'

Great Yarmouth

The bus crept along at snail's pace. The roads were jammed due to a bridge across the Yare being lifted. It allowed me another look at the docks. It was around there that Nelson had returned after his victory at the Nile and declared to the waiting crowds, 'I am a Norfolk man and glory in being so.'[1] A landlady asked if she might rename her pub The Nelson Arms, to which he gently reminded her that it might be unwise as he only had the one. More arm-related hilarity ensued during a ceremony in which the great man was granted freedom of the borough. Nelson was asked to place his hand on the bible. Which he did:
'Your *right* hand, sir,' muttered the town clerk.
'Ah,' replied Nelson, 'that is at Tenerife.'
In the distance stood the Nelson, monument: a tall column with Lady Britannia sat atop, looking peeved. It had predated London's own Nelson's Column by some twenty-four years. The idea was that Britannia would face towards Nelson's beloved Burnham Thorpe. A rather fine little legend suggests that she was supposed to face out to sea but the builders made a hash of it and came up with the Burnham theory to cover themselves. There was talk of these docklands being redeveloped. Britannia might one day overlook Comet and PC World. That's if she could survive the relentless bird crapping she was subjected to.
The Yarmouth gulls were enormous. White pterodactyls. Despite riding the bus through a busy street with the windows closed, and with a young couple behind me talking at ear-

---

[1] He said this in Gorleston, which at the time was technically in Suffolk. The cheeky so-and-so.

warping volume about phone contracts and shagging, I could *still* hear the gulls circling.[1]

The original caretaker of Nelson's monument was a man named James Sharman. He'd been aboard HMS Victory as a boy and helped carry the dying Nelson below deck. Charles Dickens visited Sharman and liked him so much that he based the character Ham from *David Copperfield* on him (those familiar with the novel will appreciate such high praise).

Daniel Defoe visited Yarmouth on his tour. He called this area 'the finest quay in England, if not in Europe, not inferior even to that of Marseilles itself.' I can only assume that when he travelled here in the early 1700s there weren't quite so many derelict premises and shops with '4 U' in their names: Insurance 4 U; Pizza 4 U; Funerals 4 U. And so on. The only flowering business endeavours I spotted were betting shops and tattoo parlours. There was also a laptop repair store. Laptops Get Repaired 4 U.

The traffic moved and the bus went back over the Yare (or was it the Bure? The Yarmouth waterways confused me greatly). During the spring of 1845, a more distressing Nelson anecdote had its birth. It involved not the long-dead Horatio Nelson, but Nelson the Clown. He attracted a crowd to a Yarmouth bridge by sailing down the river in a tub towed by four geese. As the clown approached, the crowd grew and the bridge gave way. Hundreds fell into the river. 79 lives were lost. 59 of them were children. It remains, and hopefully forever shall remain, the town's single largest loss of life in one incident. Yet it's a relatively unknown one. For an event so maddening and tragic, I don't know how. Some good souls in the town make an effort

---

[1] They were big enough to grab Lady Britannia in their claws and carry her off. They could take her to Cash Converters to sell for chip money.

each year to remember those lost. A commemorative plaque marked the site.[1]

The first thing to say about Great Yarmouth was that it was refreshing to find a place name without the words 'On-Sea' tacked on the end. Great Yarmouth *was* very much on-sea, though, regardless of whether or not its name chose to acknowledge the fact. The town was first called Great (Magna) in the 13th century to distinguish it from Little Yarmouth. (You'd think that the word 'Little' would have already performed that job, but apparently not.) Naturally, Little Yarmouth had since been swallowed whole. As was a Yarmouth man by the name of James Bartley, who, in 1891, was whale hunting near the Falkland Islands (whilst filming a *Top Gear Special*) when one of the monsters guzzled him up, Hollywood-style, like at the end of *Pinocchio*. Unlike Pinocchio, however, Bartlett wasn't sneezed out by the whale. The beast had to be captured and sliced open. The Yarmouth man fell amongst the detritus, looking understandably pale:
'Corr, boy, that whale musta swallowed you whole!'
'Can you refer to it as a Great Whale?'
'Why?'
'So I can differentiate between that and *little* whales? Where I'm from we like to label the size of things thoroughly.'
As noted, the mighty Charles Dickens stayed in the town for two days in 1849 and used the seafront as a setting for much of my personal favourite, *David Copperfield*. He is said to have

---

[1] Commemorative plaques do a hell of a job on the quiet. They're seriously unappreciated. I hope somewhere there's a commemorative plaque celebrating the birthplace of the creator of the commemorative plaque. It would only be right.

walked down the coast to Lowestoft (in Suffolk) and back. Here is David Copperfield talking about Yarmouth:

'When we got into the street (which was strange enough to me), and smelt the fish, and pitch, and oakum, and tar, and saw the sailors walking about, and the carts jangling up and down over the stones, I felt I had done so busy a place an injustice; and said as much to Peggotty, who heard my expressions of delight with great complacency, and told me it was well known that Yarmouth was, upon the whole, the finest place in the universe.'

The finest place in the universe! I'd be the judge of that.

The sun was out again. The tide of tourists pulled me along. The 'fish, and pitch, and oakum, and tar' of Dickens' Yarmouth had been replaced with amusement arcades and candyfloss shops.
 Dickens' eternal rival, Anthony Trollope, set *Can You Forgive Her?* in Yarmouth as a rumoured counterbalance for what he perceived to be his foe's gushing appraisal. 'There is an old town with which summer visitors have little or nothing to do…' he wrote. 'There is no beauty… The coast is low and straight and the east wind blows full upon it.' It didn't have the desired effect. The people came. And came. And came. Two centuries on, it remains one of Britain's top holiday destinations.
 From the top of the main thoroughfare, looking down towards the beach, I could see nothing but a sea of heads. It was like Oxford Street in the run up to Christmas. Except that it was warm and the people looked pleased to be alive.
 Oh, but how these seaside towns operate by their own rules. Nowhere else could you find so many shops within close proximity where not one of them sold essential everyday items. If this were a normal town, the shops would've been a mixture

of WHSmith, Poundland, Tesco Express, Primark et al. But here things were different. The shops were wild. This was the land of t-shirts, sweet machines, posters, Chelsea FC beach towels. Nowhere had a door. Every shop was open, frontless. Just walk right in, folks.

The shops all fascinated me, but rock shops the most. It was incredible to think that there were people out there whose careers revolved around sticks of rock. What a world to be a part of. Did they go to rock conventions? Rock fares? Rock meetings where the future trends of rock sales were discussed? One of the stores claimed to be the *World's Biggest Rock Shop*. By *World's Biggest* it meant, surely, that it was *Britain's* biggest. There couldn't be too many competitors from overseas. Did they eat rock anywhere else? Japan? Ghana? Canada? Apparently this particular store knocked out 80,000 sticks of the stuff every week. Fantastic.

It's not just rock shops that perplexed me. How many Chelsea FC beach towels did shop owners need to sell in order to pay the bills? Mind you, at least selling beach towels near a beach was hitting a target audience; I had to wonder about some of the other businesses. Outside one shop was a rail of white t-shirts with neon slogans. They said things such as 'BORN TO love NaNa' and 'If mum says NO I ask dad. If dad says NO I ask grandma'. They were £3 each. Who was snapping those up?

The thoroughfare was not only home to amazing shops, it also offered a range of equally amazing entertainments. Such as the photo booth in which you could have a black & white picture of your child superimposed onto an image of the Titanic's famous stairwell:

'Picture Yourself On Board The Titanic', cried the sandwich board.

I didn't check to see whether they also offered the opportunity to have a picture of your kids as floating blue corpses in the freezing ocean.

I thought of some new t-shirt ideas:
'BoRn TO DiE on tHe TitaNiC.'
'If mUm sAys NO, I asK Dad. IF daD SaYS No, I freEze TO deAtH iN ThE waTEr.'
On a wall outside a music venue were posters of upcoming performances. *Forever Jackson*, a Michael Jackson retrospective, led the way.[1] Also performing that month was *Kelly* Perry, the *'ULTIMATE'* Katy Perry tribute act. The images suggested that she might also be able to knock out a fairly accurate Lorraine *Kelly* tribute act in later years, should demand ever arise. At the top of the poster was the phrase *'Every Night Is Like Last Friday Night!'* which I understood to be a quote from a Perry song I'd never heard nor would ever want to hear. To think that Kelly Perry was once married to Russell Bland...

'Coming Soon: Lorraine 'Kelly' – the ULTIMATE Lorraine Kelly tribute act: Where 'every breakfast TV segment is exactly like the breakfast TV segment from the previous day!'

From the bowels of an open-fronted shop I heard the most startling recorded music. It was Irish Country & Western. I had to investigate. You can only tempt a man so much. The store sold music and DVDs. It was basically a larger version of those market stalls that sell CDs, tapes and videos by artists you've never heard of in your life. I scanned the shelves. The artists had names like Glenn Allen and Turner O'Farrell. The album covers saw their stars all leaning on farmyard gates in dazzling knitwear. The songs were spectacularly crap, neither upbeat nor down:

---

[1] Instead of having four black brothers, he had four white sisters. Mind you, as Jackson himself said: if you're thinking about being his brother, it don't matter if you're black or white. Or female.

Oh, me old mammy said, she'll die before she's done
And the singing in the fields, went on and on and on
Oh, I kissed your rosy cheeks on that summer's morn...

They were songs you'd expect to hear a drunken pirate sing to himself in the corner of aft.

I reached the Golden Mile. Great Yarmouth really was Great. Huge, in fact. It should have been called Huge Yarmouth. No wonder it swallowed so many places whole. 'The town had swollen and burst long ago,' wrote Paul Theroux, 'but it had the English seaside characteristic of being self-destructive in its own way.'

The Mile was wide and heaved with men in shorts and women in wrap-around skirts. Children ran around manically. They'd reached the promised land. I suddenly remembered visiting Yarmouth as a boy. I was about five. Timmy Mallet was there, opening some attraction or other. He said Hello to my mum. It was the talk of our family for the next ten years. A brush with fame.

If you've never seen Yarmouth's Golden Mile, it's basically the same as Blackpool's. Minus the tower. It's an assortment of gigantic amusement arcades, crazy putting and fairgrounds with any one (or two) of the following words in their names: Leisure, Pleasure, Land, Happy, Beach, Play.

At the Pleasure Beach fun fair there was a beauty of a wooden rollercoaster, one of only eight in the world. It was built by a German firm in 1932. The highest peak was 70ft. It was officially *the tallest wooden rollercoaster in Norfolk*. From the top you could see Yarmouth in all its glory. It was one of the few rollercoasters in the world still operated by a driver. It made the most wonderful, and disconcerting, rumbling as it rocketed around.

*

The Britannia was the more substantial of the town's two piers. It was stunning. Like many piers, it had spent a good deal of its time either on fire or being redeveloped as the result of a fire.[1] It had a theatre at the end, at which some of the country's top talent came to perform. Judging by the line-up, however, much of the top talent must have had prior engagements. Among the stars on show this season were Joe McElderry (*X Factor* 2009), Colin Fry (no relation to Stephen), Jethro (naturally), Jim Davidson (ditto) and the Chuckle Brothers.

The sea was out. The Britannia jettisoned far into the sands. Along the sides were rifle ranges, slot machines, cuddly toy cranes and whatnot. Down below, on the beach, children were given donkey rides. I could hear them laughing from quite a distance (the kids, not the donkeys). It was all rather fine.

I looked down the miles of flat beach towards Winterton. With the town swarming to my left, and the long, golden beach running into the distance, and the sound of children's (and possibly donkey's) laughter, it was easy to imagine Yarmouth during the Victorian and Edwardian eras. It's tempting to write that I could imagine what the town was like 'in its glory days', but in truth, I saw nothing to suggest that the place was losing its appeal. The rollercoaster thundered away in the distance.

Great Yarmouth would never be Norfolk's favourite son. But there was excitement and life there. The same couldn't always be said for some of the county's more revered haunts.

*

---

[1] The other option for pier dismantlement, as we know, is for them to be destroyed by a raging sea. Statistically, it's only a matter of time before a pier fire is extinguished by a storm.

And what history it had. The town had been home to some of the world's great shakers. John Bradshaw for one. For those of you yet to get round to reserving your copy of *Great Yarmouth Icons* from the library, John Bradshaw was Lord President of the parliamentary commission which dealt with the difficult decision of whether or not to make King Charles I considerably shorter.

The common view at that time was that Bradshaw was a bit of a tool, but one of the few people of power willing to perform the unprecedented duty. Such was Bradshaw's lack of renown, Charles cheekily claimed to have never heard of him. Bradshaw got his own back. He declared Charles guilty, adding that he was a 'Tyrant, Traitor, Murderer, and a public enemy' to boot. The rules of the day dictated that a condemned prisoner had no right to speak on appeal as they were already classed as dead. Bradshaw followed this law to the letter. Thus Charles was denied the opportunity to come up with a witty repost, should he have been in the frame of mind to drum one up. It was a shame. It could have been the best 'I know you are but what am I?' in British history.

'It will be a long time before King Charles forgets the name of John Bradshaw,' Bradshaw boasted.

'When's the beheading, Sir?'

'Tomorrow.'

'Won't he have forgotten you after that?'

'Erm.'

While Bradshaw was busy chopping off the heads of Divinely chosen royal subjects, the people of Yarmouth had threats to contend with closer to home. The Great Plague of the 1660s hit Yarmouth hard. It became the first port town in the country to refuse entry to suspect ships. The tide could only be held back for so long. By the end of 1666, close to 3,000 had died in the town. An astonishing number, but not without precedent. It had lost 2,000 people in a summer plague of 1579. And during the 14th century Black Death, up to 7,000 died in one year (the population of the town at that time was somewhere between eight and ten thousand). The Black Death almost wiped Yarmouth off the map. Only Winchester and Shrewsbury had a bigger death rate per-head. When Henry VIII commissioned a report on the place two centuries later, the writer noted that large areas still 'stood desolate' in 'utter ruin and decay.'[1]

One of the contributing factors to the spread of plague was that, for centuries, buildings were only constructed within the confines of the town's medieval walls. This meant that Yarmouth was a mixing pot for seafarers and their fashionable new viral strains from the continent.

Yarmouth was once famous for its Rows: 145 impossibly packed rows of houses and shops all squished within the medieval confines. The gaps between Rows were as narrow as 27 inches in parts. You could literally high-five your neighbour from your bedroom window. The Yarmouth Rows met their demise after a handful of Germans, who had once been so willing to build a wooden rollercoaster, flew over and gave the place the Blitz treatment. After the war, many of the remaining Rows received a similar punishment from the government.

Anyone who has ever read or seen Arthur Miller's *The Crucible* will be familiar with the heroism of Rebecca Nurse. Nurse was accused of witchcraft in Massachusetts in 1692. She was born and raised in Yarmouth and moved to the *New* - and supposedly improved - England with her family while a young adult. She married and raised a large family and became a respected figure of her community. At the age of seventy she was embroiled in the Salem Witch Hunt. She was hanged and buried with many

---

[1] Norfolk people suffered more than most during the outbreak. Upwards of sixty percent of the population were killed (compared to the national average of around thirty percent). Inexplicably, Yarmouth's neighbouring town, Acle, was one of the few in England reported to have lost no lives.

other alleged witches, including, later, her sister Mary, another Yarmouth girl.

Yarmouth's relationship with the United States didn't begin and end with the Nurse sisters. The first Mayor of New York, Thomas Willet, was the grandson of a Yarmouth man. And William Gooch, Governor of Virginia between 1727 and 1749, was also of Yarmouth stock. Gooch introduced the Tobacco Inspection Act of 1730, which increased the quality of Virginia tobacco to such a degree that it became extremely popular in Europe. And still is. It's hard to deduce whether this can be classed as a success story or not. It's likely that his reforms indirectly killed more people than all plagues combined.

Along the silent back-roads, I passed Victorian guesthouses with names like Beachyview and Seaview. The buildings, with their high windows and 'No Vacancies' signs, mostly faced one another. More accurate names would have been Beachyview-view and Seaview-view.

There was an innate Britishness to the guesthouses. Net curtains and tinned tomatoes on toast. Behind their glass porch entrances lay rooms thick with silence; furniture from the late 1970s; carpets from the mid 1980s; week-old fresh flowers; taps that needed twisting five times before water trickled out; menus with cloth-eared corners; bookshelves crammed with brown-paged Len Deighton thrillers about what would have happened if Hitler had won.

Amidst the quiet, I could hear television sets talking at me from slightly ajar upstairs windows:

'Sarah and Evelyn have been working on renovating their house in leafy Herefordshire for almost ten years. Now they need a change of scenery... And next up on the show we've got a young mother who

simply wants to know who the father... To me, then – To you... Welcome back! Still to come, music from Joe McElderry...'

The applause of a studio audience followed me on my way.

My route took me through a grand, green parkland, then round the back of a building onto which had been painted images of Charles Dickens and his *David Copperfield* characters. They were partially blocked by a row of red wheelie bins.

A better writer would have picked a metaphor out of it all. I continued pondering over the lives of rock salespeople instead.

Leg Eight

Thetford – Attleborough – Wymondham - Horning

Thetford

'O Thetford! Round thy flow'ry fields I've strolled'
George Bloomfield, *Thetford*

The weather only seemed to behave itself when I went to places of accepted beauty. Whenever I visited the supposedly less salubrious areas of Nelson's County, storm clouds gathered, giving the places an added Kitchen Sink aura. It only seemed fitting, then, that a cold morning rain began to fall as I walked through the Norwich streets on my way to Thetford.
I blustered through the train station car park. I was being spied on by a man in his forties with a pony tail.
He leapt into my path from behind a pillar.
I knew what was coming.
"Scuse me, mate. You ain't got 50p have yer? I need to get to London.'
I was sufficiently grouchy to give him a firm 'No'. The manner in which I said it contained enough gusto to let him know that I most definitely *did* have 50p but that I most definitely *wasn't* going to give it to him to buy cider with.
London indeed. And 50p! It would have taken him quite a while to collect enough coins to buy a ticket there at that time of day. A peak-time single to the capital costs somewhere in the region of £12,000 – and that's without spending £62 on a cup of

tea and a Kit Kat from the trolley. Yet, I admired the way he'd avoided the cliché destination of Peterborough. If someone stops you at Norwich station to ask for money, it's usually because they 'have to get back to Peterborough'.[1]

I thundered past him and into the station ticket kiosk, where I queued to be fleeced by a more professional act.

It was going to be a long day. I had to visit four places and, somehow, get home. I needed every train and bus to run like clockwork or the whole operation would fall apart. Each footstep had to be timed to perfection. One missed connection and the day was lost.

A voice came over the Tannoy:

'Vvvd all vvassngerrz vvr zz vvvne vvvifty-vvooo vvvrain vvv vvvvvhetvvord…'

I'd picked out the word Thetford but little else. It probably wasn't good news.

I stood in the ticket line, worried that there was something wrong with my train. As ever, the queue was being held up by an elderly couple buying tickets for a journey in six months' time. They were trying to work out how they could get into Edinburgh at four in the morning on the seventeenth and return at precisely twenty-to-six on the thirtieth. They deduced that they could save £1.20 by sitting in rear-facing, carriage class seats and agreeing not to use the toilets between Sheffield and Newcastle. I looked at the clock. My train was due to leave in four minutes. Another member of staff saw the plight of the queue and occupied a till. I performed a camp half-run towards her.

'Could I have a return to Thetford, please?'

'Certainly, Sir,' she smiled. 'The next train to Thetford has been cancelled.'

---

[1] I'd like to spend a day outside Peterborough station asking people for 50p to get to Norwich. See how they like it.

She said it as though it were good news, which, under regular circumstances, it might have been.

'When's the next?'

'In another thirty minutes. And just so you know,' she said, again chirping merrily, as though telling me they'd discovered an oil field under my house, 'there will be a *lot* of cancellations today.'

'Jeez,' I said, quietly, whilst inwardly screaming 'BASTARDS.'

She stared at me, smiling.

'Is there a reason?' I asked.

'There's a shortage of trains.'

Woah.

'Where are they? Have they run away?'

It was a genuine question. I knew my stuff. I'd seen plenty of episodes of *Thomas The Tank Engine*; trains often had mental dilemmas and dealt with them by either running away or hiding under a secret bridge.

'Sorry, Sir. I don't have any answers.'

It was checkmate. I couldn't do or say anything to change the situation. In an ideal world I could have thumped the desk and demanded to speak to the Fat Controller.[1] But, as proven by the grown men who ask for 50p to get to London (or Peterborough), the world is far from ideal. Dejected, I took my bloody expensive ticket and headed to the platform.

Train stations sound like swimming pools. You can hear whistles and shouts and echoed laughter. I love how they switch from deadly silence to absolute mayhem, and back again, in the space of about five minutes. The clientele are often an uplifting cocktail of studenty types and daytrippers. Train stations don't have that air of warped tragedy that a bus station has. You can

---

[1] The Fat Controller's real name is Sir Topham Hat. I don't know why but that always makes me laugh. Imagine him receiving his knighthood - his knees don't bend!

feel that your life has been a failure, a terrible joke, if you hang around a bus station any longer than two minutes.

I stared into space, thinking nothing thoughts. Muhammad Ali had once visited this station, which was pretty cool. What was less cool was that he'd done so as part of a promotional campaign for Ovaltine.

My reverie was broken by the sound of the voice returning over the Tannoy. Its aim was to clarify any confusion over the matter of the cancelled trains:

'Vvvd all vvassngerrz vvr zz vvvne vvvifty-vvooo vvvrain vvv vvvvvhetvvord...'

I looked at the long London Liverpool Street train. Its engine began to roar. A whistle blew.

'Wait! Hold up!' came a shout. A man ran alongside it. He had a ponytail. It was him. The 50p collector. He'd been telling the truth all along. He jumped on board just in time. I hid my face in case he looked out of a window and saw me.

Hours later, I was met off the train by Fred, a friend who happened to be part of the Thetford massif. He'd volunteered to give me a guided tour of Norfolk's largest market town, lest I miss any of the sights. With my plans in a mess, I needed his helping hand. We looked at the return train times on his phone. The next one was cancelled.

'I think we better go to the bus station.'

'Ok,' he replied, in a tone of voice which suggested that this particular area hadn't won the much-coveted Norfolk In Bloom award for a few years.

Despite the October drizzle, the streets were busy. The shops were already selling boxes of Christmas cards and tubes of wrapping paper. The posters in the windows had CGI snow in the corners. They used all the important Christmas words:

Hurry; Special; Now; Save; Extra; Shopping; This Year; Season; Buy; Today.

At the time of the Domesday survey, Thetford was the sixth largest town in England. The population currently hovered around the 20,000 mark and was comprised largely of the descendants of Londoners who were relocated in the 1950s to repopulate the town, like rabbits. They'd also been expected to bring trade and business with them, unlike rabbits.

A number of Portuguese, Latvians, Poles and Lithuanians had been arriving since the turn of the millennium. According to a newspaper report, the following sign was recently displayed in the window of a Lithuanian mini-market in Thetford:

'Two double rooms. £120 a week. Good conditions for three or four people in each room.'

Thetford had a reputation for being a rough house. Statistically, it wasn't one. Anecdotally it was. But these anecdotes have to be put into comparison with the rest of the county. Compared to Burnham Thorpe and Cley, of course Thetford seemed rowdy. Compared to Burnham Thorpe and Cley, my kitchen seemed rowdy. It didn't take much for a place to appear tough in Norfolk.

Thetford was vibrant. You can't ask for much more from a high street than for people to be using it. In a county full of people who overwhelmingly tick the 'White/British' box on application forms, the assortment of shops aimed at different international communities made the place unique. But, of course, it's hard to shed an image. Queen Boudicca had once lived in Thetford. I wouldn't be surprised if the town's hardy reputation stemmed from that fact. Norfolk people have a keen memory:

'Good Lord! Don't move to Thetford, Janet; they'll attack you with spears and make you join the Icenis!'

*

'Bus Station' was a generous term for what was no more than a bench under some tarpaulin. There was an anti-litter poster on the wall: *Don't Be A Tosser – Keep Suffolk Clean*. I hoped this was the beginning of an altogether more robust approach to public information. The softly, softly method clearly wasn't getting us anywhere:

Don't Be A Massive Prick – Get The Flu Jab

Next to the anti-tosser campaign poster were the timetables, none of which offered a bus to Norwich. I couldn't believe it. There were just thirty miles between the county's only city and its third largest town and you couldn't get a bus between them. The occasional National Express coach ran through, so Fred and I went to look at *their* timetable. We were confronted with a hollowed out casing where the timetable ought to be. Memories of 'Downham Bus Shelter' crept from the back of my mind to the very front of it.

'Sorry, Ryan, I think someone's nicked the timetable.'

He said it as though I'd held him responsible.

I was going to have to take my chances on the train. Maybe more of the engines had emerged from hiding under the secret bridge by now.

Leafy, autumnal paths ran alongside the Little Ouse. The river flowed through the town, creating surreal juxtapositions. Swans glided along, in front of kebab houses and card shops.

The downside of having the river wending its way between streets and under bridges was that it provided a stomping ground for rodents. I spotted three massive rats in the space of ten minutes. They were brazenly skirting the banks of the river, under park benches and along shop fronts.

There were also a couple of statues on show. The first we saw was of Maharajah Duleep Singh, the last Maharaja of the Sikh Empire, astride his horse. Singh was exiled to England after a string of military defeats to the British in 1854. He was fifteen at the time (if the battles had been online Playstation games, he'd have been alright). Whilst in exile, he charmed the young Queen Victoria. She went all Gok Wan on him: 'Those eyes and those teeth are *too* beautiful!' she wrote.

Victoria's opinion might have been biased. She had received some exquisite 'gifts' from Singh.[1] One of them was the Koh-i-Noor diamond which was last seen being worn to lunch by the late Queen Mother. British ownership of the diamond still touches a raw nerve in Punjab.

Singh certainly looked the part, sitting on his horse overlooking the Thetford branch of Argos. It was a wonderful, imposing statue, marred only by the fact it was surrounded by ugly makeshift fencing because it kept getting defaced by halfwits.

His statue was in Thetford because Singh bought the large country estate at nearby Elveden. He converted parts of it into a game reserve whilst also restoring many of the village's dilapidated buildings. As a hunter, he was said to have the fourth best shot in England (back in the days when people gave a hoot about that kind of thing). He still holds a record for shooting 780 birds from one gun in one day.

When he wasn't outside shooting his hunting pistol, it's rumoured that he was often inside shooting his love pistol – often at female members of his house staff. There's a common saying that 'you can see his nose in the streets of Thetford'. You can certainly see it on the statue. I'm not sure about anywhere else, though.

Singh died in Paris in 1893. It was, and is, thought by some that while in Paris he had returned to Sikhism, in which case his body should have been cremated. His family, however, had him

---

[1] In the same way her Empire took all sorts of gifts: namely, by turning up with a massive army and daring the locals to stop the gifts from being taken.

returned to Elveden for a Christian burial. (The Elveden Estate is now owned by the Guinness family. Maybe they can get Singh's bird-shooting feat in their *Book of Records*.)

Just across from Singh's monument was a lonely looking bronze Captain Mainwaring. He was sitting on a bench on his own, waiting for company to join him on either flank. Thetford had been the location for *Dad's Army's* fictional south coast resort Walmington-on-Sea. The cast and crew regularly stayed in and around the town during filming.

The statue was unveiled in 2010. On the face of it, it seemed strange to honour a fictional character. However, sitting next to him felt like an interaction with history, albeit a silly form of history. Looking into his bronze eyes, I didn't see a war hero. I saw an icon *for* war heroes.

My grandad loved *Dad's Army*. Other than England losing at rugby, it was one of the few things that made him roar with laughter. Mainwaring's statue reminded me of sitting with my sisters in front of his coal fire, eating liquorice torpedoes, wondering what was so funny (I still find myself occasionally wondering that during BBC2 repeats). I'd seen many war memorials during this tour, yet the names on them were nothing more than combinations of letters. It was hard to feel a connection. But Mainwaring, with that bushy moustache and that beautiful look of contempt, awoke the senses. He captured the elation and grief of his country's finest hour.

Comedy, eh? Write it off at your peril.

With the Thetford Traction Engine museum closed for the day, Fred and I had to look elsewhere for our kicks. We wandered past a fenced-off church by the name of St Mary The Less. It was one of three remaining medieval churches in the town. That it had been left to rot and take on a positively Hollywood horror aspect said everything about Norfolk's wealth of medieval churches. Of the thousand or so built in the county, 659 were still in use. Nowhere on planet earth could you find more medieval churches in a concentrated area. And all of them were the tallest. (Despite its abundance of churches, the 2011 census recorded Norwich as being England & Wales' 'most godless city'. Read into that what you will.)

It's hard to find a Norfolk view where there isn't at least one spire lurking in the distance. Even in the deepest haunts of the countryside, hollow churches stand proud in isolation, surrounded by nothing but fields. Many of them once supported villages since wiped out by plagues and devolving fortunes of the serfs.[1]

Visitors to Norfolk are quick to notice the churches. To locals, they are taken as a given. They are as much a part of the scenery as the farmland and the sea. Hence, an ancient building like St Mary The Less being left to fend for itself against the weeds without too much protest. In America, a building of such age would be a tourist attraction. In fact, it would be the oldest building in the country (if you took the more recently acquired state of New Mexico out of the equation).

After peering through the railings at the bent gravestones and boarded windows of St Mary, I noticed it had been at least seven minutes since I'd looked at a statue. So we went to see one of a corset maker called Thomas Paine. He stood outside the council offices. It's a location *he* may not have picked, if given the choice.

---

[1] There are over 150 deserted medieval villages in Norfolk. The Black Death alone wiped out half the county's population. Norfolk is one of the only counties in England where the population has actually decreased since the 14th century. As noted, it wasn't plague alone that created the ghost towns. John Kelly, in his book, *The Great Mortality*, claimed that 'recent research indicates that many of [these] "lost villages" actually succumbed to economic atherosclerosis.' Which, on reflection, made perfect sense. Once I'd found my dictionary.

*

The statue was a long time coming. Paine was born in Thetford in 1737. The statue was erected in 1964. It depicted Paine holding a copy of *Rights Of Man* in one hand and a quill in the other. His book was upside down. This was thought to have been done to deliberately stir conversation. (This has more of a ring of truth about it than the story of the Nelson monument at Yarmouth 'deliberately' facing Burnham Thorpe).

I patted his gilded knee. It was becoming clear just how large a role Norfolk people played in the history of America. We'd given them settlers, maps, mayors, witches, taxes, wars, Abraham Lincoln and countless place names. One of us had even inadvertently killed Pocahontas, for crying out loud. But no other Norfolk man or woman had as big an impact on the United States of America as Thomas Paine. For a start, it was he who came up with the name 'United States of America'.

Paine grew up in Thetford and was sent to the town grammar school at great expense to his corset-making father. The school building was still in operation. I stood outside it and took a picture, before Fred pointed out that that sort of thing could land me in hot water.

The population of Thetford at the time of Paine's youth was around 2,000. Only thirty people had the right to vote. It was known as a 'rotten borough'. This injustice was not forgotten by Paine in later years. Nor was the regular sight of condemned men walking past his house on their way to the gallows.

After leaving school, Paine became an apprentice in his father's trade. Melvyn Bragg once described Thomas Paine's Thetford as 'a suffocating backwater'. Well, the boy got out before he was choked. He ran away to fight at sea. On return, he moved to Kent and married, later losing his wife in childbirth. He then moved to Lewes in Sussex to become an Excise Inspector and a tobacconist. He remarried in Lewes but separated from his wife and moved to America in 1774 for fear of being imprisoned for debt. He settled in Pennsylvania and there began to write articles and pamphlets under a pseudonym.

Mr Definitely-Not-In-Debt.

Pamphlets are now more commonly made by kebab houses and companies encouraging old people to have hearing aids fitted. For Paine, they were a tool to rebuild the world. He had witnessed the flaws and hypocrisies of his land of birth: from the class system to the justice system to the royal lineage. Fortunately for him, he had just moved to a country where bad-mouthing the Brits was de rigueur - as was the use of French phrases such as de rigueur.

His first important pamphlet, which mentioned nothing of free pizza delivery after 6pm nor how much easier it would be to hear fire alarms, was *Common Sense*. Published in 1776, it was the first in a series of pamphlets labelled *The American Crises*. In proportion to the population at the time, *Common Sense* remains the bestselling book in American printing history.

Common Sense was a knockout. The thrust of its argument, for those who prefer thrusts to gists, was that it didn't make sense for Britain to rule America as Britain cared only for itself. America, Paine reasoned, would be dragged in and out of European wars with no gain. (How things have changed.)

Common Sense was read aloud in taverns. Tracts were learnt by heart:

'These are the times that try men's souls... Tyranny, like hell, is not easily conquered... The harder the conflict, the more glorious the triumph... What we obtain too cheap, we esteem too lightly: it is dearness only that gives everything its value.'

Paine's championing of the ideals of both American Independence and the French Revolution made him unpopular back home. Effigies were burnt across the country, even in

Norfolk.[1] Nelson himself, in the words of his biographer Tom Pocock, viewed Paine as 'a dangerous subversive.' Perhaps the most damning criticism came in the form of a compliment from Napoleon:

'A statue of gold should be erected to you in every city in the universe.'

'You'll be lucky,' Paine replied. 'There won't even be a statue of me in my hometown until 1964 – and even that will be a gift from America.'

Paine's perceived cosying up with Napoleon came back to bite him. He would later call the general the 'completest charlatan that ever existed.'

Thomas Paine lived in France during the Revolution, adding to his canon the *Rights of Man* (which he encouraged people to read upside down to make onlookers talk about it) and his wildly controversial *The Age of Reason*.

Amongst his unpalatable ideals were notions such as the abolition of the slave trade, equal rights for women, the end of institutionalised religion, the introduction of a minimum wage, the freedom for all to express their ideas, and a fair distribution of wealth. He derided the idea of hereditary succession, stating, 'It requires some talents to be a common mechanic; but to be a king, requires only the animal figure of a man.' Or woman. Or Anne of Cleves.

In 1802, he returned to the United States. He quietly lived out the last years of his life. His belief that the bible was a manmade oppressive tool had made him unpopular. The Thetford man, whose words inspired a nation to greatness, was buried in front

---

[1] It was in Swaffham. You can imagine the scene:
'Right, people. Get those dairy products off the Butter Cross - we've got an effigy needs burning.'

of a congregation of six. At the base of his golden statue was a quote from *Rights of Man*. It read, 'My country is the world. My religion is to do good.'

The whereabouts of Paine's bones is a mystery. They were taken from his grave in 1819 by a former foe, William Cobbett. Cobbett, himself a sturdy force of positive social change, felt Paine deserved a more fitting burial. He took the bones back to England where they remained in a trunk in his attic for 34 years. It wasn't quite the *fitting burial* he'd planned. When Cobbett died, his son auctioned off the bones. They could be anywhere.

Lord Byron, never one to let a stray thought go unrecorded, wrote:

In digging up your bones, Tom Paine,
Will Cobbett has done well;
You visit him on earth again,
He'll visit you in hell

There was just time before the next train (boldly assuming that it was going to arrive) to visit Castle Hill. It was, in summation, for those who prefer summations to thrusts, a tall grassy lump upon which used to sit a wooden 12th century motte & bailey castle. It was England's largest motte castle, built to protect Thetford from legions of invading warriors. It was now used predominantly for dog walking. There were precious visible remains of the motte (there were a fair few remains from the dog walking, though). I'm no archaeologist, but I guess this was mainly because wood doesn't tend to keep as long as stone.

We walked around the mound, sizing it up. In closer proximity, it was imposing.

'Shall we climb up?'

'Have we got time?' I asked. What I actually meant was, Won't we fall down and die?

'Yeah, come on,' said Fred. He started climbing. I followed suit.

It was a rural version of the Travelator from *Gladiators*. Except it was slippery. The ground was a mixture of wet clay and dewy grass. Neither of us had dressed appropriately.

When you're climbing, everything seems much further away than it does when you're not climbing. For example, climbing up a six-foot stepladder looks mere child's play until you reach the top and the thing starts rocking. It was the same with the hill. Yes, it looked tall, but not insurmountable by any means. But after ten or twelve big steps, I turned to look at the drop. They say that six-feet is maiming height. I was high enough to be maimed thrice over.

I turned back to face the rest of the climb. I wasn't even a third of the way up. Fred was ten-foot higher, looking decidedly less cocksure than he had two minutes prior. He had done that thing that children do when they know they've climbed too high up a rope. He had frozen.

I took another step. My foot slipped. I regained balance and lifted my other leg forward. Fred remained stationary. The hill began to feel less like a slope and more like a green wall. It was practically vertical. I stopped.

'Come on,' said Fred, beginning to ascend again.

'Sod that,' I panted. 'If my feet slip I might actually die.'

I was acutely aware of how much of a twat I must have looked to passers-by. I was one-third up a not particularly demanding hill, clinging to blades of grass and refusing to go any further.

Fred carefully slid down on his hands to join me. If we got to the top we'd never make it down without winding up in casualty, on a ward set aside for the treatment of slapstick injuries.

'No!' I yelled to myself, oddly.

I halted the expedition. It was too risky. I was both deeply concerned and laughing at the same time.

We had to get down. I felt my feet give way with each step. I took about three minutes between each movement.

Ladies, it was seriously unsexy.

There's a saying that if you walk around Castle Hill seven times at midnight you can summon the devil himself, assuming he isn't busy. I worried that I might accidentally summon him by rolling seven times.

I somehow managed to slide down the final stretch without moving my legs, riding it like the Debenham's escalator. Fred followed behind in lukewarm pursuit.

We went for a cup of tea and didn't mention any of it.

The train arrived. Hallelujah. But the following one *had* been cancelled. So I was going to have to take the train to Attleborough and hope against hope that there was a bus service to Wymondham and Norwich.

The train rode out through Thetford Forest's eighty square miles. It had been planted to create employment in the 1920s. (When was the last time a forest was planted to create employment?) The distinctive Corsican Pine dominated the landscape. You can see the forest, and the pines, during the 'You Have Been Watching' moment at the end of most *Dad's Army* episodes. After my exploits on Castle Hill, the caption should have followed me around all day.

Attleborough

My visit to Attleborough was so un-noteworthy that in my trusty book of handwritten notes there was just a blank space next to my scrawl of the word 'Attbro'.[1] I had to search the memory bank.

I certainly remember walking past a sign that said 'CIRCUS' on my way into town. I saw the Big Top through the leafless trees. It was sandwiched between 1980s detached abodes. Slightly further down the same road was a building called Connaught Hall: a cross between a leisure centre and a 1970s police station. Except that it had a large model elephant on the roof. Not since the sausage roll offer in Caister had I had so little to record.

On the side of a corner shop hung Christmas lights. It was mid-October. I marched on.

Outside another corner shop was a large picture of Guy Fawkes holding an upturned barrel, pouring out the contents carefully. He looked a bit like Russell Brand. Maybe that was where the inspiration for Katy Perry's *Firework* song came from? If only I'd had Kelly Perry, Great Yarmouth's foremost Katy Perry impersonator, on hand with the info. Or, indeed, Russell Bland, her former beau.

*

---

[1] All my notes were largely unreliable anyway. I'd get home and open the book to find what appeared to be the free association scrawls of a recently sectioned psychopath. One note, in particular, stands out. It read: 'Man with socks'. It meant nothing. I couldn't recall a thing about the man nor his supposedly sensational socks.

Attleborough was serene. There wasn't much to bemoan or excite. There were charity shops, a couple of banks, a Sainsbury's, hairdressers (plural, of course) and several newsagents. It was one of those towns where you could hear conversations in shops as you walked past:
'I said ter Shirley that oi hent done nuffun...'
'Did you see that oul plane floy oover yesterdee?...'
'Si'yalata then. Chairs, love...'
A brief moment of incongruity was afforded when a black limousine cruised through the town. Heads turned. The windows weren't tinted. Who was it? I couldn't get a good enough look. My money was on either Jennifer Lopez or Beyonce. I bet those two were always popping into Attleborough to get milk.
Even Attleborough's history was a little uneventful. Like seemingly everywhere else, the town had once been near enough wiped out by a fire (1559). It had also been a victim of Henry VIII's aversion to all things Catholic when its astounding Chapel of the Holy Cross was dismantled and the pieces used to build a road. The town claimed to have been the site of the first ever turnpike in England, which, whether true or not, was hardly likely to draw the masses.
Don't tell him your name, Turnpike.
More intriguing than its history of turnpikes, however, was Attleborough's unlikely brushes with organised crime. The Kray twins were regular visitors and invested in a local restaurant. Reggie Kray liked Norfolk so much that he ended up moving to the county on a permanent basis in his later years, staying at the nearby HMS Wayland prison.

I found a bus shelter and looked at the times. I couldn't believe it, there were loads. They ran to Wymondham *and* Norwich almost every twenty minutes. After months of being messed about by buses, the little beauties had redeemed themselves.

With the assurance of a bounty of buses, I had another jaunt around. Plonk in the centre of town was a little park over which hung brown-leafed trees. Surrounding this were handsome shops and an imposing town hall. On its wall was a sign for the Citizen's Advice Bureau and two large Christmas lights. There were even more lights across the road. Was I in Lapland? The decorations were either incredibly early to go up or incredibly late to come down. Or, maybe, the town had decided to take on Wizzard's ethos and were acting upon the wish that it could be Christmas every day.

A gust caused the trees to shake. It started snowing brown leaves. All it needed was kids to start singing and a band beginning to play.

Attleborough's pomp was arguably the 1930s when it made a name selling turkeys. Of all the poultry to specialise in, the farmers of Attleborough naturally took the festive option.

Turkeys were reared in Norfolk because the climate was closer to that of their native America.[1] The connecting railway line used to be known as the Turkey Express. It would whisk the birds off to London to be butchered. They initially thought they were being taken to see *The Lion King*. The ugly little critters would be packed in alongside regular passengers. The carriages were crammed with people and poultry: feathers flew; people shouted; birds screamed; luggage fell about the place; the conductors couldn't even get down the aisles.

I'm not entirely sure that train rides have improved since. At least the Turkey Express turned up.

---

[1] Try telling that to Pocahontas.

*

I sat on the top deck and watched the town fade from view, passing, as we went, the surprisingly spectacular replacement church built on the site of the Chapel of Holy Cross.

Formula One icon Ayrton Senna had lived in Attleborough whilst working for Norfolk-based Lotus, so it was only fitting that our bus driver took it upon himself to embody the great Brazilian's devil-may-care love of life in the fast lane.[1]

And that was Attleborough. Another town done. Another ticked off the list. It was a pleasant enough place, and although I had no concrete plans to visit it again at any time in the next forty to fifty years, it didn't feel like a wasted journey. Any wandering tourists guided towards it by the list of forty would be right to feel a little underwhelmed by its sincere normality.

Pulling away from the town (at breakneck speed, might I add), the scenery reverted to fields and crops. Something was different. The fields were smaller, more compact, incoherently divided. Were it not for the fact I was being thrust from left to right on the world's fastest double-decker, I would have said the place felt distinctly medieval.

Wymondham

The medieval landscape changed into a landscape of (rather swish) modern housing developments and (rather unswish)

---

[1] Senna referred to his time in Attleborough as the happiest of his life. (But *he* wasn't relying on public transport.)

industrial units. The bus flashed past them at a wicked pace and deposited me on the high street.

The downside of not getting the train was that Wymondham station was a famously kooky hive of activity, offering services from dog grooming to piano tuning. There was also a popular restaurant, which until recently was heavily *Brief Encounter* themed.[1]

It was market day again. Considering the fact that my journeys were timed largely at random, I seemed to have a good knack of picking market days. The high street had a festive bustle. As in Thetford, the shop windows were tinsled and fully prepped for Christmas Eve (when the Easter Egg displays were due to come out). Unlike Attleborough though, the town didn't have its lights up. The old people were walking as slowly as they possibly could, and, often, doing so just in front of me. I wasn't perturbed. Wymondham was too pretty to allow clouds of anger to form. I merely sidestepped my way around their waddling frames, whistling as I went.

I never thought I'd say this about a Tourist Information Centre, but Wymondham's was a stonker. Not only was it inside a 17th century Market Cross, it also had the unusual boast of actually being open.[2] It stood on wooden stilts with wooden steps leading up to it. On rainy days you could lay underneath and use it as a shelter – not that I imagine many people did.

The stilt-design was originally put in place to ensure that important town documents were kept safe from floods. The stilts were also useful to nail dead rats to. The idea was that other rats would see their crucified mates and think twice before

---

[1] Contrary to the belief of nearly everybody I talked to about it, the filming of *Brief Encounter* had absolutely nothing to do with Wymondham Station.

[2] Despite rarely ever being open, Norfolk Tourist Information Centres always *look* as though they are. You have to get right up close, sometimes as far as actually pushing the door, to be able to tell.

loitering. However, rather than be deterred, for a brief spell, the Wymondham rats began acting like associates of Tony Soprano. They were so incensed by seeing fellow gang members get whacked that they went to war. Instead of restaurant shootings and cheese-wire strangulations, they went on a biting spree in which at least one man was killed. His corpse was then nailed to the stilts as a deterrent to humans.

Wymondham, like everywhere else in Norfolk, had had a great fire. Entire streets were wiped out. I found out about the disaster in my non-politically correct *Penguin Guide*. It claimed the fire was 'deliberately started by some gypsies' on a Sunday morning in June 1615. The fire broke out at two separate points, suggesting arson. A register in a Norwich church stated that on the 2nd December 1615, a gypsy by the name of John Flodder, and his associates, were executed for doing the deed.

One survivor of the fire was the Green Dragon pub, located at the end of the high street. It was timber beamed and crooked. It looked immensely vulnerable. It had somehow been standing since the late 1400s. The exterior was gorgeously decorated with colourful hanging baskets. It looked like the sort of place you'd find Gandalf the Grey having a hearty piss-up with Bilbo.

Around the corner from the Green Dragon stood the imposing, mesmerising Wymondham Abbey. (The Green Dragon actually used to be part of the abbey grounds.) It dominated the skyline. It was a church-shaped monster. Imagine the largest church you have ever seen and then, rather than it having just the one tower, give it another at the opposite end. And then stick it in ancient farmland, on the edge of a squat, medieval town. Got it? Hopefully you're now visualising something you might see on the front cover of a Ken Follett novel.

One of the two towers was in ruins. Its dark, hollow windows brought to mind the *Hammer House of Horrors*; the kind of place you'd find Frankenstein skulking during a lightning storm. There was a restoration project going on. There were lots of tools and piles of wet earth. Large areas were fenced off. The plan was for the derelict tower to be brought into the 21st century, with viewing platforms and interactive experiences aimed at 'giving visitors a more enjoyable experience and connecting the church more strongly with the town.' It was a noble intention. But I was glad to have seen the tower *before* the makeover.

There'd been plenty of feuds between locals and monks about ownership of the abbey (and countless other things besides). One particular long-running 14th century row effectively centred on whose go it was to ring the bells. The solution was the building of the equally enormous second bell tower.

Well, it was either that or taking it in turns.

After the Dissolution of the Monasteries, the people of Wymondham bought the abbey from the monks. This didn't stop one of Henry VIII's loyal abbey-bashers, a local landowner by the name of Sir John Flowerdew, from tearing the place up anyway. There was an outcry in the town. *For one man, it was all getting too much.*[1]

Robert Kett was a middle class, middle-aged landowner. He was an unlikely rebel. He'd been spurred into action by peasants regularly attacking his property (they'd attacked Kett's land after being paid by Sir John Flowerdew not to attack *his*). At Wymondham's annual Feast of St Thomas, Kett spoke with the peasants. The reason for their unrest was that designated areas of common land, on which locals grew their own produce (vital, in many cases, to their survival), were being fenced off by

---

[1] That's the most exciting line I could think of. I thought it sounded like something on one of those trailers for summer blockbusters.

landowners (such as Kett and Flowerdew). The landowners wanted to use this land to graze sheep. Kett noted that feelings were so strong that it was better to side with the peasants than oppose them. He took on their plight and gathered an army of dissenters - which included his brother, William - and marched them to Norwich to see what they could do about it.

Their numbers swelled. By the time Kett settled on Mousehold Heath, a hill on the edge of the city, his army was 16,000 strong, and, importantly, largely unarmed. Armed or otherwise, their presence was enough to put the fear up anyone. Especially as the population of Norwich as a whole was hovering somewhere at the 12,000 mark. The city government amassed resistance. They sent for the Marquis of Northampton, who was a hell of a lot tougher than his name suggested.

Northampton's army fought with Kett's peasants in the Norwich streets. It was rebels who won out. They held the city for over a month.[1] While in control, Kett won over some of the gentry and attained the support of a share of Norwich men (although, it's fair to say that many of them didn't take kindly to the invasion). At their base on Mousehold Heath, Kett liaised with city officials at his meeting place under an oak tree. The tree became known as the Oak of Reformation. He used a nearby derelict house as a prison for any gentry unwilling to play the game.

Kett's gripe was exclusively with the *Norfolk* gentry, but when news of the rebellion reached London, the powers had to act. An army led by John Dudley, Earl of Warwick, arrived in Norwich on the king's commands and fought viciously with Kett's men in the streets for three days. Kett's army retreated, burning the houses of innocent people as they went. It was an

---

[1] To get into the city, hundreds had had to swim along the river Wensum whilst being shot at by archers and attacked with bricks.

ill-conceived effort to slow down their pursuers. They settled in the fields of Dussindale on the edge of the city.

The Earl's army was clinical and suitably armed. It was comprised in part by German mercenaries (and some violently angry, now homeless, Norwich men). Their numbers were great. Upon catching up with Kett's rebels, they utterly thrashed them. The number of dead is unclear but it is thought that somewhere between three and four thousand were butchered. Warwick's army lost 250.

Robert and his brother, William, were captured and taken to the Tower of London where they were found guilty of treason. They didn't even manage to do the guided tour and take a selfie with a Beefeater. They were sent to Norwich for sentencing. Execution was the outcome. They'd hoped for a slap on the wrist.

Robert Kett, 57, was hanged from the walls of Norwich Castle as a warning to anyone else out there who fancied amassing an army of 16,000 men and settling on Mousehold Heath for six weeks. His body was left to rot. William was hanged on the same day, 7th December 1549, from the recently Flowerdew-vandalised Wymondham Abbey. Many other rebels were hanged from the Oak of Reformation.

It wasn't until the 19th century that Kett's name began to be salvaged from the doldrums. Although there are few memorials to him in the county, his name is now associated with fighting for the rights of ordinary people. There's a Norwich school named after him and the hill from which he overlooked the city is now known as Kett's Hill. His Oak of Reformation was torn down to make way for a council built car park.

Wymondham was proud of the Kett brothers. Robert's presence graced the town sign (although it looked a little bit like it was depicting a biblical limbo party) and dotted about the town were commemorative plaques, including outside the abbey where William was hung.

There is an old East Anglian rhyme:

They hang the man and flog the woman
Who steals the goose from off the Common
But let the greater criminal loose
Who steals the Common from the goose

It isn't exactly Keats but it serves a purpose.

The sun shone coldly on the abbey. Here and there workmen's tools and machines stood incongruously against the backdrop of history. Behind it all rolled the same oddly proportioned green fields I'd seen from the bus window.
 Once inside, I could do nothing but swear under my breath. It was magnificent. A high, wide, golden altar screen stood as a monument to those who'd fallen in the Great War and was as stunning as anything I had seen on this trip. To think of the visitors this building had received, from Elizabeth I to the rebellious Ketts (who suddenly struck me as being Norfolk's much-searched-for answer to the Mitchell Brothers) and everyone in-between. And now *me*, standing there with a digital camera, wearing walking shoes and whistling the theme tune to *Eastenders*.

It was a sharp October afternoon but not all the market stalls had packed away. There were three or four still willing to trade. One of them sold sweets in small, transparent bags, tied at the top by red tape. The sweet stall was always the highlight of my childhood trips to the market; until the day I chose the wrong item: a bag of what I believe are called, grotesquely, Jazzies.
 Jazzies are white chocolate buttons covered in Hundreds & Thousands. They look like miniature dollops of vomit and don't

taste too dissimilar. White chocolate from markets isn't the same as the sweet and creamy white chocolate of, say, a Milky Bar. It's grey and chalky. It tastes of headaches and crumbles in your mouth. The very thought of Jazzies is always enough to make me queasy. I looked over at the sweet stand and there they were: the confectionary of the Damned.

Talking of the Damned, stuck to a window of a phone box was a poster advertising The Damned's upcoming gig in Norwich. On an adjacent railing, was a much larger poster for an upcoming production of *The Vicar of Dibley* by the Wymondham Players. Not since Walsingham had I experienced such battles in the air.

Wymondham was gorgeous; a town from a picture on a greeting card. A quick removal of the paint lines from the roads and you'd be good to start filming your adaptation of *Tristram Shandy*. The town's wealth had been built on a wool trade which near enough collapsed after the Industrial Revolution. The town had its development arrested. It was a tableau of a former world. Apart from the posters for The Damned.[1]

Horning

'Is this Horning?'
'Yep,' said the driver.

---

[1] Conversely, the town's famous boarding school was only founded in 1951. It's one of the largest in the country and, despite its relatively young age, has still managed to churn out a fair amount of MPs and crap cricketers.

I asked because on first view it appeared to be no more than a road and three trees.

'You gotta walk down there,' he added, whilst pointing down there. 'That's where the water is.'

'Oh. Ok. Thank you.'

I alighted bereft of hope. I didn't have much time to walk *down there*. The bus rides from Wymondham to Norwich and then from Norwich to Horning had taken a further ninety minutes. This wasn't the same as travelling in the summer, where the days went on until midnight. It was October. The days were wrapping up at approximately half-four. I glanced at my watch, then the sky. The sun was already falling.

The 'down there' that the bus driver had so kindly motioned towards was a downhill road. I assumed it would take me to the broads. It had been a while since I'd seen them. Wroxham was the last time. That summer morning felt a lifetime ago. To the left of the road was a hill upon which had been built an array of holiday homes. I couldn't tell if they were permanent residences, but the design - sliding glass doors and rooftop terraces, with the patio furniture long since packed away - suggested that many of the village's inhabitants paid only seasonal visits. The place had a hint of Ramsey Street, circa 1995, about it.

A flock of geese flew over, just about keeping their wobbly V-formation. The muted silence of the afternoon created the ideal environment for each individual squawk to be heard. What were they talking about 'up there'?

The driver was right: the water *was* 'down there'. There was a quay, no less. It was flat and still. The boats were moored. The sun was still dipping, drowning the village in a rich Christmassy orange. Three boys, of lower secondary school age, were casting fishing rods into the water and talking about the difficulty of catching fish one minute, and the size of Miss Watson's 'jugs' the next.[1]

A gang of geese were strutting about like they owned the joint. They stood on a patch of grass blocking my path to the water. I had to cut through them to get the sunset 'money shot' on my camera. As anyone who has ever had to walk home through East London of an evening will tell you, gangs don't appreciate you simply 'cutting through' them, especially to get so-called 'money shots' of sunsets. It doesn't matter whether the gang is made up of troubled inner-city youths or particularly large poultry: *cutting through* just isn't the done thing. The geese let me know it:

'Hownk, hownk, oi, wanker,' one of them said, racing up to me at alarming speed. 'Where'd you think your going? Hownk hownk.'

His hoodlum mates gathered around, cackling at his bravado.

'Oh, bugger off,' I said.

This created a scene. I'd started something. Never stop and respond, people. Never stop and respond.

'Hownk!' they screamed. 'Hownk, hownk, hownk!' One of them jerked his neck at my knee. 'Hownk, you cheeky fucker, hownk.'

'Oh, bloody hell,' I exhaled, trying to run away whilst giving the impression I was walking.

'Hownk, hownk, hownk. He's crying - what a wanker! Hownk, hownk.'

The boys with the fishing rods were looking now. 'Good,' I thought, '*witnesses!*' And witnesses they were. They watched the

---

[1] I've changed Miss Watson's name to protect her anonymity. Although it should be said the reviews her jugs received were overwhelmingly complimentary. And people say that the young men of today don't care about amateur pottery.

fracas intensely. Not since Miss Watson's French lessons had they seen such plump breasts in action.

The geese had me surrounded. What horrible car-horn noises they made. It was like being penned in by a fleet of Model-T Fords.

'Hownk, hownk, wanker, hownk. Give us your wallet, hownk.'

I tried to walk away. Another neck jutted out at me.

What was I going to do? I was trapped in an impossible situation. I had to either let the bastards keep pecking me or start defending myself. But what can one do to fight off wild animals? It's a problem I often face when walking home late at night and find myself in the presence of a fox. Most of the time, the brute will run away like a bolt of red lightning. But sometimes it stays and fixes its growly stare. Let me tell you, if you've never experienced the growly stare of a fox, it's not nice. You have to back off. On one occasion I walked an extra mile to avoid re-crossing a particularly wretched one's path. It's not that I fancied the fox's chances in a fight to the death: it's more that *I didn't want to get into a fight to the death with a fox.* What a surreal, disturbing occurrence it would be. Imagine witnessing the spectacle from a passing car: man vs. beast.[1]

The geese dilemma was no different. I didn't want to actually start *hitting* these birds. It would be exceptionally weird. And let's be honest, the headline 'Local Author Kicks Shit Out Of Village Geese' was hardly going to do wonders for book sales. Luckily, an angel came to my rescue.

One of the fishing boys wolf-whistled. It was loud enough to halt a cruise liner.

The geese looked at him in unison. 'Hownk?'

---

[1] The insulting thing is that, on some level, foxes must look at me and think, 'Hmm. He looks like the type of guy who enjoys rummaging through bins. Well, he's not going to do it on *my* patch. I better let him know who's boss.'

'Get out of it, yer twats,' he called.

And, remarkably, the twats got out of it. Instantly. They waddled off as though nothing had happened. 'Hownk hownk hownk....' and so on.

I looked at the boy. He winked and returned to his fishing.

I'd been rescued from embarrassment. A twelve-year-old had saved me. My dignity was intact.

Geese hoodlums aside, Horning was quite something. The buildings along the waterfront were older than those I'd passed on the way 'down there.' It was simple and homely, yet somehow spectacular.

'The breathing place for the cure of souls,' wrote the legendary Norfolk naturalist (not naturist) Ted Ellis of these waters. I both understand and *don't* understand the quote in equal measure.

The village had unexpectedly taken the brunt of Luftwaffe leftovers in 1941. They dropped fifteen bombs. Who knows why? It might have been an accident. It couldn't possibly have been part of a Nazi masterplan to wipe the symbolic stronghold of Horning off the map. Sadly, it almost did. One bomb landed at the Ferry Inn, killing 21 patrons in one blast. (The Inn reopened within three weeks.)

In each shop I was greeted with a smile. It was most agreeable. The daylight continued to twist into twilight. I took a few awful photographs and decided to call it a day. I slipped into a café and ordered tea and a lamb pie. They didn't have goose.

The day had been a success. I'd somehow made all of the connections. I could finally relax...

'Just to let you know we're closing in four minutes.'

That was the danger of visiting seasonal resorts out of season. They might look wintry and artistic, but can be quite annoying when you want to do anything after 3pm.

I had intended to see the village abbey but there were few spare minutes before the last bus of the day was due to race by. I'd been concerned about this bus all day. If I missed it I actually couldn't get home. But after the manner in which my day had started - cancelled trains to Thetford in the pouring rain - I was so relieved to have even got this far that being trapped in Horning would have only been an inconvenience, rather than the full blown Greek tragedy I'd played over in my mind the night prior. How could anyone want to leave Horning?

As a measure of its charms, I'll point out that the village's Wikipedia entry mentioned that 'the following communication services were available in Horning: Broadband, Digital TV, Digital Radio, Mobile Phone networks.'

They're available *everywhere* aren't they? What spiffing boasts. What next, tap water? Roof tiles? Cutlery?

The village website was full of equally life affirming news:

'Horning Village Fete 2013 - A Success!'[1]

It also mentioned that the village table tennis facilities were accessible to all: 'If you fancy an impromptu game, table tennis bats and balls are in a tub under the table.'

Don't tell me Norfolk isn't wonderful.

Horning's Abbey of St Benet was the resting ground of our good friend Sir John Fastolf aka Falstaff. It is also thought to be the only abbey in the country not closed by the immensely naughty Henry VIII.

The role of Horning Abbot passes by default to the Bishop of Norwich. One of the bishop's duties is to preach from the bow of a Horning wherry on the first Sunday of every August. I'm told you need to get there early to avoid the rush.

---

[1] I live for the day I see a newsletter proclaim a village fete to be a failure: 'Village Fete An Absolute Abomination – Many Dead!'

*

I walked back 'up there' on the 'down there' road. Another V of noisy birds flew over; even they were treating the area as some sort of holiday retreat. They would be back next spring. As would everyone: the boaters; the bird watchers; the walkers (walkers, as in, walking *enthusiasts*, not zombies); the families. But for now, Horning was getting ready for hibernation. It was closing in two minutes.

I sat in the bus shelter. A regular occurrence. I took a bad photograph. An equally regular occurrence. It dawned on me that I didn't have too many bus stops left. The tour was almost finished. I got strangely emotional about it. The end was coming.

'Did you find it down there?' said the driver.

He'd remembered me!

'Yes, it's lovely! I loved it.'

'It's a nice old place. It's all nice,' he said. 'All nice in Norfolk.'

And we rode away.

I didn't want the end to come.

Leg Nine

Diss – Harleston – Loddon – Norwich – Filby – Reeedham

Diss

Dr Crippen began working for a New York homeopathic pharmaceutical in 1894. That same year he married his second wife: the all-singing, all-dancing, all-shagging, Cora Turner (often known as Belle Elmore). They moved to England three years later, where, not surprisingly, Crippen's knowledge of homeopathic medicines was not considered a strong enough case for him to resume work as a British doctor. So he became a distributor of 'original medicines' instead, whilst Cora/Belle Elmore 'socialised' with the men of the London show business scene.
In response to Cora's socialising, Crippen decided to do a little socialising of his own, with his personal typist: a young lady by the name of Ethel Le Neve. They socialised each other's brains out. Ethel openly became Dr Crippen's mistress whilst Cora was gleefully socialised by a selection of other men.
Things were going so well on both the marital and extra-curricular socialising fronts that the couple regularly held parties and soirées at their Camden home:
'Now,' asked the guests upon receiving their invites, 'is this a social evening or a *social* evening? I just want to make sure I'm wearing the correct gear.'

One particularly swinging party in early 1910 went with such fizz that Cora had simply vanished into thin air by the morning. When asked of her whereabouts, Dr Crippen stated that she had gone back to America to socialise over there. When asked again at a slightly later date, he said that she had in fact died whilst in the US and that it wasn't worth looking her up because she'd been cremated and, goodness, wasn't it a frightful shame and all that? 'Of course,' he added, whilst glancing at his watch, 'these things can't be helped.'

With Cora out of the way, due to natural causes, might I add, Ethel and the doctor *officially* became an item. She moved into Cora's house, slept on Cora's side of the bed and, creepily, even wore Cora's clothes.

Such were Cora's connections with the glitzy side, it was a celebrity by the name of Vulcana who first reported the disappearance. Considering the fact Vulcana was a professional strongwoman and built like the proverbial brick outdoors-commode, the constabulary were surprisingly slow to act on her claims. It wasn't until friends of a more acceptable standing also voiced concern that the police bothered investigating the doctor's home.

The house was given a quick once over. Chief Inspector Walter Dew interviewed the doctor. He noted nothing suspicious and returned to the station to get back to work on more urgent matters i.e. that day's sudoku. However, Crippen and Ethel had thought the interview less successful. They fled. They sailed to Brussels and, at the first opportunity, boarded another ship for Canada.

Alerted by the palpable fishiness of Crippen running away at the first sign of trouble, the police conducted a thorough search of his house. Under the basement brickwork they found human remains. An abdomen: no head, no limbs, no bones. Word got out. There was a murderer on the loose.

On board their Canada bound ship, Crippen wore a false moustache and Ethel dressed up as a boy. It's never a promising sign during a mad getaway when the people being chased share similar methods of disguise as those used by the Marx Brothers. The couple were spotted by the captain. He ordered the following telegraph to be sent:

'Have strong suspicions that London cellar murderer and accomplice are among saloon passengers. Moustache taken off, growing beard. Accomplice dressed as boy. Manner and build undoubtedly a girl. Plus, I just saw them snogging.'

(I made that last line up.)

The game was up. The couple were well and truly socialised.

Inspector Dew received the telegraph with sufficient time to board an even quicker White Star Line ship and beat Crippen & Son to Canada.[1] Caught up in the excitement of it all, he too decided to dress up. He wore a pilot's uniform. It was all jolly fun stuff. The plan was for Crippen's captain to invite the doctor to meet the pilot; Dew would then whip off his disguise and surprise them all.

'He won't see this coming!' said Dew.

'Yes,' said his assistant, 'but do you really need to wear the pilot uniform? If you just approached him wearing normal clothes the result would be exactly the same.'

'Don't spoil my fun.'

Sure enough, Crippen took the captain's invite and went to meet the pilot (pilots were a rare and exciting breed in 1910). And, sure enough, the inspector whipped off his remarkable disguise.

The following exchange took place:

---

[1] Two years later, the White Star's reputation for speedy transatlantic crossings would lead to a Norfolk woman getting a free fur coat (and James Cameron winning eleven Oscars).

'Good morning, Dr Crippen. Do you know me? I'm Chief Inspector Dew from Scotland Yard.'

To which Crippen stuck out his hands for cuffing and said, 'Thank God it's over. The suspense has been too great. I couldn't stand it any longer.'

A less intimidating criminal you couldn't find. There really was no need for that pilot outfit.

Crippen was sent back to England. It was the first time in history that a criminal had been caught using the miraculous new technology of telegrams. And the ten-millionth time a false moustache had failed to fool anyone.

At the trial of 1910, it became clear that the unearthed abdomen was not necessarily going to be the dynamite piece of evidence that everyone had hoped. For a start, it was hard to judge whether it was male or female (unlike Ethel's disguise) or even how old it was. Crippen's defence said that the abdomen predated the years that the couple took residence in the building; the opposition replied that the body had a scar in the same place that Cora had a scar.

The defence said that this was, obviously, folded tissue.

The opposition replied that the body contained hyoscine in large amounts.

The defence said that, if they'd done their homework, they'd have known that Dr Crippen was into homeopathy and therefore clearly knew nothing about *actual* drugs and toxics.

The opposition asked why Dr Crippen had ordered lots of hyoscine from a chemist just before Cora went missing?

He thought it was mouthwash, came the defence.

And what, said the opposition, of the strands of bleached hair, the same as Cora's, found near the body?

Oh, she was always leaving hair about the place.

And what, pressed the opposition further, of the fragments of nightwear which matched Dr Crippen's?
It was a His & Hers matching set, m'lord...
And so on.
There was a popular song doing the rounds. It went like this:

Dr Crippen killed Belle Elmore
Ran away with Miss le Neve
Right across the ocean blue
Followed by Inspector Dew
Ship's ahoy, naughty boy!

I assume it was funny at the time.
It took the jury all of half an hour to decide on a verdict. As the rope went around her lover's neck, Ethel fled the country once again. She had been acquitted as an accomplice and sailed away on the very morning of the execution. Her innocence is often the cause of hot debate (amongst people that still give a fig, of course). There's a rumour that she spent weeks studying toxicology at the Royal College of Surgeons in the run-up to Cora's disappearance. But who knows? What *is* known is that she moved to America, then Canada, and then back to London. She lived a life of pseudonyms and alter egos; none more memorable than her schoolboy impression.
Crippen was buried with a picture of Ethel and a collection of their love letters. Ethel requested at her own burial to have a picture of the dashing doctor pressed against her heart. Whether or not this happened is not known. It's quite sad, I suppose. Until one remembers the details of Cora Crippen's burial.
Why am I telling you all this? Because Ethel Le Neve was born in Diss in 1883 and lived there briefly. It's not much of a fact but for a town that has something of a reputation in Norfolk for being unexciting, it's quite an exciting claim. To think, Diss

gave birth to the performer of the world's worst impression of a boy.

And if *that* story didn't interest you, the town had one more ace up its sleeve. Bruce Forsythe used to be the milkman.

If you'd seen how high I'd jumped when a frog leapt out at me from a hedge near the station, you'd have thought that in addition to the world's worst impression of a boy, Diss had also provided the world's worst impression of a man.

I'm not a lover of frogs and toads. I don't like their unpredictable jumping patterns, nor the way they camouflage themselves as just another leaf on the path. My ultimate fear is to stand on one and pop it. I'm rarely mistaken for a member of the SAS at the best of times, but even I must admit that the yelp I omitted as the frog pounced at me was disgraceful.

Maybe my reaction was due in part to the cosily domesticated train ride I'd just been on. I hadn't adjusted to the stark realities of nature in the raw. The carriage had been crammed with grandparents and grandchildren wearing the Marks & Spencer autumn collection. They were eating bananas and raisin bars out of neatly packed Tupperware. I overheard phrases such as 'When we get to London, can we...' and 'Doesn't Grandad look silly in his...'. It was sweet but did make me think I'd wandered onto the set of one of the railway's advertisements for their *London Attraction Two-For-One* offers.[1]

If you didn't know already, or if you're merely a trifle slow when it comes to reading between the lines, the Norwich to Diss train

---

[1] J.B Priestley wrote that Norfolk people 'go to London as a London man might go to Berlin or Rome and not hesitate to let out a good bellow of laughter at all the doings there.' I should add that lots, and I mean lots, of Norfolk people also go to *Norwich* as a London man might go to Berlin or Rome.

comes to its screeching conclusion in London. There are *two* train lines linking the capital and Norfolk. One is from King's Cross to King's Lynn and the other is from Liverpool Street to Norwich.

Regardless of how many times I've caught the London-Norwich train, pulling out of Liverpool Street, through Stratford and the sprawl, always excites me. And, Diss, dear Diss, is the first Norfolk stop of the journey. That's when you know you're back. Manningtree I view as halfway. Ipswich: touching distance. Diss: home. Nelson's County. Good old Diss. Yet I'd never stepped foot in the joint.

Aside from the deadly killer frogs that preyed around the station, the small town was probably most famous for getting the John Betjeman treatment in both poetic and, later, televisual form. His poem, *A Mind's Journey To Diss*, ends with the famous lines:

Till in the dimmest place of all
The train slows down into a crawl
And stops in silence...Where is this?
Dear Mary Wilson, this is Diss

The walk into town was as uninspiring as ever: a mixture of modern and Victorian housing along a main road.[1] I walked as far as the park and strolled across it. The town sat opulently in the background. It looked incredible. Why did Diss get such negative press?

It was still early, of course. Maybe the serial killers had yet to wake (we all know how awfully tiring it can be spending the

---

[1] That said, I did see a road named after Diss' own Thomas Manning, born 1772, who, according to the inscription on the road sign, was 'the first white man to visit the Dalai Lama.' I don't know what they spoke about, nor in which tongue. Manning must have been on a gap year.

night sellotaping photographs of future victims to the lounge window). The park was deserted except for a golden retriever that appeared to be walking itself. The only other sign of life was a man cycling along in a high-vis jacket.

High-vis jackets are designed to alert you of the wearer's presence, particularly if they're builders and road workers. 'Watch out,' says the jacket, 'there's somebody working here.' What I appreciate about the jackets, though, is that they also perform a similar function when sported by people who don't *need* to wear them but still choose to do so. 'Watch out,' warns the jacket, 'I'm insane and will probably start talking to you about my completely fictional little niece.'

Between the park and the town centre was Diss Mere: a body of water in a deep hole of which nobody could confidently explain the origins. The most sensible suggestion was that the mere sat in 'a clay filled depression in the [underlying] chalk' (the town council's words, not mine). A more fanciful myth said it was the crater of an extinct volcano. This story was most probably started by the ancestors of the chap in the high-vis jacket. Whatever the mere's origins, it was pretty. There were plenty of ducks and swans gliding about on it, looking pleased with themselves.

On a particularly biting 1827 morning, the mere froze. An eight-hour long game of cricket was played on it.[1] The whole town generally larked about. It was all very Pickwickian. At one point, a horse-drawn wagon trotted across without complaint (well, horses can't complain). It's tempting to class such bravado as 'asking for it'. But the population of 1827 had never seen an

---

[1] Talking of cricket, Diss was the childhood home of a half-decent spin bowler by the name of Thomas Lord. In 1814, Lord bought a patch of grass in St John's Wood for the express purpose of hosting professional cricket matches. He named it Lords. Despite selling the ground in old age, the name stuck.

episode of *Casualty*, so they didn't fear the consequences of such recklessness. And good on them. The ice didn't crack.

Something within a flowerbed caught mine eye. What was it? I crept closer. More rustling. A large white rabbit hopped out at me. I jumped. Why did every animal in Diss feel the need to lunge at me?

The rabbit twitched its cute little nose. It was clearly an escaped pet. I had to tell someone. But who? Where do you report rabbit dilemmas? There was a Tourist Information Centre within hopping distance. Naturally, it was closed, but there was a member of staff inside. She eventually unlocked the door after a minute or two of weighing-up whether or not I was an armed robber trying to steal pamphlets for tourist attractions. She told me that there was more than one rabbit in the flowerbed. They'd been released by somebody months ago and were making a good go of survival without the aid of a hutch. People had been feeding them and they'd taken to the area like ducks to water on the crater of an extinct volcano.

I love an uphill high street. It's how high streets should be. Diss' bobbed and bended upwards until it reached the church. I also love a church on a hill, overlooking a high street.

The church was invitingly compact and snug. The sort of thing you saw on Christmas cards from your great aunt (with a poem inside featuring the words 'fulfil' and 'dreams' at least once, often thrice). Inside, two friendly churchwardens talked about how pleasant the sunlight looked as it burst through the high windows and onto the white walls.

On one wall an inscription marked the long time passing of somebody called Elizabeth Bunny.

Diss really liked rabbits.

One of the early Diss rectors was John Skelton, tutor to a young Henry VIII. Skelton was Henry's favourite teacher and the two maintained a relationship for many years. Skelton joined Diss church after giving up teaching. Whilst there, he developed a reputation as something of a lady's man. (So *that's* where Henry got it from.) He was rumoured to have had a secret wife and to have got up to all sorts of mischief with all sorts of people. He was also a darned funny poet. He referred to himself as 'poet laureate' although nobody else did. History remains quiet when it comes to providing actual evidence that he ever held the title officially.

After his death, myths and legends circulated. The truth is nigh on impossible to separate from the fiction. His misdemeanours were circulated in a collection entitled *The Merie Tales of Skelton*.[1] According to the book, Skelton once stood in the pulpit of Diss church and held up a newborn, said to be his lovechild, and asked the shocked congregation to find fault with it. They sat in silence. Until a man in a high-vis jacket put his hand in the air and said, 'It can't talk.'

Just as one Diss man had entertained Henry VIII, so another Diss man entertained his daughter, Elizabeth. John Wilbye was born the son of Diss tanner (Wilbye was born in a village called Brome, a few miles away in Suffolk) and was a prolific writer of madrigals (those boyish choral pieces you accidentally hear two seconds of when skipping past Radio 3). His compositions were much loved by Elizabeth and her contemporaries. They allegedly remain popular to this day. Among his many chart hits were such classics as *'Yee That Doe Live In Pleasures'* and the toe-tapping *'Thus Saith My Cloris Bright'*.

*

[1] If ever a book needed to be adapted into a chirpy ITV ensemble, starring David Jason.

John Betjeman wrote of Diss that 'it would be the perfect English country town, neither too big for people to feel neglected nor too small to become a hot-bed of gossip.' He was right. The perfect English country town. It looked more like *Dad's Army's* Walmington-On-Sea than the actual Walmington-On-Sea in Thetford. And, during the war, some of the locals had behaved even more *Dad's Army*-esque than *Dad's Army*. On one occasion a suspicious item caused an almighty bomb scare until somebody noticed it was an orange. Seriously.

Diss was a timepiece. I don't mean that as a slur. It was comfortingly slow-paced and welcoming. It looked as though its last rowdy night had been when John Wilbye smashed out a few of his classic madrigals with the church choir; apparently the crowd went wild when he hit the opening chords of *'Mine Rabbit Hath Been Abandoned In Yee Hedge'*.

As ever, my bus timings had to be precise lest I remain in Diss for the next six years. My pace quickened. I now walked *down* the high street. My momentum carried me past the Tourist Information Centre, past the rabbit hedge, past the mere, past the ducks, past the swans, past the... cockerel.

Fuck me - there was a cockerel standing on a gatepost!

It was giving a morning bugle for all to hear. What was this, a town or a petting zoo? I'd seen more animals than people! And even the people had the surname Bunny. It was one big Disney film.[1] Any minute now the rabbits would run out and do a choreographed routine set to music. It was all getting too much. That golden retriever I'd seen earlier wasn't walking himself - he was on his way to the library.

---

[1] *'Where is this? Dear Mary Wilson, this is Diss-ney.'*

Harleston

The road to Harleston took me through further uncharted territory. Some of the villages sounded like they had been completely fabricated. I'd never heard anyone mention them. Ever. Billingford, Wortwell, Pulham Market and, tantalisingly, through a village called Needham. I had to get to *Reedham* by nightfall, which, since the clocks had recently gone back, was due to close in at about 2pm. I was tempted to get off the bus and adjust the village sign *N* to an *R* and get a selfie next to it.

I really had now seen most of Norfolk. There weren't many areas undetected by my radar. If only I'd kept a log of *every* place I'd been to or through. It must have been at least two hundred. I'd seen some places more than once, of course. (Mundesley springs to mind.) Some of the bus routes had been so obscure that I'm fairly certain I'd slipped into Narnia at least twice.

I don't know why, but I'd always imagined Harleston to be a bit of a dive. I envisaged a fairly large town with lots of concrete and closed-down wine merchants. It was nigh on the exact opposite. It was a fairly small town with precious little concrete.

Like Diss, it felt like a model town. There were butchers shops, bakeries, tearooms, hotels, townhouses, and a recently restored corn exchange.[1] And there were people. The shops were doing a fine trade. The tearooms rattled.

Unlike most Norfolk towns, Harleston didn't have a church in the middle. The town was built around the market place as its

---

[1] And a video shop! Hooray. I'd found one. It didn't sell trainers, though.

focal point. Once more, behind the Georgian and Victorian facades stood buildings from the times of the Tudors and Stuarts. Harleston, like Holt and Hingham, was another Lavenham with a mask on.

As fascinating as this all was, I was desperate for a wee and finding it hard to think of anything else. I nipped into a tearoom, ordered a drink, and asked where the toilet was.

'Sorry, sir, we don't have a toilet,' replied the waitress, resting the pot of hot tea on my table.

I hadn't thought this through. I now had to add a gallon of liquid to my packed bladder.

I'd ordered a sausage roll. It came with a side salad. Why, I don't know. Where would it end? The bin bags of Great Britain must be stuffed with side salad. It won't be long before we're served side salads to stir into our drinks.

I hit the streets with the low, wintry sun in my eyes and an ocean of urine in my system. My bladder was going to pop out and bounce across the street like Margaret Read's heart in King's Lynn. It was getting desperate. How had I got into this situation? It felt as though my insides were being wrung out by Hulk Hogan. I walked into the Citizen's Advice Bureau. Maybe they could help. If they were open. If not, I'd be pissing through their letterbox.

It was open. Thank God. They told me that the nearest public toilet was far away and might be closed. I visibly paled before them.

'You can use our toilet if you like,' they said.

I would like.

I left the bureau feeling like an advised citizen. Across the road was the swish looking J.D Young hotel, a 15th century coaching inn. There was a rumour, unsubstantiated, that Winston Churchill met there with General Eisenhower during World

War Two. They sat in the lounge and discussed Lord knows what. The details were exceptionally vague. I could find no evidence of the meeting other than on Harleston websites.

One recent release from the National Archives suggested that the pair met secretly to discuss a UFO that had chased an RAF pilot along the Norfolk coast. Churchill is reputed to have said, 'This event should be immediately classified since it would create mass panic amongst the general population and destroy one's belief in the church.' The details on this are even sketchier, as is often the case with alien sightings. It's almost as if the stories aren't true.

Before you judge whether or not Churchill and Eisenhower did meet in Harleston, it should be noted that the word of some local witnesses might be considered unreliable. For example, panic swept through the town in 1813 after Napoleon had also been spotted at J.D Young's hotel (formerly known as The Magpie). A small riot broke out. The people only calmed down after it was satisfactorily proven that Napoleon *wasn't* in the pub. The melee was reported by The Times as a 'Patriotic Riot'. It almost sounded fun.

I walked around the lanes, among the houses and cottages. It was all completely lovely. There is nothing finer than a blue sky on a cold morning. I could see my breath. Christmas was in the air.

I found the bus stop and waited for the ride back to Norwich. There was little margin for error. About six buses a day ran to and from Norwich. A couple of men stood talking. One was about forty, the other was old enough to have been excused from fighting in World War Two. Their discussion was heated. The cold air converted their breath to dragon smoke. The subject of debate? Cabbages.

'You only gotta sook'um erry coupla weeks,' said the old man.

'If it dunt rain,' came the reply.
'Dunt matter! They 'on't need ut. Not til the get big'
'Cuh, oi wunt loike ter not wet um. They droy up, dutt the?'
'Hent never sin one droy up yet.' This was the end of the debate. The old fella repeated the statement under his breath for good measure, 'Hent never sin one droy up yet.' The case was closed: you only had to sook'um, sorry, *soak them*, every couple of weeks, until they got big.[1]

Whilst standing at the bus stop I could have sworn I saw Barack Obama walk past. He was holding hands with David Cameron. They were talking about ghosts. But it was all Top Secret. Don't tell anyone.

Loddon

The man who is tired of Loddon is tired of life.
I wasn't tired of Loddon; I was tired of catching buses. To get to Loddon's pumping town centre (library, car park, greengrocers, some trees) I'd had to bus it back to Norwich from Harleston[2] for an hour and then catch a different bus which headed in approximately the same direction for another half hour before making a slight deviation. There must have been an easier way of doing things. I should have checked the Transport For Loddon website.

---

[1] I checked the Royal Horticultural Society's website when I got home. The old boy was right. Their wording wasn't as nice as his, though: '...a thorough soak every 10 days will be enough. When the heads begin to form, generous watering will greatly improve head size.'
[2] Via the beautiful, hilly scenery of yet more undiscovered, possibly fictitious, villages.

A sign near the bus stop proclaimed that the *town* had recently won the Eastern Daily Press *Village* of the Year award, as well as the much-coveted (I assume) 2006 Calor Gas *Village* of the Year. Possibly winning both in the 'Not Quite A Village, Not Quite A Town' category.

In the centre was a modern car park which doubled up as a market every now and then. As modern car parks go, this one was leafy and tastefully obscured. It also meant that the cute little side-streets weren't choked with parked cars. There was a smattering of elderly people wandering about. Most of them held green prescriptions tightly in their hands. Outside the Co-Op a group of primary school children were carving pumpkins and painting Halloween faces.

Talking of the occult, just off the car park stood the sort of dramatically imposing church you'd expect to see in one of the BBC's 1970s *Ghost For Christmas* episodes. It looked the ideal setting. I could already imagine the story: a recently appointed vicar refusing to acknowledge a local tradition of nailing a cross to the church door on December 1st and subsequently being hounded by a mysterious cloaked figure. The spectre not only appears in the vicar's dreams but, in the finale, is seen standing by the poor chap's sweat-soaked bed holding a dead child.[1]

In contrast to the horror façade, the sign outside read, 'Holy Trinity Church Is Open – Do Come In'. I'm a sucker for frightfully polite C of E signs, so I went inside.

There was an open door leading up a steep flight of stone stairs. Thinking back to my ascent of the Cromer spire, I approached the steps with caution. Fortunately they were few in number and led not up the tower but to an old classroom. It had a desk with two chairs either side. On the walls were black & white photographs of the town. Before it reached its current serene

---

[1] Many episodes of that terrifying BBC series were filmed in Norfolk, including the finest, *Whistle & I'll Come To You, My Lad.*

state, Loddon had a gasworks, brickworks, an industrial area, a plastics factory, a bus company, and an egg-packing factory. It's important not to forget the changing roles of the church, too. And not just in Loddon. All Norfolk churches, and all England's churches, were once vital focal points for their respective communities. It wasn't unusual for people to go to *three* Sunday services a week. Manmade rules dominated (the type of manmade rules that Thetford's Thomas Paine wanted rid of). Social classes were segregated not just by seating areas but also by the order on which they were permitted to enter the building. Children sat on pews, petrified of the consequences of looking anything other than forlorn.

'Let the little children come to me,' Jesus said.

'Ok. As long as they don't breathe too loudly or make annoying noises.'

'Sell your possessions, and give to the needy,' Jesus said.

'Nah.'

Sundays must have been horrendous for anyone with a whiff of atheism in their system. They're boring enough now: how more so when there wasn't even the *X Factor* and *Strictly* results shows to look forward to. One account of an Edwardian Norfolk Sunday reported that nobody was allowed to sew, knit or read the newspaper. It was taken as a given that they also weren't allowed to smoke, drink or think about boobies.

For all the charm of the former classroom, the combination of empty chairs and the memory of BBC ghost stories made me uneasy. I didn't want the silence broken by the sound of a dead teacher cracking his cane on the desk. I descended.

I'd left the church without seeing its infamous rood screen. According to a website about Norfolk churches, the rood depicted a politically charged image of the martyr William of

Norwich 'bound to stakes, the Jews wounding his side and collecting the blood in a basin.'

The story of William of Norwich is immensely complex. There are two options facing a writer when confronted with reporting such a complicated, sensitive narrative. They can treat it with learned, scholarly dedication, paying visits to the British Library to pore through antiquated letters in the noble pursuit of piecing together a lengthy academic discourse. Or, they can get the gist via old documentaries on YouTube and bash out a page-long summary full of crap jokes.

Guess which option I plumped for?

The body of twelve-year-old William had been discovered in a tree at Thorpe Wood, outside Norwich, during Easter, 1144. He had been gagged and stripped (and had his hair shaved off). Rather than being buried, his hanging corpse became something of a tourist attraction for the Norwich Mouth Breathers Society. Once the number of daytrippers to the site increased, rumours began circulating that the boy had been killed by Jews as a sacrificial offering. After all, the murder had happened at Easter, and didn't Jews just love sacrificing things at that time of year?

The story didn't take long to mutate. William hadn't been found hanging in the tree, he had been found *crucified*. Then it changed again. William had not only been crucified, he'd also been tortured. He had *cross-shaped scars* all over his body. The Jews, clearly, had been mocking the death of Christ.

The rumours spread throughout the country and then the world. Over the next hundred years, a myth grew that Jewish people liked sacrificing Christian children to appease their suspiciously unfriendly God. This myth, known historically as the Blood Libel, became a starting point for centuries of Jewish persecution.[1] The Black Death, two centuries after William's death, was thought to be a Jewish plot to wipe out Christianity. Even as late as the 1930s, Nazi propaganda magazines were publishing articles about the Jewish history of sacrificing innocent gentiles.

It is impossible to trace the beginnings of orchestrated, organised anti-Semitism. Of course this one event wasn't the sole cause, but the people of 12th century Norwich certainly provide a menacing presence in mankind's most shameful story.

There is little or no evidence of William's murder ever taking place, let alone that it was committed by the Jewish community. One historian wrote in 1935, 'Modern enquirers, after careful examination of the facts, have concluded that the child probably lost consciousness in consequence of a cataleptic fit.' Yet there are still people out there – sigh - who believe that those damned, sneaky Jews did indeed kill William and that the whole thing has since been 'covered-up' for no discernable reason: as though an isolated incident from 1144 was still going to rile people up.

It's queer to think of Loddon church causing heated debates on anti-Zionist websites, but it does just that. Actually, one US website says that the above quote from the historian can't be trusted because he has a Jewish sounding name. The site suggests that the Loddon rood is probably going to be removed soon by the *Power of Jewish Money*. It was very enlightening to an ignoramus like myself. I wasn't aware that Jewish money was so powerful. Was it not the same as regular money? Maybe somebody should tell the authors of the website that it's really

---

[1] Jews were also thought, by clearly *very* intelligent people, to have used the sacrifice of children as a way to alleviate haemorrhoids. The curse was believed to have stemmed from them saying to Pilate, 'His [Jesus'] blood be upon us and our children.' Apparently, dishing out sore bottoms was God's terrible judgment. Have mercy *on arseholes*.

easy to get into English village churches to take/break things. The *Power of Jewish Money* wouldn't be necessary. Loddon church is open all day, every day. The sign says 'Do Come In', for crying out loud. All any sly New World Order Jew needs to do is go in when there's nobody else around (e.g. anytime, ever) and kick the rood to pieces with the *Power of Jewish Kicking*. None of their immensely powerful money would even need to change hands.

The horrors of the post-William persecution of Jews in Norwich were made clear during the building of the Chapelfield shopping mall in 2004. A medieval well was discovered. It contained the skeletons of seventeen Jews (five of them potentially from the same family, eleven of them, children). An anthropologist noted, 'We are possibly talking about persecution. We are possibly talking about ethnic cleansing.' In terms of depicting the cold brutality of it, I can do no better than to quote the BBC report of the discovery:

'A close examination of the adult bones showed fractures caused by the impact of hitting the bottom of the well. But the same damage was not seen on the children's bones, suggesting they were thrown in after the adults, who cushioned the fall of their bodies... The team had earlier considered the possibility of death by disease but the bone examination showed no evidence of diseases.'

The crowd of pumpkin carving children had grown. Autumn was in the afternoon air. For the second time that day I was overcome with an almighty feeling of goodwill. I found everything about Loddon wonderful.

Tucked around the back of one of the stores was a charity shop. There's a modern trend for charity shops to be slick and organised. Some even sell entirely new lines of clothes, toys and, oddly, wooden footstools. Their books have stickers on the front pleading 'Please Read Me & Then Return Me'. Their CDs and DVDs are lined in alphabetical order. Well, not this one. This one was how charity shops should be. It was anarchy. The stock poured out onto the pavement. There were toys everywhere. Everywhere. Every. Where. A sign on the door read 'Enter If You Dare'. It was there for Halloween. Although it could easily not have been. I dared to enter.

Haddaway's latest hit, with the strangely philosophical title *What Is Love?*[1] crackled through the shop speakers. Amidst the chaotic bric-a-brac mountains, I found a gem: Kate Bush's *Hounds of Love*. In a more vibrant, urban charity shop, the album would have cost £3.95 and had a sticker on it pleading 'Please Listen To Me & Then Return Me'. Not in Loddon, folks. It cost me a solitary Great British Pound and was going right into my CD collection for eternity. As if to sweeten the deal, the lady who served me was dressed in full witch regalia and eating a portion of chips from her lap. With Haddaway on the hi-fi, remember.

Back outside, I noticed a table outside one of the food stores. Two items were for sale: firewood and cattle feed.[2] Loddon was that kind of place.

In Defoe's tour of Britain he said this 'side of Norfolk is very populous and thronged with great and spacious market towns, more larger than any other part of England so far.' He listed some of these greatly populated towns: 'Thetford, Dis, Hingham, Deerham, Attleboro, Windham, Harleston,

---

[1] It was released in 1993 but was still, technically, his latest hit. I'd like to have *What Is Love* sung boisterously at my funeral. Seriously. I want the lyrics printed on the order of service. Imagine walking past a church and hearing the sound of *that* coming from within.

[2] Firewood and Cattlefeed were another potential comedy duo for Cromer Pier's summer season. *I'd go and see them.*

Watton, Loddon.' He said that even the villages surrounding these towns were 'so large and so full of people that they are equal to the market towns in other counties.' Norfolk, he said, 'has the most people in the least tract of land of any county in England.'

How things change. Just because you're popular once, it doesn't mean you'll always be.

Just ask Haddaway.

Norwich: Part III

I was on the home straight. This was my last Norwich visit of the trip. Even though I knew I'd be there next week for work, it was like I was saying goodbye.

What had this trip done to me?

With Weybourne and Walsingham included, I had now visited forty towns and villages. But there were two more on the *official* list: Filby and Reedham. Both were close to one another yet worlds apart in Norfolk transport terms. Reedham was a stop on the Yarmouth train line (occasionally). Filby was accessible via a bus from Yarmouth which, from my calculations, departed once every seventh Wednesday of the month at 3am. I could never do both in a day. I had to get the journey finished by nightfall. Otherwise I'd have to wait until spring. There was only one thing to do. Get a ride. It's a form of public transport, I guess.

Chris was going to meet me in a car park on the other side of the city. I had one last walk. I went down St Stephens street: a puzzling mixture of bus lanes and pound shops. The buildings had a post-war look. This was largely due to the Luftwaffe's hatred of pre-war architecture. They disliked the stuff so much that they had a bloody good go at getting rid of most of it.

Norwich was targeted, in the words of the Nazi party, because of its 'beauty and unique historic interest' - two things they clearly felt they could do without should their invasion come to fruition. The first Norwich raid came one late afternoon in July 1940. The date was notable in that London didn't receive its first bombing campaign until the 7th of September that year. As the planes approached, the Norwich air raid siren, which had spent ten months annoying people with constant false alarms, decided, for a change, not to sound at all.[1] On that first raid, two bombers flew in and did their worst. 27 civilians were killed. One city cinema demonstrated a lack of tact by screening a film called *Dust Be My Destiny*. Ticket sales were slow. Most people had already seen the 3D version.

The bombers tore the place up. Bombing Norwich became so popular among pilots that even members of the RAF started doing it, dropping decidedly unfriendly 'friendly' bombs over Dereham Road.

When, or if, you next walk around Norwich and see an area that looks as though it was developed in the last fifty years, it's likely because what stood before it was bombed flat. The pilots flew so low that one of them managed to machine-gun a bus shelter in Hellesdon on the outskirts. (I'd considered a similar course of action in Downham Market.)

The city was often targeted by small squadrons, usually pairs, of bombers, except on two nights in April 1942. On those fateful evenings, around thirty bombers introduced Norwich to the Blitz. Two-hundred-and-thirty-one people died. Hundreds

---

[1] This became something of a deadly habit. Of the first eight raids on Norwich, the warning signal only went off once. People would find out about the raids by either the chilling hum of low flying bombers or the sound of their kitchen disappearing.

more were seriously injured. Oil bombs, sometimes up to six-feet in length were dropped on the city, leaving the sky aflame and wiping out whole streets. One account told of a mother and daughter caught in the raid. They ran down a road. The heat from the flames was such that the tarmac melted around their feet, as though they were running in scolding mud. The sky was bright orange. They saw a wild horse, foaming, galloping through the streets. As they ran they saw buildings explode, they saw firemen shoot water at unstoppable infernos, they saw neighbours pulling neighbours from smoking rubble.

As a measure of just how much clout the bombs had, one was discovered, unexploded, in a crater 35 feet below the ground. One poor soul, at the tender age of 83, got out of bed to survey the damage the next morning and realised he was in the middle of the street. His bedroom was nowhere to be seen. His dentures were later found somewhere near Aberdeen.

Lord Haw Haw found the whole thing a delightful romp. His propaganda broadcasts from Germany, when he wasn't busy bragging about the targeted bombing of Watton's chicken coups, were a hotbed of bad puns, listened to as a source of amusement by most in the region. The laughter stopped when one of his rants mentioned Norwich by name:

'The people of Norwich have a new City Hall,' he said, in his overly affected upper class tone. 'It isn't paid for yet, but never mind – the Luftwaffe will soon *put paid* to it!'

It was the kind of material you'd expect to find in a Nazi Christmas cracker.

Norwich had the last laugh. Haw Haw was captured and hanged for treason, aged 39, at Wandworth Prison.[1] His face

---

[1] Rebecca West, when not busy calling H.G Wells an 'old maid', reported on the trial for an American newspaper.

split in half due to the pressure of the noose.[1] City Hall, on the other hand, still stands tall today, its face very much intact.[2]

Although ultimately victorious, by the end of the war the city had the appearance of somebody who had gone twelve rounds with the Swaffham Gypsy (pre-boxing gloves). At the start of the war, there were 35,569 homes in Norwich. The total number of Norwich houses damaged was 30,354, of which almost 5,000 were either completely or seriously damaged. Around six out of every seven Norwich homes had taken a pasting. Added to that were the 2,025 Norfolk soldiers who left to fight and never returned.

Ah, the good old days.

On the day Victory in Europe was announced, the city burst into spontaneous celebration. RAF and US planes flew overhead (deciding not to bomb Dereham Road) as people danced in the streets. The shops and civic buildings kept their lights on into the night. It was Christmas in summer. An impromptu conga line formed, snaking at great length. Everyone was in the party mood. Although, it should be pointed out that there may have been more than one person who joined the conga assuming it was an excitable cue for powdered egg.

---

[1] Haw Haw (real name: William Joyce) was born in America and raised in Ireland. There was a strong case for him to not be charged with treason due to the fact he wasn't actually English. He had, however, considered himself English and was deputy leader of the British Union of Fascists before his escape to Germany in 1939 (after a tip-off from a friend in MI5 about his impending arrest. The MI5 agent would later become the inspiration for 'M' in the *James Bond* stories). But Churchill hated him; the PM may have rollicked around like an enormous drunken baby in a top hat, but he had a ruthlessly keen memory. Haw Haw was *put paid* to.

[2] A long-running unsubstantiated rumour is that Hitler himself had earmarked Norwich's art deco City Hall as the place to deliver his first address to the British people after his successful invasion. It's also claimed that the building would have been the Nazi party's British HQ.

I've lost count of the amount of times old people have talked to me about subjects of stultifying historical dullness. They're more than happy to tell me about how much bread *used* to cost or how polite the postmen *used* to be, yet they seldom mention these enthralling stories of the war. Even if you try and gently encourage the conversation onto that particular subject, they still manage to shift onto their more favoured subjects: namely, which shops *used* to be butchers. It may be painful for them to talk, but that's why they need to do so. Otherwise we risk becoming desensitised by programmes like *Home Fires*.

It's vital that we're not led into clouding the reality of war with vague notions of swing parties and hip vintage clothing. I'm just as guilty as anyone. Mention the war and the first thing I think of is a friendly ARP warden conducting stocking-legged typists in a rousing underground sing-a-long of *Run, Rabbit, Run*. We need the truth. How had I gone so long without knowing of Norwich's trauma?[1] It's our duty to spread the word. Everyone must know that, some nights, the fires were so fierce that the roads melted.

I careered through Castle Meadow at breakneck speed. The sun illuminated the castle on the hill. It's hard to imagine it was ever used for anything other than a museum. Obviously, this wasn't what the original architects had in mind.

Norwich Castle was built in the 11th century on the command of William the Conqueror, who was new to the country and wanted holiday homes in as much of it as possible.[2] It was an imposing fortification, with commanding views of the distant

---

[1] Even when the Germans switched from pilot bombers to V2 rockets, the county wasn't spared. They were aimed almost exclusively at London and Norwich. Luckily, most of them were wayward.

[2] That sounds like a joke. It isn't.

landscape. It was used mainly as a palace and was largely unvisited by the royals. William only went there once, to quell some Norwich rebels by cutting their eyes out. His son, Henry I, stayed there for Christmas in 1121 (and generally left people's eyes alone).

The castle was as a gaol for more than 600 years and was a renowned site for public hangings. You might recall that the Wymondham rebel Robert Kett was hanged there. He was one of countless thieves, crooks, and blasphemers sent there to receive similar punishment. Many were hanged, many were burnt.[1] Crowds of spectators would sometimes reach 30,000. In fact, the hanging of James Blomefield Rush in 1849 was so hotly anticipated that extra trains were laid on for daytrippers. Funny lot, the Victorians.

Rush was a tenant farmer who'd got himself into financial difficulty and, in the days before payday money lending websites, decided that his only option was to shoot his landlord, and his landlord's son, on their doorstep at Stanfield Hall, near Wymondham. Aware that he may have perhaps taken up a rather drastic method of debt management, he decided to put on a disguise. He donned a wig and false beard.

He was recognised and arrested about twelve seconds later. The disguise fooled nobody. Even two-year-olds were leaning out of their perambulators and pointing him out. Norfolk didn't have a good track record when it came to inventive disguises. Ask Dr Crippen.

The double murder created a national furore. Rush defended himself at the trial. He delivered a *fourteen-hour* closing speech,

---

[1] One man 'openly avowed' that 'the New Testament and Gospel of Christ, [were] but mere foolishness, a story of man, or rather a mere fable' and was duly 'burnt in the Castle Ditch' in 1583. He was a known troublemaker. He'd already had his ears chopped off in the marketplace for bad-mouthing Queen Elizabeth.

by the end of which *everybody* wanted him dead. 'His death was greeted with loud applause by an immense crowd who had assembled to witness the execution,' read the official notice. (The executioner hadn't dared ask if Rush had any final words. They'd have been there until nightfall.)

In the crowd that day was Charles Dickens. Despite being an advocate for the cessation of public hangings, calling them an 'ugly, filthy, careless, sickening spectacle', he certainly went to a fair few. He described the location of Rush's hanging as 'a grand place for a scoundrel's exit'.

Rush's notoriety reached sufficient heights for him to have a waxwork effigy in the Chamber of Horrors at Madame Tussauds. It stayed there from 1849 until 1971, when, judging by the photos of it, it may have been remoulded into Fred Elliot from *Coronation Street*.

The castle and gaol became a museum in 1894 (public hangings were, like, *so* 1867). It's typical of Norfolk that even its museums belonged in a museum. No longer a place for criminals to be detained and tortured, the castle was now home to butterfly collections and Anglo-Saxon pottery.[1] The cries of prisoners had been replaced by the sound of children on school trips. Evolution, my dears.

But it's not just renowned murderers that Norwich had attracted down the years. Many of the world's most famous

---

[1] The castle also held many works of the artists of the celebrated Norwich School of Painters (1803 – 1834). It was the fact that J.J Colman (of the mustard empire) had generously bought so many of their paintings, for displaying in the castle, that the school's members took so long to gain wider recognition. It wasn't until 2001 that many of the works were displayed outside of Norwich for the first time.

people had visited the Fine City.[1] The Beatles played and queued for chips here in 1963 and later referenced Britain's first black circus master, Pablo Fanque, a Norwich man.[2] Laurel & Hardy performed at the Hippodrome ('The pair so resembled their film-selves that when the curtain went up the audience took a minute or two to realise they were seeing their childhood comedy favourites in the flesh,' said the local press review), as did Charlie Chaplin, Cary Grant, Morecambe & Wise, and The Goons. The Hippodrome survived the Blitz but couldn't survive the council. It was replaced by a multi-story car park. It seemed a good idea at the time. Devolution, my dears.

But Norwich's most famous face, was, arguably, Elizabeth Fry (no relation to Stephen - also a famous Norwich face). Fry was born in Norwich in 1780 (Elizabeth, not Stephen) and became known as the 'Angel of Prisons' after implementing reforms to the conditions and segregations of cells.

If you're wondering what Elizabeth Fry looks like, she's on the opposite side to the queen on every £5 note. She fought off competition for the honour from the more popularly revered Jane Austen and Elizabeth Barrett Browning. Fry may have received a leg-up onto that particular pedestal. Her family were the founders of Barclays.

'It's *who* you know,' fumed Jane Austen, throwing her bonnet to the floor and generally causing a scene.

One last walk through the city (until work next week). One last look at the market place (until work next week). One last look

---

[1] That's what it says on the signs on the way in: 'Norwich – A Fine City.' It's unclear where the quote came from. Both George Borrow and William Cobbett said something similar.

[2] Everybody sing along, *'The Hendersons will all be there, late of Pablo Fanque's fair, what a scene!'*

at the twisting alleys of independent shops (until work next week). One last look at the cathedral (until work next week). One last walk down cobbled Elm Hill, under the bending Tudor houses (until work next week).

Ah, Elm Hill. Norwich's beauty spot. Now a dainty collection of antique shops and boutiques running alongside the river. Just one hundred years ago it was a scene of squalor. For once, rather than knocking it down, it was decided that the area be renovated and restored to former glory. It's an almost perfect city street. The shine is taken off by the fact it leads to a Wetherspoons. I resisted the temptation to get annihilated for £6 on Bulgarian lager. I didn't want to fund their demolition project in Dereham. Instead I found the car park, and Chris.

'Come on, then. Let's futtun goo to Filby,' he said, doing his best Norfolk impression. It was better than Alan Bates' effort.

Filby

Filby is noted for its raspberries, so says my *Penguin Guide*. It says little else. There isn't much *to* say. My other Norfolk guides ignore the place altogether.

We drove through expecting at some point to find the thriving epicentre. We found a village sign. And a flowerbed. And a tree. I got out of the car and took photos of them. It was getting desperate.

'Where the hell is everything?' I shouted.

The tinge of regret I felt about not getting the bus was replaced with an overwhelming sense of relief. I would have been fuming if I'd spent four hours on the bus to find that Filby was, of all the places I'd visited, the least worthy of inclusion on the list.

Worse still, I would have been walking around it for hours in vain. It appeared nothing more than a long main road with some houses on the side of it.

We drove down unmade roads, looking for something, anything, of note.

'There's the church!' I yelped, in the style of a child who'd just seen Alton Towers from the car window. Never had I been so excited to see a church.

I walked around the graveyard alone. The sky was turning red on the horizon. I counted four stars. Half of the grass had been freshly cut; the rest grew ankle height around weathered headstones. It hadn't rained for a few days but the ground was damp and soft. I zipped up my jacket. There was an abandoned lawn mower behind one of the gravestones. It was still plugged in. The gardener had vanished. A strange and thankless job, to mow a village churchyard. I can see myself doing it one day. It might add a touch of mystique to my character. I always think people who work the church gardens have a sad tale to tell, that there's a reason why they're doing good deeds deliberately in front of God's house. Maybe it's atonement for an old transgression. Maybe it's to feel closer to a recently buried partner. Maybe it's just Community Service for flashing their willy at a family of four in an Esso forecourt. Whatever it is, I want in.

I took a deep breath. Autumn afternoon air is my cocaine. I'd gladly pay a dealer for an out-of-season snort. There's something about that part of an October day that throws me into my past. Looking at the darkening sky, I was taken back to the end of the school day: getting on the coach, my chubby hands stuffed with reading folders and pasta artwork and letters home, for *your parents or guardians*, printed on green paper.

Standing in the sunlight, I had one of those moments where the heart swells and you feel as though everything is fine and will be fine forevermore. I could hear the car running above the silence. I couldn't keep Chris waiting. We had to get to Reedham.

Reveries must be short. That's the rule.

I checked the lawn mower model before leaving. I was right. It was an *Atonement 4000*.

One article described Filby as 'a picturesque village tucked away in the heart of the broads featuring a wealth of pretty chocolate-box cottages surrounded by spectacular scenery'. I couldn't see any of this. Had I gone to the right place? We drove up and down every road we could find. There was nothing. Where were the chocolate boxes?

We parked on the edge of the broads. In the distance were wind turbines and southward flying birds. The scenery was a cross between *Dawson's Creek* and the end of the first *Lord of the Rings* when (spoiler alert) Sam and Frodo bugger off in that little boat.

We were the only people. Six empty wooden boats rocked gently in their moorings. I walked along the boardwalk and posed for photographs. I became one of the models in the *Next Directory*, one minute looking out across the water, the next, ruminating moodily on the changing of the seasons.

The best time to visit Filby, says all available literature, is the summer. That's when the village goes full throttle into the heady business of flower arranging. It performs admirably in many national and regional 'In Bloom' competitions. Summer also brings rare birds, which, in turn (forgive the pun), attract birdwatchers. It is all immensely fascinating if you happen to be interested in either flowers or birds, which, if you've learnt nothing else from this book, you'll be well aware that I don't.

Filby was done. Tick. One more to go. One more: Reedham. The last station stop. The end of the line and so forth. Maybe I would get my chance to use the joke I'd been lining up since day one of the tour.

'Come on,' Chris said as I got in the car. 'Let's go to Reedham and weep.'

'*I* was going to say that!' I said.

And with that, I wept.[1]

Reedham

Since I'd found out that there was a pub in Reedham named The Lord Nelson, I'd had it in mind that it ought to be my final port of call. What better way to end the trip, I reasoned, than with a pint and a pie in a pub named after the man whose final words helped give this book its name?

I'd visualised it all in advance: I'd sit by a roaring fire, maybe patting the friendly pub dog (called Bernard or Charlie), sipping an ale whilst looking out onto the river in a state of whimsical reflection and sense of achievement at a job well done. Think of the symbolism, dear reader. What a grand finale it was going to make!

Except that the pub was shut. It was as shut as a pub could possibly be. Windows boarded, paint faded, wheelie bins blocking the front door, junk mail sticking out of the letterbox.

---

[1] I'd also been desperate to find out about a love triangle between two people from Holkham and one person from Burnham. It would have been a case of, wait for it, *Holkham Holkham Burnham love*. Annoyingly, such a trio didn't appear to exist and the joke had to be squeezed in here instead.

'Oh, for f...' I said, not feeling the need to bother finishing the sentence with *uck's sake*.

In a way, the pub being closed *was* symbolic. It symbolised the dark side of the trip: the closed museums; the stealth bus stops; the driving rain; Ray Winstone's twin sister; the sweat; the confused conversations; Downham Market Bus Shelter; *Need*ham.

If Reedham was my Trafalgar, then the pub was the French sniper bullet through my left shoulder, bringing me to my glorious end.

I wasn't the first Reedham visitor to get a raw welcome. The hilariously named Viking chieftain, Lodbrog, beat me to it. Whilst out looking for interesting Danish birds and wildlife in his boat, the wind became so fierce that he was whisked further out to sea than one generally likes to be whisked. By the time the breeze had stopped whisking, Lodbrog was 700 miles away in Reedham. As if things couldn't get any worse, Edmund, Saxon king of the Angles, was on holiday in Reedham at the time. And he just so happened to have packed a spare pair of shackles.

Edmund was initially wary of the captured Dane (and his incredibly suspicious story about how he got to Reedham) but they ended up forming an unlikely friendship. This didn't sit well with Edmund's associate, Bern, who viewed the Dane as a threat. Bern took Lodbrog to the woods and killed him.[1]

---

[1] There are so many stories in which people were led to the woods to be killed (*Babes in the Wood*, for instance). How were the victims tempted there in the first place? It's not exactly the most enticing place, is it?
'Fancy a trip to the woods, mate?'
'Definitely! I hear the orchids are in bloom!'
Woodland murders don't happen so much now. Maybe people wised up.

Edmund was devastated and packed Bern off on a boat to be 'committed to the mercy of the winds and the waves.' Remarkably, Bern's boat somehow caught the same breeze to the one Lodbrog travelled in on. Except it was the return service. His boat wound up in Denmark. And it just so happened that they had a spare pair of shackles.

Bern was tortured for information about the whereabouts of good old Lodbrog. Good old Lodbrog, lied Bern, had been killed by King Edmund. The Danish torturers almost choked on their bacon sandwiches. They amassed an army of 20,000 men and invaded East Anglia, using the traitorous Bern as their guide. The directions weren't difficult:

'Just lay back and wait for the wind to do the work,' Bern said, getting out his iPod.

When the Danes caught Edmund they tied him to a tree and used him as a target for archery practice. They then chopped off his head. The legend goes that his head was later discovered in the woods, protected by a wolf. This might not be true. What was true, however, was that Edmund, for whom Bury St Edmunds was named, no longer had a head, and neither did East Anglia. The Viking army wiped out the remaining Saxon dynasty with ruthless aggression.

Birdwatching can have terrible consequences.

Unlike *real* sniper bullets, of the kind that brought Nelson to his fate, *metaphorical* sniper bullets only wound the soul; they still allow you to walk freely without much fuss. So, rather than keeling over and saying 'fan, fan, rub, rub' to myself, I took a roam around the shops.

Reedham was similar to Horning in that its main street ran alongside a body of water, in this case the Yare. Aside from the locked and bolted Lord Nelson, there were a few shops still open. But it was almost dark and the season all but over. There was nothing to see. The village did have a Grade II listed wind-pump, but you'll forgive me if I tell you that I wasn't quite in the mood to be dealing with that level of excitement.

I got back into the warmth of the car and we drove around the village. Was this really the end of my trip? Reedham was the 42nd place I'd visited since the spring. I'd gone beyond the list of forty. I'd done most by public transport. I'd seen it all. I'd taken terrible photographs. I'd studied. I'd made notes. I was fully prepped. I was ready to contribute my effort to the 'Local Books' sections of Nelson's County.

Fan, fan, rub, rub.

Epilogue

I'd been sent to Birmingham for training. I'd left Norwich at 5.30am. By the time I arrived, I felt like I'd been awake since the Dawn of Man, or, if not exactly then, certainly the Elevenses of Man.

My brain was pounding. Prolonged travelling always throws me into a stupor. It's like getting up in the night to go for a wee; I stumble around looking confused and saying random words out loud.

I didn't know where I was. The room was lit by white electric lights. There were no windows. The walls were white. The projector screen was white. Words were being said. Blue Sky Thinking under a white ceiling.

'You might want to take notes,' we were advised.

Some had their pens pre-clicked and ready for action. Clipboards and notebooks in pristine condition. I was caught out. I was no better than the students I regularly berated:

'Why come to college without pen and paper?'

I rummaged through my bag long after everyone else had begun scrawling. I couldn't find a pen. I tried to search discreetly but that made the noise worse, like when you try to eat crisps slowly. Every slight movement drew glares.

Damn. What was I going to do? I didn't want to ask for a pen. It would look unprofessional. (I am unprofessional. But I never want to *look* it.)

Then I remembered. The front compartment of the bag! That's where I kept all of my... I felt something in my hand and pulled it free, into the electric light.

It was my North Norfolk Railway pen. The one I'd bought all those months ago in Weybourne. The first day of the trip. The pen that didn't have a price sticker.

I looked at the logo and I was there again, strolling in the sun with my backpack on. Riding steam trains and miniature trains. Talking to people I'd never normally approach. Walking through woods. Sitting on beaches. Listening to birds. Thinking about blue skies.

'We'll be working a little later than projected today as we've got a lot to get through. It's all very important.'

I clicked my pen.

'Well,' I thought, 'nobody told *me*.'

Acknowledgements

There are many people to thank. I'd best get stuck in.

Firstly, to those who helped me on the journey, allowing me to arrive in a messy heap at their doorstep and scoff their vittles: David and Sue (the Hunstanton wing of the McLeod hospitality suite), and Chris (the Norwich wing). Tony and Lydia Byrne for buying a property in the centre of the Norfolk countryside (no doubt doing so with the express purpose of giving me a helpful halfway-house on my travels). Thanks to Norfolk Tourist Information and to all the mighty fine bus and train drivers in the county (and the grumpy ones).

To those who have helped with promoting my work. Gay and the team at *Just Regional*, *BBC Introducing* and *BBC Radio Norfolk*. Donna Bishop at the *Eastern Daily Press*. To Michael Palin (not *the* Michael Palin) for creating an unlikely readership for me in and around Wigan (I've shot myself in the foot with a book about Norfolk. Sorry, Wigan. I hope you forgive me).

To Sarah, for another excellent job on my front and back covers. And to her husband, Dan, for his juicy, idea-heavy brain. Dressing up as Nelson and dicking around Hunstanton on one of the busiest Saturdays of the year is an experience I shall never forget (regardless of how much counselling I receive).

To Rosie Johnson for her proofreading skills. If there are any mistakes in here, *its orl her folt*. After reading the draft she came to the conclusion that my diet was a cause for concern. She now thinks I'm in danger of getting scurvy. She gave me some tangerines to combat the onset. I dipped them in chocolate.

Thanks to Norfolk Library Services for stocking my work and generally being brilliant. Also to Jarrolds, the Holt Bookshop, and Katie's Gifts & Accessories for being equally helpful.

Thanks also to: Robert Lockwood (I've remembered you this time), Alex Jones, Bill and Mike, Georgie Kuna, James Groves, Tim & Jackie G, Ian Johnson, Abbie Panks, Maria Pavledis, Arriarne Pugh, Kirsty Raby, Jared Carpenter, Chris Beckett, Laura Bailey, Julie & Tim, Julie & Tim (a different one), Clare Rose, Chris Marshall, Wayne Craske, James 'Fred' Threadwell (Thetford massif) Tom & Sue Roche (suppliers of books by Buttercup Joe), David Langrish (hope you enjoy the film references), Karen Youngs, Alan, Christopher Whitfield (now I'll never forget in which drawer the butter knife is kept!), Dana Ellsworth (my US fan club), Mark Narayn, Katie Porter, Ian O'Brien, Kate Ross and all my regular readers. You really are swell.

Lastly, my greatest thanks go to the many, many writers of Norfolk books, past and present. May the world continue to churn out more Buttercup Joes and Margaret Looses.

This book has taken the best part of two years to plan and complete. It has been, to quote UB40 for the first and last time in my life, a labour of love. I adore Norfolk. If it were a girl, I'd fancy her.

For new articles visit

ryantpugh.co.uk

To see my terrible photographs and read additional notes to Kismet Quick, visit www.flickr.com and search for Ryan T. Pugh. You can also follow me on Twitter and Facebook.

Made in the USA
Charleston, SC
01 September 2015